The Plays of Girish Karnad

Series on Indian Drama

General Editor: **R.K. Dhawan**

The Plays of Girish Karnad

critical perspectives

edited by

Jaydipsinh Dodiya

PRESTIGE

Published by
Prestige Books
3/28, East Patel Nagar
New Delhi 110 008
Ph. 9818755529
email: prestigebooks@gmail.com
website: asiabookclub.com
ISBN: 81-7551-061-7

Rs. 600

Printed at Chaman Offset Press, New Delhi 110 002

CONTENTS

Preface

Girish Karnad is perhaps the most renowned media personality in the contemporary India. He is India's leading playwright and an adept practitioner of the performing arts. His first play *Yayati* (1961), a retelling of a myth from the *Mahabharata* won critical acclaim. But it was his second play *Tughlaq*, that established him as one of the foremost playwrights of India. It is a historical play in the manner of the nineteenth-century Parsee theatre. It deals with the tumultuous reign of the medieval Sultan, Muhammad-bin-Tughlaq, a visionary, a poet, and yet most eccentric individual to ascend the throne of Delhi. His next play *Hayavadana* (1971) won the Sahitya Akademi Award and the Natya Sangh Award. It was one of the first modern Indian plays to employ traditional theatre techniques. The play *Naga-Mandala* (1988) turns to oral tales, usually narrated by women while feeding women in the kitchen. *Tale-Danda* (1987), which means death by beheading, has been acclaimed widely for its brilliant analysis of the ills that plague Indian society today. His latest play *Fire and Rain* treats the contemporary problematic of a-moralism as its central theme. As the title suggess, Karnad places *Yagna* the fire, in opposition to rain the life.

The present volume comprising more than thirty scholarly papers offers a critical appraisal of Karnad as a dramatist and gives varied and analytic interpretations of his plays.

I cannot close these prefatory remarks without expressing my gratitude to all those who have contributed to the making of this book: to all the contributors of this anthology for their scholarly papers; to Dr. R.K. Dhawan for his editorial help; to my colleagues Prof. M.G. Machhar, Dr. K.K. John, Prof. I.G. Purohit and Prof. Sheetal Takore; to my wife Jignasha, my son Kuldeep and my daughter Bhargavi without whose co-operation and encouragement this anthology would not have seen the light of the day. And lastly, I must thank Prestige Books for bringing out this publication so elegantly and promptly.

Jaydipsinh Dodiya

For my mother

Girish Karnad: The Man and the Writer

R.K. DHAWAN

The theatre in India is still amateurish. Largely speaking, there are two types of theatre in India, one which is performed in the villages, the various *jatras*, *mandalis* etc. These have been evolved through the centuries. But the plays of other type, performed in cities, need to develop more. The biggest problem is that it is very difficult to make a decent living from theatre and that is the reason why it has not become professional.

The growth of Indian theatre has a queer history. Modern Indian theatre emerged under British influence in three cities that were founded by the British and had no previous Indian history, namely Calcutta in the East, Bombay in the West and Madras in the South. It was but natural that theatre in these cities followed the British legacy. The entire system of stage and performance as also of selling the tickets made its way.

An appraisal of Indian drama shows that while drama in various Indian languages has shown a marked development, it has not done so in Indian English. In this literature, drama is a plant of poor growth. The first and the foremost reason is the want of a living theatre. It is a well-known fact that the real success of a play can be tested only on stage. A playwright needs a living theatre to put his work on acid test, evaluate its total effect on the audience and thereby get a chance to improve upon his performance. This handicap has not allowed him to pursue playwriting in a systematic and comprehensive way.

Very recently Indian English drama has shot into prominence. Younger writers like Mahesh Dattani and Manjula Padmanabhan have infused new life into this branch of writing. The thiry-eight-year-old Bangalore-based Dattani has published forceful plays like *Where There is a Will*, *Final Solutions* and *Tara*. Padmanabhan's Onassis award-winning *Harvest* has achieved worldwide acclaim.

Incidentally, both Dattani and Padmanabhan do not write on the traditional subjects. Dattani writes about mean, ugly, unhappy things of life; Padmanabhan projects a dehumanized, terrifying world in which mothers sell their sons for "the price of rice." Her play *Harvest* is about an impoverished family living in a single room in a chawl of Bombay. Population explosion has rendered the city dwellers into helpless, poor, dehumanized lot struggling for their survival. In this scenario, driven by hunger and unemployment, twenty-year-old Om Prakash decides to become an organ donor and mortgages his body to a white First-World buyer. Padmanabhan projects in her play a more serious, grim and unpalatable world than Dattani. But her play is rather intellectual and not suited for stage, unlike the plays of Dattani which have been quite successful on the stage and have captured the imagination of the middle-class audience.

English plays are occasionally staged, especially in big cities like Bombay, Delhi and Calcutta. Visits of foreign troupes are arranged from time to time by the British Council and the American Center. In Delhi, Yatrik group has actively staged several plays. Barry John, the renowned director, has made a significant contribution to the Delhi theatre. It is a matter of great satisfaction that some of the Indian English plays like Gurcharan Das's *Mira*, Pratap Sharma's *A Touch of Brightness* and Asif Currimbhoy's *The Dumb Dancer* have been staged in the West.

It is mainly then Indian drama in Indian languages and the drama in English translation which has registered a remarkable growth in the recent decades. During the last few years, several plays originally written in the regional languages have been translated into English. Today, a sizeable number of such plays exist, and it is possible for the scholars to assess and evaluate Indian drama in its totality. Many academics have felt the need for English translations of literature in the Indian languages. English translations of classics in the Indian languages should form an important component of Indian English literature and if these are taught to our students, it will engage their attention fully and meaningfully. The translations have forged a link between the east and west, north and south, and contributed to the growing richness of contemporary creative consciousness. Thus regional drama in India is slowly paving way for a "national theatre" into which all streams of theatrical art seem to converge. The major language theatres active during the Sixties, Seventies and Eighties that rejuvenated and consolidated are those of Hindi, Marathi, Bengali and Kannada. A study of Vijay Tendulkar, Badal Sircar and Girish Karnad clearly shows that they are the symbols of the new resurgence in their own areas and have made bold innovations, fruitful experiments and given new directions which go in the history of Indian drama as a significant mark of achievement.

II

Girish Karnad is the foremost playwright of the contemporary Indian stage. He has given the Indian theatre a richness that could probably be equated only with his talents as an actor-director. His contribution goes beyond theatre: he has directed feature films, documentaries and television serials in Kannada, Hindi and English, and has played leading roles as an actor in Hindi and Kannada art films, commercial movies and television serials. He has represented India in foreign lands as an emissary of art and culture.

Karnad was born on 19 May 1938 in Matheran, a town near Bombay. His childhood was spent growing up in a small village in Karnataka where he had first-hand experience of the indigenous folk theatre. His encounter with the Natak companies at the early stage of his life made a lasting impression on the mind of Girish Karnad. Says he: "It may have something to do with the fact that in the small town of Sirsi, where I grew up, strolling groups of players, called Natak Mandalis or Natak companies, would come, set up a stage, present a few plays over a couple of months and move on. My parents were addicted to these plays. That was in the late 1940s. By the early 1950s, films had more or less finished off this kind of theatre, though some Mandalis still survive in North Karnataka in a very degenerate state. But in those days they were good or at least I was young and thought so. I loved going to see them and the magic has stayed with me." (*NTQ*, 360)

During his formative years, Karnad went through diverse influences. He was exposed to a literary scene where there was a direct clash between Western and native tradition. It was India of the Fifties and the Sixties that surfaced two streams of thought in all walks of life—adoption of new modernistic techniques, a legacy of the colonial rule and adherence to the rich cultural past of the country. Karnad's position was akin to that of John Dryden, the seventeenth-century British dramatist who, while writing his plays, had to choose between the classical tradition and native tradition. In the first, norms had been set rigorously by Aristotle, the second was a more liberal, native approach that was practised by Shakespeare. Dryden evaluated the merits and demerits of both the traditions in his famous critical treatise *Essay on Dramatic Poesy.* Karnad was fascinated by the traditional plays, nonetheless the Western playwrights that he read during his college days opened up for him "a new world of magical possibilities."

After graduating from Karnatak University, Dharwad, in 1958, Karnad moved to Bombay for further studies. In the meantime, he received the prestigious Rhodes scholarship and went to England to do his Master's degree. During his stay at Magdalen College, Oxford, Karnad felt immensely interested in art and culture. On his return to India in 1963, he joined Oxford University Press, Madras. This offered him an opportunity to get exposed to various kinds of writing in India and elsewhere. Such influences made an indelible mark on the creative genius of Girish Karnad. In 1974, he received an important assignment and was appointed Director of the Film and Television Institute of India, Pune. In 1987, he went to the U.S.A. as Fulbright Scholar-in-Residence at the Department of South Asian Languages and Civilizations, University of Chicago. From 1988 to 1993, he served as Chairman of the Sangeet Natak Akademi (National Academy for the Performing Arts), New Delhi. In 1994, he was awarded Doctor of Letters degree by the Karnatak University, Dharwad.

III

When Karnad was preparing to go to England, amidst the intense emotional turmoil, he found himself writing a play. One day as he was reading the *Mahabharata* just for fun, he read the story of Yayati. It clicked in his mind. He started writing. It came as a 'play.' He suddenly found he was a playwright and a Kannada playwright at that. This was so sudden and so natural. The play was in Kannada, the language of his childhood. And the theme of the play *Yayati* was taken from ancient Indian mythology. While the theme and language was typically native, the play owed its form, not to numerous mythological plays he watched, but to Western playwrights whom he had read. While the subject matter was purely native and traditional, the form and structure were essentially western.

Karnad's writing of the play *Yayati* without any premeditation, set things straight. He was to write plays, not poetry which he aspired to write, and that the source of his inspiration was native stuff, history, mythology and folklore. Even at the age of twenty-two, he realized that he could not be a poet, but only a playwright. Until he wrote this play, Karnad fancied himself a poet. During his teens, he had written poetry and had trained himself to write in English. "The greatest ambition of my life was to be a poet," says Karnad. By the time he was in college, he wanted to write in English, become a novelist and be internationally famous. There have been more poets and more novelists, but there have been very few playwrights and very few good plays. Karnad further realized that the art of a poet or a novelist was easier than that of a dramatist. As he says:

> The subject that interests most writers is, of course, themselves and it is easy subject to talk about. But you know it is always easier if you are a poet or a novelist because you are used to talking in your voice. You suspend your whole life talking as writer directly to the audience. The problem in being a playwright is that everything that you write is for someone else to say.

A playwright has many problems. What is upsetting for a playwright is the total lack of plays in India, although the company Natak tradition made a major contribution that flourished since the early decades of the eighteenth century. Where does the playwright look for the sources? And why does one write plays at all?—questions Karnad. There is hardly any theatre in the country. Karnad got into films in an effort to find some kind of a living audience. And perhaps to earn his livelihood.

Karnad has always found it difficult to find a suitable, rich subject for writing plays. For instance, after writing *Yayati*, he read all kinds of books in an effort to find a plot, some plot that would truly inspire. He read the history of Kanada literature by Kirtinath Kurtkoti and learnt from him that Indian history has not been handled by any Indian writer the way it has been done by Shakespeare or Brecht. Greatly impressed by this statement, Karnad went through a book of Indian history. And when he came to Tughlaq, he said, "Oh! Marvellous. That is what I wanted." That was a subject in tune with the times. In those days, existentialism was quite in fashion. Everything about Tughlaq seemed to fit into what Karnad had surmised from Kurtkoti. He felt that in Tughlaq he had hit upon a fantastic character. He realized that he had absorbed this character and it was growing in front of him. Tughlaq was the most extraordinary character to come to the throne of Delhi: in religion, in philosophy, even in calligraphy, in battle, warfield, and all other areas, he was unsurpassable; no other ruler could match his capability. Writing on such a subject seemed challenging and rewarding.

Karnad's *Tughlaq* bears several resemblances with Shakespeare's *Richard II*. Like King Richard, Muhammad-bin-Tughlaq is temperamental and whimsical. Events in both the plays centre around the eccentricities of their protagonists. Again, like Shakespeare, Karnad presents the historical events and complexities of the time with perfect objectivity of a true historian, throwing upon them the beautiful colouring of art. He exhibits without concealment the weakness of the king's character but spares no pain to evoke our whole-hearted pity for him in his fall.

Tughlaq had a tremendous success with the reading public and it achieved greater popularity on the stage as actors have liked to do the role of the emperor. As opposed to the first play, Karnad wrote this one in the convention of the Company Natakas. For form of the play, Karnad was no more interested in John Anouilh. He divided the play into scenes in the indigenous fashion of the natakas.

The political chaos which Karnad depicts in *Tughlaq* reminded many readers of the Nehru era in Indian history. Karnad finds this similarity accidental. Says he, "I did not consciously write about the Nehru era. I am always flattered when people tell me that it was about the Nehru era and equally applies to development of politics since then. But, I think, well, that is a compliment that any playwright would be thrilled to get, but it was not intended to be a contemporary play about a contemporary situation."

IV

The publication of *Yayati* in 1961 and especially of *Tughlaq* in 1964 established Karnad as a master dramatist. Subsequently he published *Hayavadana* (1971), *Angumalige* (1977), *Hittina Hunja* (1980), *Naga-Mandala* (1988), *Tale-Danda* (1990) and *Agni Mattu Male* (1995). Karnad wrote all his eight plays in Kannada; these have been translated into major Indian languages including the national language Hindi. Five of his plays—*Tughlaq*, *Hayavadana*, *Naga-Mandala*, *Tale-Danda* and *The Fire and the Rain*—have been translated into English. The first three of these have been published by Oxford University Press in India and the remaining two by Ravi Dayal Publishers, New Delhi.

Karnad is a skilful translator. He writes his plays in Kannada; English is the language of his adulthood. He writes articles, essays, film scripts in English but not plays. When he translates his own work, he has a great advantage. He has a lot of freedom that another translator will not have. A translator has to be faithful to the text and he does not have the freedom to make changes if it is somebody else's text. "My translation," says Karnad, "must therefore, be seen as approximation to the original." (*Translation*, 218) To begin with, he was quite reluctant to translate his own plays. He realized that translating from Kannada into English required a great deal of re-writing—a kind of transcreation. He translated *Tughlaq* when Alyque Padamsee was to stage it and then *Hayavadana* for the Madras Players. He feels that translating from one regional language to another is easier than translating into English. The basic problem for the translator lies in his search for appropriate cultural equivalents.

Besides his own plays, Karnad has translated Badal Sircar's *Evam Indrajit* which was well-received in literary circles. He found translating the play very enjoyable and rewarding. As a translator, he kept in mind the utterance value of the dialogue. He also conveyed appropriate rhythm and pace of the original language. Karnad has an immense faith in the discipline of translation. It is the only way for creative writers to reach a wider audience. How else, wonders Karnad, should one experience world theatre!

V

Karnad's plays have been performed on stage, directed by eminent directors. The historical play *Tughlaq*, in particular, has stood the test of time. B.V. Karanth's 1966 Kannada production in Bombay, Om Shivpuri's Hindi production in Delhi the same year and Alyque Padamsee's English production in Bombay in 1970 are some of the memorable performances of the play. In 1974, the National School of Drama Repertory Company mounted a memorable revival of the play at the Old Fort in Delhi under E. Alkazi's direction.

Karnad's plays have received an international recognition. These have been widely performed in Europe and America. The play *Tughlaq* has been translated into Hungarian and German. The B.B.C., London, broadcast it in 1979 and *Hayavadana* in 1993. Directed by E. Alkazi, *Tughlaq* was presented in London by the National School of Drama Repertory Company as part of the Festival of India in 1982. Karnad's mythical play *Hayavadana* was presented at the Berlin Festival of Drama and Music in Germany in 1985. Directed in German by Vijaya Mehta, it was part of the Repertoire of the Deutsches National Theatre, Weimar, in 1984-86. It was rechristened as "Divided Together" and presented at the Ark Ensemble in New York in 1993.

The play *Naga-Mandala*, directed by Vijaya Mehta in German, was presented by the Leipziger Schauspielhaus at Leipzig and Berlin for the Festival of India in Germany in 1992. Again, it was performed at the University Theatre at Chicago and subsequently at the Gutherie Theatre in Minneapolis as part of its thirtieth anniversary celebrations in 1993. In the same year, Gutherie Theatre commissioned Karnad's latest play *The Fire and the Rain*.

Karnad has received wide recognition for his plays. He got Mysore State Award for *Yayati* in 1962; Kamaladevi Award of the Bharatiya Natya Sangh for the Best Indian Play of the Year for *Hayavadana* in 1972. For *Tale-Danda*, he won a number of awards: B.H. Sridhar Award in 1992, Karnataka Nataka Akademi Award for the Best Play of 1990-91 in 1992, Karnataka Sahitya Akademi Award in 1993 and Sahitya Akademi Award in 1994. He was honoured in 1990 by *Granthaloka*, Journal of the Book Trade, as "The Writer of the Year" for his play *Tale-Danda*. In 1992, he received Karnataka Sahitya Akademi Award for the Most Creative Work of 1989 for *Naga-Mandala*. He has also received Govt. of Mysore Rajyotsava Award in 1970; Sangeet Natak Akademi's Award for playwriting in 1972; Karnataka Nataka Akademi Award in 1984; Nandikar, Calcutta, Award for playwriting in 1989; Booksellers' and Publishers' Association of South India Award in 1992.

Karnad is an important film-maker and writer of film scripts. He has written the script and dialogues for the film *Samskara* (1960) in Kannada based on the novel of the same name by U.R. Anantha Murthy, and played the lead role in it. With B.V. Karanth, he has co-directed the film *Vansha Vriksha* (1971) in which he has also acted, and *Godhuli* (Hindi), *Tabbaliyu Ninade Magane* (Kannada) in 1977. He has also directed films like *Kadu* (1973) and *Ondanondu Kaladalli* (1978) in Kannada, *Utsav* (1984) and *Cheluvi* (1992) in Hindi. His roles in *Manthan* (1976) and *Swami* (1978) are among his best in Hindi art cinema.

Between 1963 and 1970, Karnad was an active member of an amateur group called "Madras Players." He worked as actor and director, in such plays as *Evam Indrajit*, *Six Characters in Search of an Author*, *Uncle Vanya*, *The Caretaker*, *The Crucible* and *A View from the Bridge* in English during 1964-69. He also acted the lead roles in *Oedipus Rex* and *Jokumaraswamy*, directed in Kannada by B.V. Karanth, for the Open-Air Festival in Bangalore in 1972.

Karnad has also published a number of articles, the most significant being "In Search of a New Theatre" in *Contemporary Indian Tradition*, ed. Carla Borden (Washington: Smithsonian Press, 1988) and "Theatre in India," in *Daedalus*, Vol. 118, No. 4, pp. 331-52.

VI

Whileas Karnad is a multi-faceted personality, it is essentially as a playwright that he is at his best. He confesses, "I have been fairly lucky in having a multi-pronged career. You know, I've been an actor, a publisher, a film-maker. But in none of these fields have I felt quite as much at home as in playwriting." (*NTQ*, 362) In India, unfortunately, the writers cannot live on their writingg alone; it does not yield enough royalties for sustenance. Says Karnad, "One can't earn a comfortable living even from a successful play. Take *Tughlaq*. As you know, it's been enormously successful—critically as well as in performance. Playwrights in the West have been able to retire on such successes—or at least, to devote themselves to that activity entirely. I can't." (*Ibid*)

Today Girish Karnad is considered one of the most significant Indian dramatists. He has enriched the Indian literary scene by his contribution to art, culture, theatre and drama. It is most befitting that Karnad has been conferred by the President of India, the prestigious awards, Padma Shri in 1974 and Padmabhushan in 1992. Also, he received the Gubbi Veeranna Award from the Government of Karnataka in 1997.

Karnad is based in Bangalore and lives with his wife, a medico, and his two children—a daughter and a son—both in their teens. He keeps shuttling between Bangalore, Bombay and Delhi as the three metropolitan cities abundantly offer him opportunities for creative writing, acting in films, and directing serials for national television.

Karnad is not impulsive by temperament, and does not resort to writing just at the flash of an idea. He follows a golden mean of thought and action when he launches on a new play. Commenting on the character of Horatio, Hamlet says that those persons are indeed blessed in whom "blood and judgement are so well commingled" that they are not treated by fortune as a musical instrument on which Fortune may play at will and from which Fortune may be able to produce whichever tune she wishes to produce. The classical qualities of balance and restraint are true of the person of Karnad too. He is a genius as a writer, man of excellent disposition. And one in whom all the four elements, to use a Renaissance analogy, are so well-mixed that Nature may stand up and say "Here's a man."

Bibliography

Crow, Brian and Chris Banfield. *Postcolonial Theatre*. Cambridge University Press, 1996.

Dharwadker, Aparna. "Historical Fictions and Postcolonial Representation: Reading Girish Karnad's *Tughlaq*," *PMLA*, 110:1, January 1995, pp. 43-58.

Karnad, Girish. Interview by Aparna Dharwadker. "Performance, Meaning and the Materials of Modern Indian Theatre." *New Theatre Quarterly*, Vol. XI, No. 44, November 1995, pp. 355-70.

________. "Acrobating between the Traditional and the Modern," *Indian Literature*, May-June 1989, pp. 85-99.

________. Introduction to *Three Plays*: *Hayavadana*, *Naga-Mandala*, *Tughlaq*. Pages 21-37 in this book.

Mullick, Ritu. "Karnad's Unrealised Dream," *Evening News*, Nov. 22, 1988.

Raju, Anand Kumar. "A Genius Born out of His Time?" *The Hindu*, Aug. 23, 1992.

Wasi, Jehanara. "A Dramatic Talent," *Economic Times*, July 3, 1988.

Introduction to *Three Plays*
Naga-Mandala, Hayavadana, Tughlaq

GIRISH KARNAD

My generation was the first to come of age after India became independent of British rule. It therefore had to face a situation in which tensions implicit until then had come out in the open and demanded to be resolved without apologia or self-justification: tensions between the cultural past of the country and its colonial past, between the attractions of Western modes of thought and our own traditions, and finally between the various visions of the future that opened up once the common cause of political freedom was achieved. This is the historical context that gave rise to my plays and those of my contemporaries.

In my childhood, in a small town in Karnataka, I was exposed to two theatre forms that seemed to represent irreconcilably different worlds. Father took the entire family to see plays staged by troupes of professional actors called *natak companies* which toured the countryside throughout the year. The plays were staged in semipermanent structures on proscenium stages, with wings and drop curtains, and were illuminated by petromax lamps.

Once the harvest was over, I went with the servants to sit up nights watching the more traditional *Yakshagana* performances. The stage, a platform with a back curtain, was erected in the open air and lit by torches.

By the time I was in my early teens, the *natak companies* had ceased to function and *Yakshagana* had begun to seem quaint, even silly, to me. Soon we moved to a big city. This city had a college and electricity, but no professional theatre.

I saw theatre again only when I went to Bombay for my postgraduate studies. One of the first things I did in Bombay was to go and see a play, which happened to be Strindberg's *Miss Julie* directed by the brilliant young Ebrahim Alkazi.

I have been told since then that it was one of Alkazi's less successful productions The papers tore it to shreds the next day. But when I walked out of the theatre that evening, I felt as though I had been put through an emotionally or even a physically painful rite of passage. I had read some Western playwrights in college, but nothing had prepared me for the power and violence I experienced that day. By the norms I had been brought up on, the very notion of laying bare the inner recesses of the human psyche like this for public consumption seemed obscene. What impressed me as much as the psychological cannibalism of the play was the way lights faded in and out on stage. Until we moved to the city, we had lived in houses lit by hurricane lamps. Even in the city, electricity was something we switched on and off. The realization that there were instruments called dimmers that could gently fade the lights in or out opened up a whole new world of magical possibilities.

Most of my contemporaries went through some similar experience at some point in their lives. We stepped out of mythological plays lit by torches or petromax lamps straight into Strindberg and dimmers. The new technology could not be divorced from the new psychology. The two together defined a stage that was like nothing we had known or suspected. I have often wondered whether it wasn't that evening that, without being actually aware of it, I decided I wanted to be a playwright.

At the end of my stay in Bombay, I received a scholarship to go abroad for further studies. It is difficult to describe to a modern Indian audience the traumas created by this event. Going abroad was a much rarer occurrence in those days; besides, I came from a large, close-knit family and was the first member of the family ever to go abroad. My parents were worried lest I decide to settle down outside India, and even for me, though there was no need for an immediate decision, the terrible choice was implicit in the very act of going away. Should I at the end of my studies return home for the sake of my family, my people and my country, even at the risk of my abilities and training not being fully utilized in what seemed a stifling, claustrophobic atmosphere, or should I rise above such parochial considerations and go where the world drew me?

While still preparing for the trip, amidst the intense emotional turmoil, I found myself writing a play. This took me by surprise, for I had fancied myself a poet, had written poetry through my teens, and had trained myself to write in English, in preparation for the conquest of the West. But here I was writing a play and in Kannada, too, the language spoken by a few million people in South India, the language of my childhood. A greater surprise was the theme of the play, for it was taken from ancient Indian mythology from which I had believed myself alienated.

The story of King Yayati that I used occurs in the *Mahabharata*. The king, for a moral transgression he has committed, is cursed to old age in the prime of life. Distraught at losing his youth, he approaches his son, pleading with him to lend him his youth in exchange for old age. The son accepts the exchange and the curse, and thus becomes old, older than his father.[1] But the old age brings no knowledge, no self-realization, only the senselessness of a punishment meted out for an act in which he had not even participated. The father is left to face the consequences of shirking responsibility for his own actions.

While I was writing the play, I saw it only as an escape from my stressful situation. But looking back, I am amazed at how precisely the myth reflected my anxieties at that moment, my resentment with all those who seemed to demand that I sacrifice my future. By the time I had finished working on *Yayati*—during the three weeks it took the ship to reach England and in the lonely cloisters of the university—the myth had enabled me to articulate to myself a set of values that I had been unable to arrive at rationally. Whether to return home finally seemed the most minor of issues: the myth had nailed me to my past.

Oddly enough the play owed its form not to the innumerable mythological plays I had been brought up on, and which had partly kept these myths alive for me, but to Western playwrights whom until then I had only read in print: Anouilh (his *Antigone* particularly) and also Sartre, O'Neill, and the Greeks. That is, at the most intense moment of self-expression, while my past had come to my aid with a ready-made narrative within which I could contain and explore my insecurities, there had been no dramatic structure in my own tradition to which I could relate myself.

One of the first plays of post-independence India to use myth to make a contemporary statement was Dharamvir Bharati's *Andha Yug* ('The Blind Age'). The play is about the aftermath of the Kurukshetra War, which forms the climax of the epic *Mahabharata*. The entire epic is in fact a build-up to this great confrontation between Good and Evil, in which God himself participated in the form of Lord Krishna. It was during this war that Krishna expounded the *Bhagavadgita*, a discourse on the ethics of action and knowledge that has exercised the most profound influence on Indian thought through the ages. Yet this fratricidal war left in its wake nothing but desolation and a sense of futility. No 'new world' emerged from the wholesale massacre of the youth of the country. Arjuna, the hero, became impotent. Lord Krishna himself meekly accepted a curse and died an absurd death. In his play, Bharati used the myth to give voice to the sense of horror and despair felt in India in the wake of the partition of the country and the communal bloodbaths that accompanied it.

Although later Satyadev Dubey's production proved that it was genuine theatre, *Andha Yug* was actually written for the radio, as a play for voices. It was as if, at the time of conceiving the play, the playwright could imagine no stage on which to place it.

Indeed this contradiction haunts most contemporary playwrighting and theatre in India. Even to arrive at the heart of one's own mythology, the writer has to follow signposts planted by the West, a paradoxical situation for a culture in which the earliest *extant* play was written in A.D. 200! The explanation lies in the fact that what is called 'modern Indian theatre' was started by a group of people who adopted 'cultural amnesia' as a deliberate strategy. It originated in the second half of the nineteenth century in three cities, Bombay, Calcutta and Madras. None of these seaports built by the British for their maritime trade had an Indian past of its own, a history independent of the British. These places had developed an Indian middle class that in all outward respects aspired to 'look' like its British counterpart. The social values of this class were shaped by the English education it had received and by the need to work with the British in trade and administration.

Inevitably the theatre it created imitated the British theatre of the times, as presented by visiting troupes from England. Several new concepts were introduced, two of which altered the nature of Indian theatre. One was the separation of the audience from the stage by the proscenium, underscoring the fact that what was being presented was a spectacle free of any ritualistic associations and which therefore expected no direct participation by the audience in it; and the other was the idea of pure entertainment, whose success would be measured entirely in terms of immediate financial returns and the run of the play.

Until the nineteenth century, the audience had never been expected to pay to see a show. Theatre had depended upon patronage—of kings, ministers, local feudatories, or temples. With the myth-based story line already familiar to the audience, the shape and success of a performance depended on how the actors improvised with the given narrative material each time they came on stage. Actors did not rehearse a play so much as train for particular kinds of roles, a system still followed today in folk and traditional theatre forms. The principle here is the same as in North Indian classical music, where the musician aims to reveal unexpected delights even within the strictly regulated contours of a raga, by continual improvisation. It is the variability, the unpredictable potential of each performance that is its attraction. The audience accepts the risk.

With the new theatre, in conformity with the prevailing laissez-faire philosophy, risk became the producer's responsibility, the factor determining the company's investment policy. The audience paid in cash to see a show guaranteed as a 'success' and in return received as much entertainment as could be competitively fitted within the price of a ticket. A performance became a carefully packaged commodity, to be sold in endless identical replications.[2]

The proscenium and the box office proclaimed a new philosophy of the theatre: secularism—but a commercially viable secularism.

The secularism was partly necessitated by the ethnic heterogeneity of the new entrepreneurial class. In Bombay, for instance, the enterprises were financed by the Parsis, who spoke Gujarati. But the commonly understood language was Urdu, popularized by the Muslim chieftains who had ruled over most of India since the sixteenth century. Naturally many of the writers employed by the Parsi theatre were Muslim. And the audience was largely Hindu!

The consequences of this secularism were that every character on stage, whether a Hindu deity or a Muslim legendary hero, was alienated from his true religious or cultural moorings; and myths and legends, emptied of meaning, were reshaped into tightly constructed melodramas with thundering curtain lines and a searing climax. Unlike traditional performances, which spread out in a slow leisurely fashion, these plays demanded total attention, but only at the level of plot. Incident was all. Even in *natak* companies run entirely by Hindus, the basic attitude was dictated by this Parsi model.

There was, however, a far more important reason for the superficiality of the fare. The audience that patronized the Parsi theatre professed values it made no effort to realize in ordinary life. Whereas in public it accepted the Western bourgeois notions of secularism, egalitarianism, and individual merit, at home it remained committed to the traditional loyalties of caste, family, and religion. Only a society honest enough to face squarely the implications of this division within itself could have produced meaningful drama out of it. But as the new bourgeoisie claimed to be ashamed of the domestic lifestyle to which it nevertheless adhered tenaciously, the theatre certainly would never be allowed to acknowledge and project these contradictions.

It is possible to argue, as Ashis Nandy has done, that this inner division was not psychologically harmful at all but was a deliberate strategy adopted by this class to ensure that its personality was not totally absorbed and thereby destroyed by the colonial culture. Whatever the case, the effect on drama was to render it sterile. Despite its enormous success as spectacle over nearly seventy years the Parsi theatre produced no drama of any consequence.

With the advent of 'talking' films in the 1930s the Parsi theatre collapsed without a fight. In the West, movies diminished the importance of theatre but did not destroy it. In India, professional theatre was virtually decimated by the film industry, which had learned most of its tricks from the theatre and could dish out the made-to-order entertainment on a scale much larger than the theatre could afford and at cheaper rates. India has not seen a professional theatre of the same proportions since.

In the process of settling down, the Parsi theatre had absorbed several features of traditional or folk performing arts, such as music, mime, and comic interludes. In Maharashtra, for instance, where this theatre flourished and continues to survive, its greatest contribution was in the field of music, in the form of a rich and varied body of theatre songs. However, to my generation of playwrights, reacting against memories of the Parsi stage in its decadence, music and dance seemed irrelevant to genuine drama. The only legacy left to us then was a lumbering, antiquated style of staging.

Yet there was no other urban tradition to look to, and in my second play, having concluded that Anouilh and Co. were not enough, I tried to make use of the Parsi stagecraft. This time the play was historical and therefore, perhaps inevitably, had a Muslim subject.

(I say inevitably, for the Hindus have almost no tradition of history: the Hindu mind, with its belief in the cycle of births and deaths, has found little reason to chronicle or glamorize any particular historical period. Still, independence had made history suddenly important to us; we were acutely conscious of living in a historically important era. Indian history as written by the British was automatically suspect. The Marxist approach offered a more attractive alternative but in fact seemed unable to come to terms with Indian realities. Even today Marxist ideologues are lost when confronted with native categories like caste. It was the Muslims who first introduced history as a positive concept in Indian thought, and the only genuinely Indian methodology available to us for analyzing history was that developed by the Muslim historians in India.)

My subject was the life of Muhammad Tughlaq, a fourteenth century sultan of Delhi, certainly the most brilliant individual ever to ascend the throne of Delhi and also one of the biggest failures. After a reign distinguished for policies that today seem far-sighted to the point of genius, but which in their day earned him the title 'Muhammad the Mad,' the sultan ended his career in bloodshed and political chaos. In a sense, the play reflected the slow disillusionment my generation felt with the new politics of independent India: the gradual erosion of the ethical norms that had guided the movement for independence, and the coming to terms with cynicism and realpolitik.

The stagecraft of the Parsi model demanded a mechanical succession of alternating *shallow* and *deep* scenes. The shallow scenes were played in the foreground of the stage with a painted curtain—normally depicting a street—as the backdrop. These scenes were reserved for the 'lower class' characters with prominence given to comedy. They served as *link* scenes in the development of the plot, but the main purpose was to keep the audience engaged while the deep scenes, which showed interiors of palaces, royal parks, and other such visually opulent sets, were being changed or decorated. The important characters rarely appeared in the street scenes, and in the deep scenes the lower classes strictly kept their place.

The spatial division was ideal to show the gulf between the rulers and the ruled, between the mysterious inner chambers of power politics and the open, public areas of those affected by it. But as I wrote *Tughlaq*, I found it increasingly difficult to maintain the accepted balance between these two regions. Writing in an unprecedented situation where the mass populace was exercising political franchise, in however clumsy a fashion, for the first time in its history I found the shallow scenes bulging with an energy hard to control. The regions ultimately developed their own logic. The deep scenes became emptier as the play progressed, and in the last scene, the 'comic lead' did the unconventional—he appeared in the deep scene, on a par with the protagonist himself. This violation of traditionally sacred spatial hierarchy, I decided—since there was little I could do about it—was the result of the anarchy which climaxed Tughlaq's times and seemed poised to engulf my own.

(An aside: whatever the fond theories of their creators, plays often develop their own independent existence. In his brilliant production of *Tughlaq*, E. Alkazi ignored my half-hearted tribute to the Parsi theatre and placed the action on the ramparts of the Old Fort at Delhi; and it worked very well.)

Another school of drama had arisen in the 1930s, at the height of the struggle for national independence. When social reform was acknowledged as a goal next only to independence in importance, a group of 'realistic' playwrights had challenged the emptiness and vapidity of Parsi drama. The contemporary concerns of these playwrights gave their work an immediacy and a sharp edge lacking in the earlier theatre, and a few plays of great power were written. While trying to awaken their audience to the humiliation of political enslavement, many of these new playwrights made a coruscating analysis of the ills that had eaten into Indian society. This was essentially the playwright's theatre; the plays were presented by amateur or semiprofessional groups and were mostly directed by the playwrights themselves. Unlike in the Parsi theatre, where a hard-headed financial logic was the guide, here the writers, the actors, and the audience were all united by a genuine idealism. They created a movement, if not a theatre, for the times.

Although its form aimed at being realistic, it must be pointed out at once that this drama concentrated on only a small corner of the vast canvas explored by Western realistic theatre.

The door banged by Nora in *The Doll's House* did not merely announce feminist rebellion against social slavery. It summed up what was to be the main theme of Western realistic drama over the next hundred years: a person's need to be seen as an individual, as an entity valuable in itself, independent of family and social circumstance. Indian realism, however, could not progress beyond analyses of social problems, for in India, despite the large urban population, there really has never been a bourgeoisie with its faith in individualism as the ultimate value. 'Westernization' notwithstanding, Indians define themselves in terms of their relationships to the other members of their family, caste, or class. They are defined by the role they have to play. In Sudhir Kakar's words, they see themselves in 'relational' terms in their social context, and they naturally extend the same references to theatre as well.

Let me give an example. A few years ago Arthur Miller's *A View from the Bridge* was presented in Madras. Eddie Carbone, the play's protagonist, is an Italian dock worker. He is a good man, but tragedy is brought about by his incestuous passion for his orphaned niece. He harbours two young, illegal Italian immigrants in his house, one of whom falls in love with the niece. Consumed by jealousy, Eddie breaks his code of honour, betrays the immigrants to the authorities, and is killed by one of them.

The audience watching the play in Madras was English educated, familiar with Western literature. Many of them frequently were abroad and had a living contact with the Western way of life. The production was a success. But most of the audience entirely missed the element of incest in the play; rather, they chose to ignore it as an unnecessary adjunct to an otherwise perfectly rational tale. After all, Eddie was his niece's guardian, a surrogate father. It was only right that he should be interested in her welfare. You certainly could not blame him for trying to safeguard her future. On the contrary, the illegal immigrants emerged as unsympathetic, for they had betrayed their host's confidence by seducing the niece's affections.

Even apart from consideration of social roles that led the Madras audience to write its own *A View from the Bridge*, Eddie Carbone perfectly fits an Indian archetype: the father figure aggressing toward its offspring. Our mythology is replete with parental figures demanding sacrifices from their children—as in my own *Yayati*—Eddie's position was not one in which the Indian audience was likely to find any tragic flaw.

To get back to realistic theatre, its great improvement over the Parsi theatre was that it took itself seriously both as art and as an instrument of social change. Yet it remained saddled with the European model. Bernard Shaw was its presiding deity. The proscenium continued, only now the grand spectacles gave way to the *interior set* with the invisible fourth wall. And that three-walled living room succinctly defined the basic limitation of this school of writing.

From Ibsen to Albee, the living room has symbolized all that is valuable to the Western bourgeoisie. It is one's refuge from the sociopolitical forces raging in the world outside, as well as the battleground where values essential to one's individuality are fought out and defended. But nothing of consequence ever happens or is supposed to happen in an Indian living room! It is the no-man's-land, the empty, almost defensive front the family presents to the world outside.

Space in a traditional home is ordered according to the caste hierarchy as well as the hierarchies within the family. Whether a person is permitted inside the compound, allowed as far as the outer verandah, or admitted into the living room depends on his or her caste and social status. And it is in the interior of the house, in the kitchen, in the room where the gods are kept, or in the backyard, where family problems are tackled, or allowed to fester, and where the women can have a say. Thus the living room as the location of dramatic action made nonsense of the very social problems the playwright set out to analyze, by distorting the caste dimensions as well as the position of women in the family.

How could these playwrights have so misunderstood the geography of their own homes? The three-walled living room was a symptom of a much more serious malaise: the conceptual tools they were using to analyze India's problems were as secondhand and unrealistic as the European parlour. The writers were young, angry, and in a hurry. The concepts defined for them by their English educators were new and refreshing and seemed rational. If the tools didn't quite fit the shifting ambiguities of social life, reality could be adjusted to fit these attractive imports. It may also be said that the refusal to go beyond the living room exactly mirrored the reluctance of these Westernized, upper-caste writers to go to the heart of the issues they were presenting.

To my generation, a hundred crowded years of urban theatre seemed to have left almost nothing to hang on to, to take off from. And where was one to begin again? Perhaps by looking at our audience again, by trying to understand what experience this audience expected to receive from theatre? This at least partly meant looking again at the traditional forms that had been sidelined by the Parsi theatre. The attempt, let me hasten to add, was not to find and reuse forms that had worked successfully in some other cultural context.

The hope, rather, was to discover whether there was a structure of expectations and conventions about entertainment underlying these forms from which one could learn.

The most obvious starting point should have been the Sanskrit theatre. *Sakuntala* and *Mrcchakatika*, two Sanskrit masterpieces, had been presented successfully on the Marathi stage in the early part of this century. Recently, Ratan Thiyam, K.N. Panicker, and Vijaya Mehta have brought Sanskrit plays alive again for today's audience. But no modern playwright has claimed, or shown in his work, any allegiance to Sanskrit sensibility. Sanskrit drama assumed a specific social setting, a steady, well-ordered universe in which everyone from the gods to the meanest mortals was in his or her allotted slot. Even in its heyday it was an elitist phenomenon, confined to a restricted group of wealthy and educated courtiers, remote from the general populace.

Along with this court theatre there had existed other, more popular forms—more flexible, varying in their emphasis on formal purity. The exact relationship between Sanskrit theatre and these popular forms is of course difficult to determine. Sanskrit was not a language spoken in the homes; it was the language of courtly, literary, and philosophical discourse. The popular forms, on the other hand, used the natural languages of the people. Further, most of these languages came into their own as vehicles for artistic expression only about A.D. 1000, by which time Sanskrit literature particularly drama—was already moribund. Even the aesthetics of these two theatre traditions differed. Sanskrit drama underplayed action and emphasized mood. It avoided scenes that unduly excited the audience. The popular forms wallowed in battles and hard-won marriages, blood and thunder. The biggest hurdle from our perspective is that unlike in Sanskrit, in which plays were written as independent works of art, this class of performing arts eschewed written texts and depended on improvisation within limits prescribed by their separate conventions, making it difficult to trace their historical growth. But in India, as has often been pointed out, the past is never totally lost; it coexists with the present as a parallel flow. A rich variety of regional theatre forms still exists, with a continuous history stretching over centuries, though through these centuries they have undoubtedly undergone changes and even mutilations.

For the first two decades after independence, how traditional forms could be utilized to revitalize our own work in the urban context was a ceaseless topic of argument among theatre people. The poet Vallathol had given a new identity to *Kathakali*, Shivaram Karanth a new lease of life to *Yakshagana*. Habib Tanvir has gone to areas in which the traditional troupes operate, taking with him his urban discipline. He has taught, lived, worked, and toured with the local troupes and evolved through them a work that is rich, vital, and meaningful.

But what were we, basically city-dwellers, to do with this stream? What did the entire paraphernalia of theatrical devices, half-curtains, masks, improvisation, music, and mime mean?

I remember that the idea of my play *Hayavadana* started crystallizing in my head right in the middle of an argument with B.V. Karanth (who ultimately produced the play) about the meaning of masks in Indian theatre and theatre's relationship to music. The play is based on a story from a collection of tales called the *Kathasaritsagara* and the further development of this story by Thomas Mann in "The Transposed Heads."

A young woman is travelling with her insecure and jealous husband and his rather attractive friend. The husband, suspecting his wife's loyalties, goes to a temple of Goddess Kali and beheads himself. The friend finds the body and, terrified that he will be accused of having murdered the man for the sake of his wife, in turn beheads himself. When the woman, afraid of the scandal that is bound to follow, prepares to kill herself too, the goddess takes pity and comes to her aid. The woman has only to rejoin the heads to the bodies and the goddess will bring them back to life. The woman follows the instructions, the men come back to life except that in her confusion she has mixed up the heads. The story ends with the question: who is now the real husband, the one with the husband's head or the one with his body?

The answer given in the *Kathasaritsagara* is: since the head represents the man, the person with the husband's head is the husband.

Mann brings his relentless logic to bear upon this solution. If the head is the determining limb, then the body should change to fit the head. At the end of Mann's version, the bodies have changed again and adjusted themselves to the heads so perfectly that the men are physically exactly as they were at the beginning. We are back to square one—the problem remains unsolved.

As I said, the story initially interested me for the scope it gave for the use of masks and music. Western theatre has developed a contrast between the *face* and the *mask*—the real inner person and the exterior one presents, or wishes to present, to the world outside. But in traditional Indian theatre, the mask is only the face 'writ large'; since a character represents not a complex psychological entity but an ethical archetype, the mask merely presents in enlarged detail its essential moral nature. (This is why characters in *Hayavadana* have no real names. The heroine is called Padmini after one of the six types into which Vatsyayana classified all women. Her husband is Devadatta, a formal mode of addressing a stranger. His friend is Kapila, simply 'the dark one.') Music—usually percussion—then further distances the action, placing it in the realm of the mythical and the elemental.

The decision to use masks led me to question the theme itself in greater depth. All theatrical performances in India begin with worship of Ganesha, the god who ensures successful completion of any endeavour. According to mythology, Ganesha was beheaded by Shiva, his father, who had failed to recognize his own son (another aggressive father!). The damage was repaired by substituting an elephant's head, since the original head could not be found. Ganesha is often represented onstage by a young boy wearing the elephant mask, who then is worshipped as the incarnation of the god himself.

Ganesha's mask then says nothing about his nature. It is a mask, pure and simple. Right at the start of the play, my theory about masks was getting subverted. But the elephant head also questioned the basic assumption behind the original riddle: that the head represents the thinking part of the person, the intellect.

It seemed unfair, however, to challenge the thesis of the riddle by using a god. God, after all, is beyond human logic, indeed beyond human comprehension itself. The dialectic had to grow out of grosser ground, and I sensed a third being hovering in the spaces between the divine and the human, a horse-headed man. The play *Hayavadana*, meaning 'the one with a horse's head,' is named after this character. The story of this horse-headed man, who wants to shed the horse's head and become human, provides the outer panel—as in a mural—within which the tale of the two friends is framed. Hayavadana, too, goes to the same Goddess Kali and wins a boon from her that he should become complete. Logic takes over. The head is the person: Hayavadana becomes a complete horse. The central logic of the tale remains intact, while its basic premise is denied.

The energy of folk theatre comes from the fact that although it seems to uphold traditional values, it also has the means of questioning these values, of making them literally stand on their head. The various conventions—the chorus, the masks, the seemingly unrelated comic episodes, the mixing of human and nonhuman worlds—permit the simultaneous presentation of alternative points of view, of alternative attitudes to the central problem. To use a phrase from Bertolt Brecht, these conventions then allow for 'complex seeing.' And it must be admitted that Brecht's influence received mainly through his writings and without the benefit of his theatrical productions, went some way in making us realize what could be done with the design of traditional theatre. The theatrical conventions Brecht was reacting against—character as a psychological construct providing a focus for emotional identification, the willing-suspension-of-disbelief syndrome, the notion of a unified spectacle—were never a part of the traditional Indian theatre. There was therefore no question of arriving at an 'alienation' effect by using Brechtian artifice. What he did was to sensitize us to the potentialities of nonnaturalistic techniques available in our own theatre.

How invigorating this legacy of traditional theatre has proved for Indian theatre can be illustrated by two other plays, which appeared soon after *Hayavadana.* In his *Ghasiram Kotwal*, Tendulkar uses *Dashavatara*, a traditional semiclassical form, to investigate a contemporary political problem, the emergence of 'demons' in public. These demons are initially created by political leaders for the purposes of their own power games, but ultimately go out of control and threaten to destroy their own creators. It is a theme recurrent in Indian mythology: the demon made indestructible by the boon of gods and then turning on the gods themselves. (A decade after the play was written, in Punjab, Sant Bhindranwale and Mrs. Indira Gandhi seemed to be re-enacting the theme in real life in horrifying detail.)

The central theatrical device in the play is the use of about a dozen singers who start conventionally enough as a chorus. But as the play progresses, they become the human curtain alternately hiding the action and revealing bits of it as in a peep show. From neutral commentators, they slide into the roles of voyeurs who enjoy the degeneration they condemn, of courtiers who perpetrate atrocities, and of the populace that suffers the harassment. In the final scene the demon is ritually destroyed, torn limb from limb; the city is exorcised, and the now-purified stage is filled with revellers led by the politician who initially created the demon.

In Jabbar Patel's production, music and dance become the instruments of comment and analysis. Ritualistic movements turn imperceptibly into an orgy or a political procession; the music by Bhaskar Chandavarkar, based on traditional devotional tunes, continually turns upon itself, sometimes indulgently, sometimes critically. Unexpected breaks jangle the nerves of the audience. There is no explicit political analysis, but the matrix of the myth and the ironic use of *Dashavatara* drive the point home.

Unlike most Indian playwrights writing today, Chandrasekhar Kambar does not come from an urban background. As he was born and brought up in the country, there is no self-consciousness in his use of *Bayalata*, a secular folk form of his region. He draws upon the rich resources of popular speech and folklore with an effortlessness that conceals a rare sophistication of sensibility and technique. He is a poet at ease with the ballad, and his approach to poetry on stage is through the ballad rather than the lyric; the imagery is the action, the metaphors serve to resonate the narrative at different levels of meaning.

Jokumaraswamy starts with a fertility rite in honor of the phallic deity Jokumara, who is worshipped in the form of a snake gourd and then consumed by those desirous of bearing children. The basic situations as well as the music are all traditional, in the sense that they are set pieces, familiar in *Bayalata* drama. The impotent chieftain's virgin wife feeds the snake gourd by mistake to the village rake and has a child by him. The rake's death at the hands of the chieftain's men is a kind of gang rape-cum-fertility offering. The chieftain himself is literally left holding a baby he cannot disown.

Through this semicomic tale, Kambar makes a very Brechtian statement about the right of the peasants to the land on which they work virtually as series for an absentee landlord. But the analysis goes beyond this rather obvious political manifesto to a complex exploration in action of political power as a compensation for sexual inadequacy, of philandering as a psychosexual equivalent of anarchism, which can be controlled by love and responsibility. By working out the psychological, social, and political implications of the concept of virility, the play brings out the ambiguous nature of the very fertility rite it had set out to celebrate.

It must be admitted that the popularity of traditional forms on the urban stage has much to do with the technical freedom they offer the director. Music, mime, and exotic imagery open up vast opportunities for colorful improvisation, which nevertheless can—and alas! all too often does—degenerate into self-indulgence. While there are productions today which combine traditional theatre techniques with modern choreography and visual design to an effect unimaginable in the '60s, most such efforts tend to be imitative and soul-less. It is as though now that the problem has found a technical solution, the spirit of the quest has been lost.

Naga-Mandala is based on two oral tales I heard from A. Ramanujan. These tales are narrated by women—normally the older women in the family—while children are being fed in the evenings in the kitchen or being put to bed. The other adults present on these occasions are also women. Therefore these tales, though directed at the children, often serve as a parallel system of communication among the women in the family.

They also express a distinctly woman's understanding of the reality around her, a lived counterpoint to the patriarchal structures of classical texts and institutions. The position of Rani in the story of *Naga-Mandala*, for instance, can be seen as a metaphor for the situation of a young girl in the bosom of a joint family where she sees her husband only in two unconnected roles—as a stranger during the day and as lover at night. Inevitably, the pattern of relationships she is forced to weave from these disjointed encounters must be something of a fiction. The empty house Rani is locked in could be the family she is married into.

Many of these tales also talk about the nature of tales. The story of the flames comments on the paradoxical nature of oral tales in general: they have an existence of their own, independent of the teller and yet live only when they are passed on from the possessor of the tale to the listener. Seen thus, the status of a tale becomes akin to that of a daughter, for traditionally a daughter too is not meant to be kept at home too long but has to be passed on. This identity adds poignant and ironic undertones to the relationship of the teller to the tales.

It needs to be stressed here that these tales are not left-overs from the past. In the words of Ramanujan, 'Even in a large modern city like Madras, Bombay or Calcutta, even in western-style nuclear families with their well-planned 2.2 children, folklore . . . is only a suburb away, a cousin or a grandmother away.'[3]

The basic concern of the Indian theatre in the post-independence period has been to try to define its 'Indianness.' The distressing fact is that most of these experiments have been carried out by enthusiastic amateurs or part-timers, who have been unable to devote themselves entirely to theatre. I see myself as a playwright but make a living in film and television. There is a high elasticity of substitution between the different performing media in India; the participants—as well as the audiences—get tossed about.

The question therefore of what lies in store for the Indian theatre should be rephrased to include other media as well—radio, cinema, audio cassettes, television and video. Their futures are inextricably intertwined and in this shifting landscape, the next electronic gadget could easily turn a mass medium into a traditional art form.

Perhaps quite unrealistically, I dream of the day when a similar ripple will reestablish theatre—flesh-and-blood actors enacting a well-written text to a gathering of people who have come to witness the performance—where it belongs, at the centre of the daily life of the people.

NOTES

1. In the *Mahabharata*, King Yayati has five sons; after the elder four refuse their father, the youngest yields to his entreaties.
2. Interestingly, although in Bombay ticketing of shows was the logical result of bringing theatre within the free market economy, in Bengal, where the Anglophile landed gentry had immediately made theatre their exclusive privilege, ticketing was the means by which this privilege was attacked and the form made accessible to the middle class.
3. A.K. Ramanujan, "Introduction," *Folktales fiom India* (New Delhi: Viking, 1993), p. xiii. A.K. Ramanujan, "Two Realms of Kannada Folklore," Stuart H. Blackburn and A.K. Ramanujan, ed., *Another Harmony* (Berkeley: University of California Press, 1987). A.K. Ramanujan, 'Telling Tales,' *Daedalus*, Fall, 1989.

This is a considerably revised and expanded version of the author's paper, "In Search of a New Theatre," in Carla M. Sorden, ed., *Contemporary India* (Delhi: OUP, 1989). Published as "Author's Introduction" in Girish Karnad, *Three Plays* (Delhi: OUP, 1994). Reprinted here with his kind permission.

Experiment and Innovation in Modern Indian Drama: The Plays of Mohan Rakesh, Badal Sircar, Vijay Tendulkar and Girish Karnad

VEENA NOBLE DASS

Modern Indian drama reveals two main tendencies, both natural to a historical development. One is, Indian playwrights have gone back to tradition for their themes and techniques and the other is, making use of what are considered modern trends in the theatre. These two tendencies are specially seen in theatrical events in the 1960s and 1970s which led to an unconscious awareness of the oneness or "Indianness" of Indian theatre, though such terms as Hindi theatre, Bengali theatre, Marathi theatre or Kannada theatre are still used.

Plays written in various Indian languages are being translated into English and other languages as they are produced and appreciated in the various parts of the country. A closer contact is being established between the theatre workers from different regions and languages through these translations.

Thus regional drama in India is slowly paving a way for a "national theatre" into which all streams of theatrical art seem to converge. The major language theatres that are active all through the turbulent years of rejuvenation and consolidations are those of Hindi, Bengali, Marathi and Kannada. Not that there are less number of great dramatists in other areas, or less important dramatic activity in other languages, but these four have initiated in the fifties and sixties, a new experimental theatre which has cross-cultural manifestations. They also paved the way for the emergence of important writers in these four major languages.

A brief study of a few of these, namely Mohan Rakesh, Vijay

Tendulkar, Badal Sircar and Girish Karnad, shows clearly that they are the children of the new resurgence in their own areas and have established that, by translating and performing the translated plays in other language areas than their own, they are marching towards the possibility of building a national theatre movement. Hence a study of these four representative writers becomes inevitable to students of culture in general and students of drama in particular, if they want to know how the contemporary Indian drama has made bold innovations and fruitful experiments which go in the history of Indian drama as a significant mark of achievement.

Mohan Rakesh was one of those rare literary personalities who never accept the traditional set up but always aspire to find and project something which is challenging and new. Rakesh's language separates him from other Hindi playwrights and puts him on a higher level of competence. His plays—*Ashadh Ka Ek Din* (One Day in Ashadha), *Lehron Ke Rajhans*[1] (Great Swans of the Waves), *Adhe-Adhure*[2] (Half-Way House)—show that his dialogues have a smooth flow, a meaningful depth and an elemental naturalness suitable to his characters. They express the characters's mental conflict, frustration, dissatisfaction and the resulting anger in a unique manner. Though some of the dialogues between Mallika and Kalidasa in *One Day in Ashadha* tend to be longer than required and seem to be a little heavy on the audience, they are necessary to the play. As Kalidasa says in the play, "people think that living in that life and atmosphere I have written a great deal. But I know that while living there I wrote nothing. Whatever I wrote was a recollection of life here."[3] This lengthy dialogue is necessary for the reader to understand the feelings and moods of the characters. But Rakesh became conscious of this and made an effort to reduce the length of the dialogues in his other plays namely *The Great Swans of the Waves* and *Half-Way House*. Though in the former play, the dialogues between Nand and Sundari tend to become longer, in *Half-Way House* the playwright seems to be completely in control of the situation. Here the dialogues are short, suitable and to the point. They hit at the subject immediately. It cannot be denied that Rakesh contributed much to the enrichment of the language.

One aspect of his plays is that he pays much attention to the internal conflict in the minds of his characters. He has made an effort to come to grips with the problem of man-woman relationship. The irony and tragedy of this problem on different levels has been treated in his plays. Nand, Kalidasa, Man I in *One Day in Ashadha, Great Swans of the Waves* and *Half-Way House* run away from Sundari, Mallika and Savitri respectively. But do they succeed in doing so? Neglected by man and left alone are Mallika, Sundari and Savitri, but are they able to face the new situation? These are the problems that Mohan Rakesh tackled in his plays. The depiction of the complexity of the human heart, man's helplessness and the chains of relationship attract the audience and keep them enthralled.

Rakesh's technique of taking support from historical themes and then throwing light on the realities of life is quite his own. He has explained the dilemma of this problem by saying that to some people the word "contemporary" has meaning only in terms of consciousness. But he really was not aware of having written anything that is not contemporary because history as such has fascinated him much for creative interpretation. Therefore this technique would be understood only by those who knew that in the context of creative writing the meaning of the word "contemporary" is not the same as in journalism.

It may however be argued as to why a writer should choose the historical or semi-historical background for interpreting contemporary life. To this, Rakesh replies: "I know the force of this argument and can only say that I have no prejudice in the matter. I do mean to write plays with a contemporary background, but the point I wish to emphasize is that background itself is no criterion."[4]

While Rakesh uses historical characters to project the breakdown of communication, Badal Sircar, the great Bengali playwright, uses contemporary situations and social problems to project the life-in-death attitude of modern life. The central theme of many of his early plays is a sense of utter meaninglessness in our existence which leads to a state of metaphysical anguish.

This anguish is in fact closely embedded in the Bengali middle-class psyche, the tearing up of which was Sircar's constant concern since his early theatre career. It is an irony that early Bengali drama of the mid-nineteenth century has strong social moorings, but could not lead the middle-class man towards a self awareness. The drama of 1880s bears testimony to this attitude of the middle-classes towards social responsibility.

Sircar's early plays *Evam Indrajit*[5] (And Indrajit), *Baki Itihas*[6] (The Other Side of History) and *Sheish Nei*[7] (There is No End) are based on political, social and psychological problems. *Evam Indra-*

jit is about the residue of the middle class who have failed to adjust, align and cease to aspire among the intellectually alive urban middle-class.

Evam Indrajit was not the only play written by Sircar when he was away from India. A particularly prolific period in his playwriting career occurred between 1966 and 1967 when he wrote six plays while working as a town-planner in Nigeria. Three of these plays are *Bagh* (Tiger), *Jadi Aur Ekbar* (If there were other Chances) and *Pralap*[8] (Mad Speech). Though these plays are not inconsequential, they are far from what Sircar believes is his central concern as a playwright, nothing less exciting than "the responsibility of mankind for the events of our times."[9] The horror of Hiroshima, in particular, obsessed Sircar in two of his plays—*The Other Side of History* and *There is No End.*

These plays are not only stylistically similar but have a thematic continuity. The framework within which this act of synthesis is made possible is a strong sense of the frustration of the intellectual aspiration, the failure to get involved and the resultant feeling of guilt. The self-surging of the heroes might often provoke discomfort among the readers or the audience. But it is more the chill of being forced to look at something asked, in which they often discover themselves than any strong feeling of embarrassment.

The plays after all the ruthless exposure of responsibility for guilt in personal and social relations end with feeble apologies for a continuation of the conventional mode of living. Perhaps Sircar wants to leave his heroes to suffer from the awareness of the responsibility. He seems to prefer a sort of self-flagellation to any positive action. A life-long nagging reminder of guilt can be the only consolation for the Indrajits, Sharadindus and Sumantas, who are too sensitive and individualistic to choose any path of action to put an end to Hiroshimas.

These questions, which are difficult to answer, Sircar continues to grapple with in his exploration of the *Third Theatre*.[10] The Third Theatre is an outcome of his interest in involving himself in theatre. Not satisfied with being a playwright, Sircar wanted to do "theatre." He was at this time influenced by his tours to the U.S.A. and Czechoslovakia. Sircar's "Satabdi" was the first group in the Bengali theatre that recognized the validity of a "poor" theatre. Grotowski's concept of the need to renounce all outward technique and concentrate on analyzing the closeness of the living organism struck a synonymous chord in Sircar's imagination. His theatre gradually minimized its use of sets, costumes, background, music, tape recorders and projectors. The body of the actor and its relation to the space on stage were Sircar's most immediate concern as a director. Sircar also attempted to break down barriers in theatrical time and space by emphasizing the simultaneous action of his play and its non-sequential mode of narration.

Along with *Spartacus*, Sircar's later plays *Micchil* (Procession), *Bhoma* and *Basi Khabar* (Stale News) are based on the concepts of Third Theatre. *Procession* is one of Sircar's most intricately structured plays with innumerable transactions and juxtapositions. The relentless flow of events in the text is most skilfully concretized in the choreographic movement of the scenes. The actors are constantly on the move, walking, running, dancing and jogging through the room. The benches in the room are placed in such a way that the spectators feel that they are part of a maze. Sircar creates a most bewildering environment with the bodies, backs, faces and profiles of the spectators. When the actors begin to move between and around the environment created by the spectators, the effect is startling. One can almost see a procession winding its way around the streets in Calcutta.

These plays of Sircar have placed him on a pedestal higher than other contemporary playwrights of Indian drama. His time of entry into Indian drama was very appropriate. Perhaps he made the final breakthrough when a considerable amount of modernity had already been ushered in and the new directors who responded so happily to him had already achieved an identity.

In his first three plays the protagonists are writers, searching for poets to write their stories. This is Sircar's own search for plots to write his plays. But the characters in his later plays which were written after he formulated his Third Theatre are not individualized at all. They can be seen as what Sircar himself has said, "I can be taken as a prototype of a particular class in a society at a particular period."[13] The spectator assumes a protagonist's role in the theatre of Sircar, making the theatrical incident experimental, indeterminative and open-ended.

There are three strands in Badal Sircar's life which mesh well to give a striking texture to his work and introduce a new value to Indian theatre. These strands are his professional career as an urban planner, plus his training as a civil engineer, his inner life as a playwright and its outward expression in his role as a theatre director and actor. More than writing, Sircar prefers doing theatre. This he wants to accomplish by what he said "trekking to the villages and rural areas"[14] in the near future. Sircar wants to go from village to village even to the remotest of them and do theatre and at the same time involve the people. If there is any playwright in the contemporary Bengali theatre who is capable of creating a genuine people's theatre, a theatre supported and created by the people and not merely performed by the people, it is Badal Sircar.

While Badal Sircar makes the society, specially the middle-class, feel guilty for being indifferent towards man and his problems, Vijay Tendulkar, the avant-garde Marathi playwright, harps upon the theme of isolation of the individual and his confrontation with the hostile surroundings. Both these playwrights express their anguish at the prevailing social condition and the role man has to play in these conditions.

Tendulkar stands on a different pedestal from that of the other contemporary Marathi playwrights because of his innovations of style in presenting a large variety of themes. Most of Tendulkar's full-length plays which concentrate on the travails of the little man essay a more or less conventional dramatic form. The plays *Shantata Court Chaloo Aahe*[15] (Silence! The Court is in Session), *Giddh*[16] (Vultures), *Sakharam Binder*[17] and *Ghasiram Kotwal,*[18] which made Tendulkar a popular playwright, are experiments of an intense and deeper impulse and not just a matter of superficial innovation. A kind of new freedom and conviction is seen in these plays. The phrase "sex and violence" is very loosely attributed to in the discussion of these plays. But in none of these, the theme of sex and violence is superficial, as it forms an important part of the content of the plays. These four plays are considered as representative plays of the Marathi theatre of cruelty. Many of Tendulkar's plays show his concern for modern man's anguish. That these plays, so different in content and form, point towards an important human predicament is itself a tribute to the questioning, probing spirit of Tendulkar. The controversies that arose after the performance of many of his plays is a clear proof of his unconventional attitude towards human problems. The theme of violence pervades quite blatantly in most of his plays. Tendulkar was influenced by Artaud's idea of relating the theme of anguish to the theme of violence.

When he was awarded a fellowship by Nehru Memorial Fund

Committee, Tendulkar elaborated the theory of violence in his project "Emerging Pattern of Violence," structuring his theory on the concept of the theatre of cruelty. He does not consider the occurrence of human violence as something loathsome or ugly as it is innate in human nature.

Ever since he wrote *Silence! The Court is in Session*, Tendulkar has discovered that violence makes man fascinating and there are many variations in the way violence manifests itself in the way man expresses it. Its various manifestations and how they are moulded by each person are important for a study of human nature. He believes that violence is a basic quality.[19] When this understanding of human nature is translated into a play, it not only becomes an explosive piece of art but a thesis. Tendulkar unabashedly presents and defends it. According to him the most important point is to keep the violence raw while depicting it on stage, not to dress it up with any fancy trapping and not to make it palatable.

Unlike Badal Sircar and Vijay Tendulkar who delved into the problems of the middle-class man, Girish Karnad, the noted Kannada playwright, went back to myths and legends and made them a vehicle of a new vision. By using these myths, he tried to show the absurdity of life with all its elemental passions and conflicts and man's eternal struggle to achieve perfection.

Karnad has won an All-India recognition with his plays *Yayati,*[20] *Tughlaq,*[21] *Atte Ka Kukkut*[22] (The Dough Cock) and *Hayavadana.*[23] He has been in the west and has been attracted by the drama of Giradoux, Anouilh, Camus and Sartre in his search for new forms of drama. Yet he is essentially in the Kannada tradition. His reworking of myths, Puranic, historical and literary, relates him to Kailasam and Rangacharya as much as it does to those European dramatists who remake their myths.

Karnad in his plays tries to evolve a symbolic form out of a tension between the archetypal and mythic experience and a living response to life and its values. Contemporaneity in Karnad's plays manifests itself through his operative sensibility in his attempt to give new meaning to the past from the vantage point of the present.

Karnad does not take the myths in their entirety. He takes only parts of them that are useful to him and the rest he supplements with his imagination to make his plots clear. Thus in *Yayati* he has taken the myth partially. The characters in *Tughlaq* particularly Barani, Najib, Aziz and the stepmother are seen in a new context. In

Hayavadana the discussion between Devadatta and Kapila is at variance with the myth. Karnad has read extensively Shakespeare, Brecht, Anouilh, Camus, Sartre and to a considerable extent, Pinter, and is influenced by them. Structurally, the plays offer interesting studies. *Yayati* is the best in this respect. Every character is fully realized and has a clear solidity. This cannot be said of all the characters in *Tughlaq*. Except for Tughlaq and Aziz there is hardly any character that is growing. *Yayati* takes place between sunset and sunrise. Tughlaq is in the epic scenes and takes place in a period of five years or more. *Hayavadana* takes place in several years.

There is one drawback in Karnad's characters. All of them are intelligent. There is hardly any who is less than intelligent. Aziz and Tughlaq appear as one. There is nothing that really makes them what they are individually. Individuality is missing. This defect is seen in Devadatta and Kapila also. They lack an individuality that is theatrically essential to their characters holding sustained interest. We see them as chess pieces moved to definite purposes by the playwright.

Karnad remains the most important dramatist of the contemporary Kannada stage. He has given the Kannada Theatre a richness that could probably be equated only with his talents as an actor-director. He has shown the Indian stage as to what depths the mythical themes could be taken to in order to recreate a contemporary consciousness. Karnad's advantages are many—his expert knowledge of contemporary European theatre, his exposure to the Western dramatic literature and more importantly his theatrical sensibility—all these certainly sharpened by his thorough knowledge of the stage. He has shown to the Indian theatre community and to the world theatre community how our past and present can coalesce to give to our present day existence meaning and to theatre activity a direction.

Thus we find that today when the modern Indian playwright wants to express himself, all existing dramatic forms fail him. This necessitates him to find a new form and this urge induces him to begin the search of all traditional theatre forms in his own state or elsewhere. This forces him to examine all the aspects of the folk and classical tradition where it was not difficult to find answers to his questions but the real difficulty was to synthesize them in order to create a new form. What the modern playwright has achieved is a thorough synthesis of all the three traditions—classical, folk and contemporary western, which when used discriminatingly and intelligently, leads to a discovery of a new form and as a result a new style of production—leading to the evolution of "Indian" drama.

NOTES

1. Mohan Rakesh, *The Great Swans of the Waves*, trans. Paul Jacob and Meena Williams, *Enact*, No. 73-74 (Jan.-Feb. 1973).
2. Mohan Rakesh, *Half-Way House*, trans. Bindu Batra, *Enact*, No. 53 (May 1971).
3. Mohan Rakesh, *One Day in Ashadha*, trans. Sarab K. Ehslay, *Enact*, No. 32-33 (Aug.-Sept. 1969).
4. Mohan Rakesh, "Why Plays," *Enact*, No. 13-14 (Jan.-Feb. 1968). Unpaginated.
5. Badal Sircar, *Evam Indrajit*, trans. Girish Karnad (Calcutta: Oxford University Press, 1974).
6. Badal Sircar, *Baki Itihas*, trans. Vinod L. Doshi, *Enact*, No. 165-66. (Sept./Oct. 1980).
7. Badal Sircar, *Sheish Nei*, trans. K. Raha, *Enact*, No. 59 (Nov. 1971).
8. Badal Sircar, *Bagh*, *Jadi Aur Ekbar* and *Pralap*. Not translated into English.
9. Rustum Barucha, *Rehearsals of Revolution* (Calcutta: Seagull Books, 1983), p. 138.
10. Badal Sircar, *The Third Theatre* (Calcutta, 1978).
11. Badal Sircar, *Spartacus*. Not translated into English.
12. Badal Sircar, *Michhil* (Procession), trans. Samik Bandyopadhyay, *Bhoma*, trans. Badal Sircar and Kalyani Ghosh, *Bashi Khabar* (Stale News), trans. Samik Bandyopadhyay, in *Three Plays* (Calcutta: Seagull Books, 1983).
13. Badal Sircar, "Azad Memorial Lectures," 1982, quoted by Ella Dutta in the Introduction to *Three Plays*, p. v.
14. Veena N. Dass, "An Interview with Sircar," Hyderabad, 1985. Unpublished.
15. Vijay Tendulkar, *Silence! The Court is in Session*, trans. Priya Adarkar (Calcutta: Oxford University Press, 1978).
16. Vijay Tendulkar, *The Vultures*, trans. Priya Adarkar (Delhi: Hind Pocket Books, 1974).
17. Vijay Tendulkar, *Sakharam Binder*, trans. Shanta Shahane and Kumud Mehta (Delhi: Hind Pocket Books, 1973).
18. Vijay Tendulkar, *Ghasiram Kotwal*, trans. Jayant Kurve and Eleanor Zellot (Calcutta: Seagull Books, 1984).

19. Veena N. Dass, "Interview with Tendulkar," Bombay, 1984. Unpublished.
20. Girish Karnad, *Yayati*, trans. into Hindi by S.R. Narayana (Dharwad: Manohar Granth Mala, 1978).
21. Girish Karnad, *Tughlaq*, trans. Girish Karnad (Delhi: Oxford University Press, 1971).
22. Girish Karnad, *Atte Ka Kukkut*. Not translated into English.
23. Girish Karnad, *Hayavadana*, trans. Girish Karnad (Calcutta: Oxford University Press, 1975).

New Directions in Girish Karnad's Plays

P.H. SETHUMADHAVA RAO

Girish Karnad was born in Matheran near Bombay. He was a Rhodes scholar at Oxford during 1960-63 and Bhabha Fellow during 1970-72. Karnad is today one of the foremost playwrights in India and writes in Kannada. His first play *Yayati*, written in 1961, is retelling of the Hindu Myth on the theme of responsibility. This play was a major success. Karnad's second drama *Hayavadana* written in 1970 was given the Natya Sangh award for the best play of 1971.

Karnad's play *Yayati* is a self-consciously existentialist drama on the theme of responsibility. The theme of the play is based on the *Mahabharata* where Puru as an obedient son accepts his father's old age—a great sacrifice indeed. Yayati wanted someone else in his kingdom to accept his old age in exchange for money, land and even part of his kingdom. But no one is prepared for the sacrifice. Ultimately, Puru accepts with a great sense of respect to his father. But alas! his wife Chitralekha cannot bear this. She drinks poison and ends her life. At the end of the play, Yayati takes back the old age from his son and Puru has to witness the death of his wife.

Hayavadana is based on *Kathasaritsagara—Vetal-Panchavinshati*, an ancient collection of stories in Sanskrit. But Karnad has borrowed it through Thomas Mann's retelling of the story in "The Transposed Heads." The Sanskrit tale told by a ghost to an adventurous king, gains further mock-heroic dimensions in Mann's version. The original play poses a moral problem while Mann uses it to ridicule the mechanical conception of life which differentiates between body and soul. He ridicules the philosophy which holds the head superior to the body. The human body, Mann argues, is a fit instrument for the fulfilment of human destiny. Even the transposition of heads will not liberate the protagonists from the psychological limits imposed by nature.

Karnad's play poses a different problem, that of human identity in a world of tangled relationships. When the play opens, Devadatta and Kapila are the closest of friends—one mind, one heart, as the Bhagavata describes them.

At the beginning of the performance, one can observe that Karnad has used the old conventions and motifs of folk tales and folk theatre—masks, curtains, dolls, the story-within-a-story to create a bizarre world.

At the beginning of the performance, a mask of Ganesha is brought on the stage and kept on the chair. Lord Ganesha is worshipped. The Bhagavata sings verses in praise of Ganesha accompanied by his musicians. Then the mask is taken away. The opening speech of the Bhagavata describes indirectly the main theme of the play:

> May Vigneshwara, the destroyer of obstacles, who removes all hurdles and crowns all endeavours with success, bless our performance now. How indeed can one hope to describe his glory in our poor, disabled words? An elephant's head on a human body, a broken tusk and cracked belly—whichever way you look at him he seems the embodiment of imperfection, of incompleteness. How indeed can one fathom the mystery that this very Vakratunda-Mahakay, with his crooked face and distorted body, is the Lord and Master of success and perfection? Could it be that this Image of Purity and Holiness, this Mangalamoorty, intends to signify by his very appearance that the completeness of God is something no poor mortal can comprehend? Be that as it may. It is not for us to understand this mystery or try to unravel it. Nor is it within our powers to do so. Our duty is merely to pay homage to the Elephant-headed god and get on with our play.

Karnad then introduces the two characters—Devadatta and Kapila. Devadatta is the only son of Vidyasagar. The other youth is Kapila. He is the only son of Lohita. The world sees these two young men wandering down the streets of Dharampura, hand in hand and remembers Lava and Kush, Rama and Laxmana, Krishna and Balrama. Two friends they were—one mind, one heart. Later, Karnad introduces another character namely, Hayavadana, who has a man's body but a horse's head and is sitting on the floor hiding his head between his knees. The Bhagavata cannot believe that there can be a human body with horse head. He feels that perhaps a person might be using a mask during the course of the dialogue. It is very clear that Hayavadana really has the head of a horse. Hayavadana requests the Bhagavata to help him in getting rid of the horse head. The Bhagavata feels that it may be due to the error committed in the last birth which is responsible for such a shape. Hayavadana says that it has nothing to do with the last birth and further narrates that his mother was a princess of Karnataka, who was a beautiful girl. When she came of age her father decided that she should choose her own husband. So Princes of other kingdoms in the world were invited and they all came from China, from Persia, from Africa but she did not like any one of them. The last one to come was the Prince of Araby. Hayavadana's mother took one look at the handsome prince sitting on the great white horse and fainted. Her father at once decided that this was the man and all arrangements for the wedding were made. When Hayavadana's mother woke up she said that she would not marry the prince but marry the horse. No one could dissuade her. Ultimately, she was married off to the white horse. She lived with him for fifteen years. One morning she woke up and there was no horse, in his place stood a beautiful celestial Gandharva. Apparently, this celestial being had been cursed by Kubera to be born as a horse for some act of misbehaviour. After 15 years of human love he had become his original self again. Released from his curse Gandharva asked Hayavadana's mother to accompany him to the Heavenly Abode. But she did not agree. So he cursed her to become a horse herself. Hayavadana's mother became a horse and ran away happily and his father went back to his Heavenly Abode. Only the child of their marriage was left behind and that was Hayavadana himself.

Karnad depicts the mythological legend in a very interesting and humorous manner. What is more significant is to describe the feeling of Indians who try to believe that they can achieve anything if they visit sacred places like Banaras, Rameshwar, Gokarn, Haridwar, Gaya, Kedarnath, etc. Accordingly, Hayavadana informs the Bhagavata that he visited all these places and tried other means such as magicians, mendicants, maharshis, fakirs, saints and sadhus etc. In spite of all these he could not get rid of his horse head and become a complete man. Towards the end of the play Karnad describes the horse-man searching for completeness in a very comic vein. Ultimately Hayavadana becomes a complete horse. The animal body triumphs over what is considered the best in man, the human head.

The main plot is equally interesting. The relationship between Devadatta and Kapila was complicated when Devadatta married Padmini. Kapila falls in love with Padmini and she too starts drifting towards him. The friends kill themselves in a scene, hilariously comic but at the same time full of profound dramatic implications. Padmini transposes their heads, giving Devadatta Kapila's body and Kapila Devadatta's. The result is a confusion of identities which reveals the ambiguous nature of human responsibility.

Initially, Devadatta—actually head of Devadatta on Kapila's body—behaves differently from what he was before. But ever so gradually he changes to his former self. So does Kapila. But there is a difference. Devadatta stops writing poetry while Kapila is haunted by the memories in Devadatta's body. Padmini, after the exchange of heads, feels that she has the best of both of them, but slowly she gets disillusioned. She has the capacity for complete experience. Her situation is beautifully summed up by the images of the river and the scarecrows in the choric songs. The end of the play is quite interesting. A duel leaves both the friends dead and subsequently Sati of Padmini has been presented. But this end is not tragic. The deaths serve the absurdity of the situation. What Karnad wants to convey is that the world is of incomplete individuals, indifferent dolls that speak. The world is indifferent to the desires and frustrations, joys and sorrows of human beings.

Karnad has the genius and the power to transform any situation into an aesthetic experience. This is the main theme of the play *Hayavadana*. Karnad has rendered the story of the completeness of Hayavadana in a lighter tone but the pathos of it is touching. The superiority of the primitive force in a horse rather than in the intellect is implied through this.

Hayavadana sings national songs to get his neighing back. The dramatist, perhaps, wants to criticize the impropriety of people singing national songs without realizing the spirit of those songs. But it appears very awkward on the stage. The dramatist has artistically implied the monotony of contemporary life by showing Hayavadana—now a neighing horse—circling the stage.

Uniting the narration of the Bhagavata (which is interspersed by Yakshagana) with the characteristic masks of the three characters and the talking puppets, Girish Karnad successfully utilises the various facets of the folk theatre. That Devadatta gradually becomes lean and regains his original form is suggested casually through the dialogue of the puppets.

Karnad's play *Tughlaq* is the first in 'New Drama in India'—a series which will comprise outstanding, contemporary Indian plays. The play explores the paradox of the idealistic Sultan Muhammad Tughlaq, whose reign is considered one of the more spectacular failures in Indian history. Tughlaq was an immediate success on the stage. It was first produced in Kannada in 1965 and was also done about the same time in Hindi by the National School of Drama. Bengali and Marathi productions followed, and in 1970 there was an English production in Bombay which was a major success.

One can enjoy the play on the stage without paying much attention to its rich and complex symbolism and the subtle weaving of its different motifs. The play has an interesting story, an intricate plot, scope for spectacle and has dramatic conventions like the comic pair, Aziz and Aazam, to which theatre audiences respond readily. Another reason for *Tughlaq*'s appeal to Indian audience is that it is a play of the sixties, and reflects as no other play perhaps does the political mood of disillusionment which followed the Nehru era of idealism in the country.

What is more striking in *Tughlaq* historically is the fact that Tughlaq is the most intelligent king ever to come on the throne of Delhi and one of the greatest failures also. Within a span of 20 years this tremendous man had gone to pieces. This was due to both his idealism as well as his shortcomings within him such as impertinence, cruelty and the feeling that he had the correct answer.

The play is more than a political allegory. It has an irreducible, puzzling quality which comes from the ambiguities of Tughlaq's character, the dominating figure in the play. The play is about an 'interesting' character for the play relates to the character of Tughlaq to philosophical questions on the nature of man and destiny of a whole kingdom which a dreamer like him controls.

Although the theme of the play is from history—there are many such plays in Kannada—Karnad's treatment of the theme is not historical. The use Karnad makes of the leitmotif of the play, 'Prayer', in the scene where the Muslim chieftains along with the Shaikh-ud-din, a pacifist priest, conspire to murder Tughlaq while at prayer. The use of prayer for murder is reminiscent of what Tughlaq himself did to kill his father. That prayer, which is most dear to Tughlaq, is vitiated by him as well as his enemies, is symbolic of the fact that his life is corrupted at its very source. The whole episode is ironic. It involves Shihab-ud-din, an idealist, who has put great trust in Tughlaq's rule and is himself ultimately betrayed by Ratansingh who masterminds the entire plan of murder for his own ends. The intrigue here not only enhances the theatrical interest of the play but is a dramatized projection of Tughlaq's tortured, divided self. Thus, the external action throughout enacts the inner dream of Tughlaq. Both Tughlaq and his enemies initially appear to be idealist; yet in the pursuit of the idea they perpetrate its opposite. The whole play is structured on these opposites: the ideal and the real; the divine aspiration and the deft intrigue. Tughlaq is what he is in spite of his self knowledge and an intense desire for divine grace. He is aware of the irony of his life when Aziz, the only character in the play who has skilfully used all the schemes of Tughlaq for his own designs, kills Ghiyas-ud-din and comes in his guise as a holy messenger of peace to purify the land and revive the banned prayer. The irony is deeply chaos, as he knows it. No play in Kannada is comparable to *Tughlaq* in its depth and range. It is a classic in Kannada literature.

Karnad has completely rejected the professional stage established by Kailasam and Sri Ranga. He has tried to bring in his play a first-hand knowledge of practical demands of the stage and a better understanding of dramatic style and technique.

In his works, Karnad has moved away from the regionalist tradition that had given Kannada literature its idealism in the early years of the century. None of his three plays has a specifically Kannada theme. *Yayati* reinterprets an ancient myth. *Tughlaq* is based on history and the plot of *Hayavadana* comes from *Kathasaritsagar* in Sanskrit.

Thus Karnad's plays have new directions as compared to other playwrights in Kannada literature.

Thematic Concerns and Technical Features in Girish Karnad's Plays

A.K. SINHA

Girish Karnad (b. 1938) is one of the foremost playwrights in India who writes in Kannada and yet has moved away from the regionalist tradition to make fresh raids on the inarticulate. His first play *Yayati* (1961) re-interprets an ancient Hindu myth on the theme of responsibility and emerges almost like a self-consciously existentialist dream. Regarding this play, Karnad frankly confessed in an interview that he "wanted to tell people I had read Sartre, Camus and others."[1]

Karnad's second play *Tughlaq* (1964) explores the paradox of the idealistic Sultan Muhammad Tughlaq whose reign is considered to be one of the spectacular regimes of history. In connection with this play, Karnad has also revealed in course of the same interview that "he read a work of Kannada criticism which proved that many historical plays written earlier were costume plays and that no one attempted to relate a historical episode to modern sensibility like Shaw. This inspired me to write such a play in Kannada."[2] His third play *Hayavadana* (1970) presents the theme of human beings aspiring for the unattainable in the Brechtian pattern. And in his fourth play *Naga-Mandala*, Karnad weaves two Kannada folk tales together; the first one comments on the paradoxical nature of oral tales, and the other is the story of Rani whose predicament reflects the human need to live by fictions and half-truths.

In all his plays—be the theme mythical, historical or legendary—Karnad's approach is modern. He uses the conventions and motifs of folk art, like masks and curtains to project a world of intensities, uncertainties and unpredictable denouements. He rightly believes that the energy of folk theatre comes from the fact that although it seems to uphold traditional values, it also has the means of questioning these values. The various conventions—the chorus, the music, the apparently unrelated comic interludes, the mixing of the human and the non-human worlds—permit a simultaneous presentation of alternative points of view. Like Bertolt Brecht, Karnad strives to break the "illusion" of the theatre by which the spectators become so engrossed in a play that they forget, for the time being, what they are. Therefore, like Brecht, Karnad leaves the stage apparatus visible, presents synoptic announcements, has narrators directly talking to the audience. All this compels the audience to respond intellectually to the action of the play and to question it, instead of responding emotionally and merely accepting it.

In *Yayati*, Karnad takes liberty with the original myth and invents some new relationships to make it acceptable to modern sensibilities. In the Puranic story, Yayati marries Devayani, daughter of the sage Shukracharya, and also takes Sharmishtha, a low-born girl as his wife under certain niceties of *dharma*. Devayani, furious and seething with jealousy, brings a curse on Yayati, of course with a saving clause that if he desired, anybody else could also bear that curse for Yayati. Drenched in sensual pleasures, Yayati promptly asks his son to exchange his youth with him. Puru willingly offers his youth as filial devotion, and Yayati shuns carnality only after indulging in it for a thousand years. In Karnad's play, Yayati has already married Devayani, and marries Sharmishtha during the action of the play. Karnad invents two characters—Puru's wife Chitralekha and confidant Swarnalata. In Karnad's play, the whole action takes place in one night. Puru is shown coming home after his marriages and the bed is being prepared for the newly-wedded couple. The same bed is used for Yayati to solemnize Sharmishtha. The curse falls and Puru loses his youth and suddenly grows old. Chitralekha (Puru's wife), who wants to bear a child, is disillusioned. She decides to offer herself to Yayati and then she commits suicide. This shakes Yayati and acts as an eye-opener. In a moment of genuine remorse, he takes back the curse from his son.

Karnad's interpretation of the familiar old myth on the exchange of ages between father and son seems to have baffled and even angered many of the conventional critics. But to others, who are trying to root their contemporary concerns in old myths, Karnad's unheroic hero Puru is a challenging experience. Karnad places the individual person at the centre of his picture of the world and shows that each man is what he chooses to be or makes himself. In his psychological exploration, the playwright shows an impressive insight and introduces concepts which greatly extend the area of moral self-knowledge and self-awareness. Yes, Karnad has indeed read wisely Sartre, Camus and others.

In fact, his *Tughlaq* has been compared by critics to Camus's *Caligula*, for both the plays present a tyrant using his power absolutely, indulging in wanton and senseless cruelty. In both the plays, the king appears as a "carnivorous animal" paying an unexpected penalty at the end. Yet neither play aspires to be historical drama and liberties are taken with historical fact in both of them. Karnad adds a sub-plot with purely imaginary characters and ignores historical truth in showing a close bond between Tughlaq and his step-mother. Both the plays have been invested by critics with urgent topical significance and have been generally described as political allegories. But to do this, asserts M.K. Naik in his book *Studies in Indian English Literature*, will be to divert attention from both the works. Although Karnad himself admits that what struck him about Tughlaq's history was that it was contemporary, it has to be affirmed that *Tughlaq* is basically concerned with the tragedy of the limits of human power in a predominantly psychological context. In *Tughlaq*, the focus is on the psychological implication of the theme of human power in respect for a self-righteous idealist (the most dangerous combination possible) armed with absolute power over his subjects. In this play, Karnad, like Shaw, emerges as a playwright who is historically awake. Karnad, Shaw and Brecht share a healthy courage by which their drama is committed to a higher didacticism. Each one of them devises a dramatic art that utilizes parable to please and to teach simultaneously.

Tughlaq begins with a scene that presents a Shakespearean exposition of characters and human motives. Somewhat like Gloucester and Kent in Shakespeare's *King Lear*, secondary characters introduce the king:

Young Man: This King now, he isn't afraid to be human—
Third Man: But does he have to make such a fuss about being human?[3]

The scene goes on to hint at the lurking suspicion between the Hindus and the Muslims during that period (1327 A.D.), and makes it clear that while Tughlaq is deeply religious, he strives for Hindu-

Muslim unity and that he has no partiality for any particular community. That all are equal before justice is evident from the announcement to restore the property of Vishnu Prasad, a Brahmin of Shiknar whose land has been illegally seized by the officers of the state. The Sultan's sense of justice and fair play is so strong that besides restoring the land to Vishnu Prasad he announces his decision to appoint the Brahmin in the service of the state. When the king himself appears on the scene, he makes yet another startling announcement:

> Later this year the capital of my empire will be moved from Delhi to Daulatabad. . . . Your surprise is natural, but I beg you to realize that this is no mad whim of a tyrant. . . . But for me the most important factor is that Daulatabad is a city of the Hindus and as the capital it will symbolize the bond between Muslims and Hindus which I wish to develop and strengthen in my kingdom. (3-4)

The assembly is stunned and the words "mad whim of a tyrant" are so suggestive that they are taken up by a crowd once the King leaves. The people gathered there indulge in gossip and the third man refers to Sheikh Imam-ud-din as the King's arch-rival who has publicly proclaimed in Kanpur that the Sultan was guilty of killing his father and brother. The third man, significantly enough, points at the certain physical resemblance between the King and the Sheikh—similar mannerisms, similar gestures. Thus the King and the Sheikh are drawn with subtle parallelisms and contrasts between them. The crowd disperses. Only Aazam remains hanging around; for he wants to see the Brahmin Vishnu Prasad. After some time, the Brahmin appears and Aazam is stunned to discover that this Brahmin is Aziz, a clever and cunning "dhobi" (washerman) who has only disguised himself as Vishnu Prasad because he has suddenly realized that there was no future in being a "dhobi." Aazam is a pick-pocket and Aziz persuades him to be his assistant, for he believes that the Sultan would welcome a Brahmin officer with a Muslim assistant (and the tongue-in-the-cheek irony is so evident here). The scene ends with an anti-climactic bang:

Aziz: Come along. It won't be long. I don't intend to be a Brahmin all my life! There's money here and we'll

make a pile by the time we reach Daulatabad.
Aazam: And then?
Aziz: How should I know! (8)

Does not Aziz remind us of both Falstaff and Iago at the same time? Does not Aazam appear to be a Roderigo in the hands of an ever planning Iago!

Scene Two presents the Sultan theatrically confiding to his stepmother: "I pray to the Almighty to save me from sleep. All day long I have to worry about tomorrow but it's only when the night falls that I can step beyond all that." (10) The King wants to climb up the tallest tree in the world and ask his people to confide in him their worries. As the Sultan prepares to leave for Kanauj, news arrives regarding the twin danger, that of the march of Ain-ul-Mulk with his powerful army and that of the arrival of Sheikh Imam in Delhi. Najib, a politician and Barani a historian, two confidants of the Sultan, brief him on the support the Sheikh has already been getting from the people. Muhammad is apparently unruffled and he decides to start for Kanauj the day after the next day. Najib will look after the administration in his absence. Besides, he has invited Shihab-ud-din, Prince of Sampanshahr to be there when he goes out to Kanauj.

In the third scene, we find Muhammad and Sheikh Imam-ud-din in front of the Big Mosque. The clever manipulator that he is, the Sultan has arranged a prayer meeting here in honour of the Sheikh and also to listen to him. It is actually a trap laid cleverly by the Sultan and the people, seeing through this, stay away from the meeting. When the Sultan asks his servant to tell the Vizier to call the Khans, Amirs and Sardars to the meeting, Imam-ud-din remarks that he has not come there to speak to a collection of courtiers. The Imam observes: "What's the point in my addressing a gang of bootlickers? I want to speak to the people who are willing to act, who are willing to do something." (19) The Sultan, however, persuades the Imam to go as his envoy and dissuade Ain-ul-Mulk of Avadh who is marching on Delhi at that very moment. The Imam accepts this request, although he does not trust the motives of the King and feels that he is left with no other alternative.

Scene Four takes us back to the Sultan's palace where Muhammad returns. When his stepmother asks the Sultan about Sheikh Imam-ud-din, the Sultan freezes and then speaks: "It was a terrible sight. They brought his body into my tent and I felt—as though it was I who was lying dead there and that he was standing above me looking at me." (27) This is a unique example of a Brechtian "complex seeing" and it subtly brings out the parallelism and contrast between the Sultan and the Sheikh. The Sultan is indeed a master tactician, for he just does not set Ain-ul-Mulk free but gives him back the kingdom of Avadh and even promises not to send him to Deccan. He also announces a state mourning for Imam-ud-din, observing that when men like him die, it is a sin to be alive.

In Scene Five, Ratan Singh, the adopted brother of Shihab-ud-din, who has been with the Sultan in the "peace mission" and has survived and Shihab-ud-din attend the secret meeting arranged by the Amirs and the royal courtiers. The scene reminds one of the persuasion scene in Shakespeare's *Julius Caesar*: Shihab-ud-din appears as Brutus who has to be persuaded. The Amirs feel that the Sultan is taking them to Daulatabad just to weaken them, because they are strong in Delhi. The conspiracy is hatched. The Sultan is to be killed at the meeting of the courtiers next Tuesday and the Muezzin's call to prayer will be the signal of attack.

Scene Six takes us back to the palace of the Sultan. Barani informs the Sultan that a descendant of the last Khalif is going to visit him and Shihab-ud-din compliments Muhammad on his wisdom. When Amir I observes that the sins of Delhi will be washed clean by the visit, the Sultan observes that by then they will be in Daulatabad. This makes Shihab-ud-din implore His Majesty not to move the capital to Daulatabad. But the Sultan will not budge. In fact, he gives yet another piece of information. From next year, they shall have copper currency in their empire along with silver dinars and a copper coin will have the same value as a silver coin. The hour of prayer arrives. As soon as the Muezzin's call begins, Muhammad unbuckles his sword and places it on the throne. Half-way through the prayer, a commotion is heard off-stage. Taking this as a cue, Shihab-ud-din and the Amirs get up and pull out their daggers. But suddenly from behind the curtain, about twenty Hindu soldiers rush in with spears and surround the Amirs and drag them away—all except Shihab-ud-din. While all this is going on, the Sultan goes on praying unconcerned. Muhammad steps down from the throne only after completing his prayer. He stabs Shihab-ud-din to death, telling him that he liked him "too much." He orders Najib to see that all those involved in the conspiracy are caught and beheaded, their bodies stuffed with straw and hanged up in the palace yard. He further orders that a public announcement should be made in which it should be made known that a rebellion had taken place in the palace and that the nobles of the Court had tried to assassinate the Sultan during prayer. He was saved by Shihab-ud-din, who died a martyr's death. The father of Shihab-ud-din, a powerful man, is to be invited to the funeral. And the Sultan wants Delhi to be vacated immediately. Every living soul in Delhi will leave for Daulatabad within a fortnight. There will be no more praying in the kingdom.

Scene Seven takes us to a camp on the Delhi-Daulatabad route. Aziz (still dressed as the Brahmin) and Aazam fleece people mercilessly (reminding us of Falstaff extracting a thousand pounds from Justice Shallow in Shakespeare's *Henry IV Part II*). When Aazam warns Aziz that they will be ruined ultimately, Aziz retorts:

> You are a hopeless case, you know. Pathetic! You've been in Delhi for so many years and you're as stupid as ever. Look at me. Only a few months in Delhi and I have discovered a whole new world—politics. My dear fellow, that's where our future is—politics. It's a beautiful world—wealth, success, position, power. (50)

The scene ends with Aziz telling Aazam that instead of stealing copper coins, they will make counterfeit copper coins.

In the eighth scene, we are taken to 1332 A.D. Five years have passed. The shifting of the capital from Delhi to Daulatabad has been a painful experience for everybody. The Sultan cannot sleep and he is fully aware that only one industry flourishes in his country—and that is of making counterfeit copper coins. His subjects even call him "Mad Muhammad," and the Sultan wants to become "wise" again. But he also cannot admit that he has been wrong all those years, for he still feels that he has something to give, something to teach. The scene ends with the Old Man coming to inform the Sultan that Vizier Muhammad Najib has been found murdered in his bed.

Scene Nine offers some dramatic relief in which Aziz (very much like Falstaff in Shakespeare's *Henry IV Part I*) tells some "honest" things to Aazam: "If you remain virtuous throughout your life no one will say a good thing about you because they won't need to. But start stealing—and they'll say: 'What a nice boy he was. But he's ruined now.'" (57) This apparently jovial remark can also be taken as an indirect comment on the fall of the Sultan himself. Aziz in some ways reminds us of the Fool in Shakespeare's *King Lear*. Ghiyas-ud-din, a descendant of Khalif Abassid is on his way to Daulatabad. Aziz and Aazam happen to see him and they murder him. Aziz opens Ghiyas-ud-din's bundle and prepares to make his entry into Tughlaq's palace as the "grandson of the Khalif."

Scene Ten takes us back to the palace where the Sultan realizes that if he does not withdraw the copper coins now, the whole economy of his dilapidated kingdom will be in a shambles. His stepmother shocks Muhammad when she tells him that it was she who had got Najib murdered. She makes him conscious of his degeneration when she says: "It's only seven years ago that you came to the throne. How glorious you were then, how idealistic, how full of hopes. Look at your kingdom now. It's become a kitchen of death." (65) The Sultan orders that he wants her stoned to death publicly the next day. Barani brings some joyful tidings—Ghiyas-ud-din Abbasid is to arrive within the next month or so.

In the eleventh scene, we are taken to a plain outside the fort of Daulatabad where crowds of dejected citizens have gathered. They do not want prayer now, they want some food. Just then Aziz (disguised as Ghiyas-ud-din) and Aazam and their entourage enter and Muhammad steps down from the fort welcoming His Holiness as the only person who can save him now. Trouble starts when a Hindu woman identifies Aziz as the one who killed her son. People shout that they want food—not prayer. The riots begin and the scene ends.

Scene Twelve takes us to the palace where Aazam wants escape and Aziz knows that he cannot get on without him. Aazam asks Aziz to come along with him too but Aziz does not budge.

Scene Thirteen concludes the play. Aazam has been found murdered at the mouth of the secret tunnel from the palace. Sultan is stunned. The famine riots have already spread. Daulatabad is in a shambles. Even Barani wants to leave the place. In a sudden flash of realization, Muhammad asks Aziz who he is. Aziz is obviously frightened and confesses his guilt but adds with his characteristic wit and humour: "What if I am a dhobi. Your Majesty? When it comes to washing away filth no saint is a match for a dhobi." (82) Muhammad laughs and acknowledges that the man is a genius. When the Sultan asks Aziz what punishment should be given for his crimes, Aziz replies that he should be made an officer in his state. The Sultan appoints Aziz as an officer in the army in Deccan, saying that perhaps a State office really would be the best punishment for him. Muhammad also announces his decision to shift the capital back to Delhi. He suddenly feels tired and sleepy. For five years, sleep has avoided him and now suddenly it is coming back. The Muezzin's call to prayer is heard and as that call fades away, the Sultan suddenly opens his eyes and looks around, dazed and frightened, as though he cannot understand where he actually is. The play ends.

Thus it is evident that *Tughlaq*'s thematic concerns have a universal significance. Karnad here grapples with fundamental human motives with a distinctive, masterly control. There is a critical exploration of the psychic structure of the characters. The moral and manners of the political world of power have been sensitively commented upon. The struggles of the Sultan have been forcefully brought out and the play ends with time pleasantly flowing at its own sweet will. *Tughlaq* presents a rich orchestration of themes subtly interlocked with one another, with a rapid progression of events.

In his next play, *Hayavadana*, Girish Karnad poses the problem of human identity in a world of tangled relationships. He deftly uses the conventions and motifs of folk tales and folk theatre—masks, curtains, dolls, the story-within-a-story—to create a bizarre world of incomplete individuals, indifferent gods, dolls that speak and children who cannot—world which appears to be indifferent to the desires and frustrations, joys and sorrows of human beings. In fact, the central episode in the play—the story ot Devadatta and Kapila—observes the playwright—is based on a tale from *Vetalpanchavimshika* (also known as *Vetal Pachisi*). But he has drawn heavily on Thomas Mann's re-working of the tale in *The Transposed Heads*.

While the Sanskrit tale poses a moral problem, Mann uses the story to ridicule the philosophy which holds the head superior to the body. For Mann, the human body is a fit instrument for the fulfilment of human destiny and even the transposition of heads will not liberate the protagonists from their natural psychological demands. For Karnad, the confusion of the identities reveals the ambiguous nature of the human personality. *Hayavadana*, in many ways, reminds us of Shakespeare's *A Midsummer Night's Dream* where a comedy of errors takes place so hilariously.

When *Hayavadana* begins, a mask of Ganesha is brought on the stage and the Bhagavata (the Sutradhar or Commentator) sings verses in praise of "Vakratunda-Mahakaya" with the crooked face and distorted body who is the Lord and Master of Success and Perfection. The story-within-the-story starts when the Bhagavata takes us to the city of Dharmapura where live two friends—Devadatta, comely in appearance, unrivalled in intelligence, the only son of the Revered Brahmin Vidyasagar and Kapila, dark and plain to look at, having no equal in strength and in physical skills, the only son of an ironsmith Lohita. The Bhagavata's narration is interrupted by a Nata (Actor) who rushes on to the stage in fear and informs the Sutradhar that outside in the street he has met a talking horse. This is Hayavadana, who has a man's body and a horse's head who has all his life been trying to get rid of his head and become a complete man.

In the central episode, Kapila promises Devadatta to be his cloud messenger who will find out the house and also the name of the lady Devadatta has fallen in love with. Devadatta swears that if he ever gets her as his wife, he will sacrifice his arms to goddess Kali and his head to Lord Rudra. So Kapil finds his way to Pavan-Veethi, the street of merchants, and meets Padmini, who is the girl Devadatta has fallen in love with. But Kapila too falls in love with Padmini, observing that she is not for the likes of Devadatta. However, Padmini is married to Devadatta, settles in his house and is soon to deliver their first baby.

However, we soon discover that on their way to Ujjain, Devadatta becomes suspicious of the relationship between Padmini and Kapila (somewhat like Leontes being jealous of the relationship between Hermione and Polixenes in Shakespeare's *The Winter's Tale*). Padmini, however, is different from Hermione because secretly Padmini is wonderstruck by the swaying body of Kapila and his curving limbs. Kapila informs Devadatta that there is a temple of Rudra nearby and beyond the hill is a temple of Kali. Devadatta suggests to Padmini and Kapila to go and visit the Rudra temple while he will stay back and watch their cart. Immediately afterwards, we see Devadatta swearing in front of Kali: "Forgive me, Mother. You fulfilled the deepest craving of my life—you gave me Padmini—and I forgot my word. . . . Here Mother Kali. . . . My Head. Take it."[4]

Devadatta has sacrificed his head to Kali, the mask rolls off and blood flows. Padmini and Kapila return to the cart. After looking for and waiting for Devadatta for some time, Kapila finds his footprints leading to the Kali temple. When on reaching the temple Kapila finds the body of Devadatta with his head truncated, he moans: "Devadatta, I can't live without you. . . . You spurned me in this world. Accept me as your brother at least in the next." (30) Kapila cuts off his head. Now Padmini finds her way to this temple, stares at the two bodies and picks up the sword to kill herself. Just then goddess Kali drops her arms, shuts her mouth (for she has been yawning) and intervenes: "The rascals! They were lying to their last breaths. That fellow Devadatta—he had once promised his head to Rudra and his arms to me! Think of it—head to him and arms to me! . . . Then this Kapila. Died right in front of me—but 'for his friend.' Mind you! Didn't even have the courtesy to refer to me." (33) The subtle humour in such a description is so evident. Kali asks Padmini to put the heads of the two friends back properly, attach them to their bodies and then press the sword on their necks. They will come up alive. Padmini puts these heads back, but in her excitement she mixes them up, so that Devadatta's head goes to Kapila's body and Kapila's finds its way on Devadatta's body. This takes us to a really overwhelming question: Whose wife is Padmini? When Devadatta (with the body of Kapila) says that the head is the sign of a man, Kapila (with the body of Devadatta) claims that he has the body she has lived with all these months and the child she is carrying is the seed of his body. Act One ends with the Bhagavata throwing the same question to the audience (somewhat like Vetal of *Vetalpanchvimshika*): who is the rightful husband of Padmini?

Act Two begins with the Bhagavata announcing the answer to the question he has raised at the end of the first Act. As the heavenly Kalpa Vriksha is supreme among trees, so is the head among the human limbs. Therefore, according to a great rishi, the man with Devadatta's head is indeed Devadatta and he is the rightful husband of Padmini. So the roads diverge and Kapila goes into the forest and disappears. Devadatta and Padmini return to Dharmapura and plunge into the joys of married life. Time passes. Events so conspire that Padmini with her child in her arms loses her way in the forest. And there she meets Kapila, whose arms, once so slender and fair, have become tough and rough. Devadatta, whose palms, which were so rough, have become soft like a young girl's, also comes here in search of Padmini and the child. Kapila suggests a compromise: "Devadatta, couldn't we all three live together—like the Pandavas and Draupadi?" (60) But Devadatta's stand is clear, for, according to him, there are no grounds for friendship now. They must fight like lions and kill like cobras. The fight begins. Kapila wounds Devadatta who falls to his feet and stabs Kapila. Both fall and die. Padmini entrusts her son, who is sleeping in Kapila's hut, to the Bhagavata and even asks him to make a large funeral pyre for the three of them. She will perform *Sati*: "Kali, Mother of all Nature, you must have your joke even now. Other women can die praying that they should get the same husband in all the lives to come. You haven't left me even that little consolation." (63) But the play does not end even here, for a scream is heard in the wings. Hayavadana has at last emerged not as a complete man but as a full-fledged horse. He too had gone to the goddess and implored to her that he would kill himself if she did not help him. The goddess had appeared and had said rather peevishly why people did not go somewhere else if they wanted to chop off their heads. She, however, has said "So be it" to Hayavadana and has disappeared even before he could ask her to make him a complete man. Thus Hayavadana's dream of becoming a complete man remains unfulfilled. (And this picture of the complete horse takes us back to the houyhnhnms presented by Swift in *Gulliver's Travels*). The play ends with the Bhagavata's prayer:

> Grant us, O, Lord, good rains, good crop,
> Prosperity in poetry, science, industry and other affairs.
> Give the rulers of our country success in all endeavours
> and along with it, a little bit of sense. (71)

The theme of this play thus is a complex one and Karnad good humouredly yet critically evaluates the very concepts of the rational and the physical. The multiplicity of the characters and their individual psychic circles playing into each other build up a complex pattern of human relationships. And by projecting these interlocked human sympathies against a gradually intensifying clash of personalities, Karnad presents a comprehensive picture of the human living. Indeed, Karnad's work has the tone and expression of great drama. He has the genius to transform any situation into an aesthetic experience, with his tongue-in-the-cheek humour and irony.

Girish Karnad bases his next play *Naga-Mandala* (Play with a Cobra) on two folk tales from Karnataka, which he acknowledges to have heard several years ago from A.K. Ramanujan. This play begins with a Prologue in which one is taken to the inner sanctum of a ruined temple, in which the idol is broken and therefore cannot be identified. It is night and a man is sitting in the temple, yawning involuntarily (reminding us of Kali yawning in *Hayavadana*). He turns to the audience and confides:

> I may be dead within the next few hours. . . . I asked the mendicant what I had done to deserve this fate. And he said, 'You have written plays. You have staged them. You have caused so many good people, who came trusting you, to fall asleep twisted in miserable chairs, that all that abused mass of sleep has turned against you and become the Curse of Death.'[5]

So the man with a self-directed irony swears that if he survives that night he will have nothing more to do with themes, plots or stories. He abjures all story-telling, all play-acting. Suddenly he is shocked to see naked lamp flames entering the temple, talking to each other in female voices. Then a new flame enters and is enthusiastically greeted by the other flames. This new flame tells the others: "My mistress, the old woman, knows a story and a song. But all these years she has kept them to herself. . . . This afternoon. . . . The moment her mouth opened the story and the song jumped out." (4) The story took the form of a young woman and the song became a sari: this young woman wrapped herself in the sari and stepped out.

And so soon arrives in this very temple this story with the song. The story, however, looks despondent because she feels that there is no point in the flames listening to her, because they cannot pass it on. The Man, in spite of his vow not to do any more story-telling, ultimately agrees to help the Story and the Prologue ends.

Act One begins with the Story addressing the audience: "A young girl. Her name . . . it doesn't matter. But she was an only daughter, so her parents called her Rani. Queen." (6) Rani is the Queen of the long tresses. When her hair is tied up in a knot, it is as though a black King Cobra lies curled on the nape of her neck. Her fond father finds her a suitable husband, Appanna (any man) who soon comes and takes her to his village. Here Appanna maltreats Rani, coming home only for lunch which the wife cooks with great pains and then going away to a concubine, leaving Rani alone and locked up for the night.

One day it so happens that Kappanna (the dark one) enters the street carrying his mother Kurudavva (the blind one) on his shoulders. As Appanna's mother is the best friend of Kurudavva, the latter has to visit the new daughter-in-law who has arrived in the house. When Kurudavva meets Rani and finds about her sorry state of affairs, the elderly lady bursts out: "I'll tell you. I was born blind. No one would marry me. . . . One day a mendicant came to our house. . . . He was pleased with me and gave me three pieces of a root. 'Any man who eats one of these will marry you,' he said." (12) So Kurudavva used the middle-sized root and got her loving husband. Kurudavva now gives Rani the smaller one of the roots and asks her to give it to Appanna and win him over. But even this charm does not work, for Appanna only feels giddy. Kurudavva now gives Rani the bigger piece, which Rani grinds into a paste and pours it into the curry. The curry boils over, red as blood. Rani is so terrified that she goes out and pours the entire curry into the ant-hill where lives King Cobra. The charm has worked now. King Cobra lifts its hood, sees Rani and follows her at a distance. When it is totally dark, the Cobra enters Rani's house through the drain in the bathroom. As the Cobra is supposed to assume any form it likes, it takes the shape of Appanna and Act One ends.

Act Two continues with the same scene. Rani is naturally surprised to find Appanna coming to her in the night. These meetings at night continue and Rani tells Appanna (who actually is Naga): "You talk so nicely at night. But during the day I only have to open my mouth and you hiss like a . . . stupid snake." (22)

Rani is pregnant and Appanna (the actual husband) is furious. The Village Elders sit in judgement and Rani confesses, swearing by King Cobra: "Yes, my husband and this King Cobra. Except for these two, I have not touched any one of the male sex. Nor have I allowed any other male to touch me. If I lie, let the Cobra bite me." (33) At this, the Cobra slides up her shoulders and spreads its hood like an umbrella over her head. The crowd gasps and the Elders declare that it is a miracle and that Rani is not a woman but a divine being—a goddess. Even Appanna asks her forgiveness and gently takes her into his arms. Appanna's concubine volunteers to do menial work for Rani. And Rani gives birth to a beautiful son. But Appanna knows that he has not slept with his wife. And on that night of the village court when her true husband climbed into bed with her, how could Rani fail to realize it was someone new? Still, Rani and Appanna come together, smile, embrace each other and plunge into darkness. And Naga, who has brought all the happiness and glory to Rani, wants to take a look at her. Finally, he ties a tress of Rani's hair (introduced so symbolically at the beginning of Act One) into a noose and places it around his neck and strangles himself. When Rani combs her hair, a dead cobra falls to the ground.

Realizing it all, Rani wants the Cobra to be cremated and the fire should be lit by their son and on every year on that day their son should perform the rituals to commemorate this death. Appanna admits that there is no question of saying no because Rani is the goddess herself incarnate. The play ends.

Thus it is obvious that in *Naga-Mandala*, Karnad has cut below the surface to reveal the burning core of mental or spiritual reality. The main concern of the playwright here becomes centred on human (and non-human) beings in combination, interacting, entering into one another's lives, becoming part of one another. What Karnad seems to be primarily interested in is a real contact, a real meeting of the selves, depending on mutual knowledge. The abandonment of realism in this play takes us to a world that appears to be weird and even metaphysical. The primarily psychological treatment of character seems to embody a philosophy of life which emphasizes that events have meaning only in relation to the characters. And yet there is a patterning of human affairs by an agency which remains inscrutable. Karnad here presents a world where things happen inexplicably and the schemes and intentions of people do not seem to control the action. Indeed, Girish Karnad's art can be described as a vision of reality.

NOTES

1. Meenakshi Raykar, "An Interview with Girish Karnad," *New Quest*, Nov.-Dec. 1982, p. 340.
2. *Ibid.*
3. Girish Karnad, *Tughlaq* (Oxford University Press, 1972), p. 1.
4. Girish Karnad, *Hayavadana* (Oxford University Press, 1975), p. 28.
5. Girish Karnad, *Naga-Mandala* (Oxford University Press, 1990), pp. 1-2.

A Psycho-Cultural Study of Karnad's Plays

M. SARAT BABU

Girish Karnad is a great bureaucrat, famous TV and film artiste and director, and successful playwright. He wanted to become a poet in English. But instead he wrote a play in Kannada. This play, *Yayati*, emerged out of his sublimated protest against his being suffocated by the responsibilities thrust on him by his parents. His other plays also betray his rebellion against hegemonic culture. He borrows his themes from Indian myth, folk tales and history. He employs in his plays the techniques of classical and folk theatre of India. He makes use of the devices of culture to expose its retrogressive values. So he argues, "The energy of folk theatre comes from the fact that although it seems to uphold traditional values, it also has the means of questioning these values, of making them literally stand on their head." (back cover, *Naga-Mandala*) He shares the disillusionment of modern Indian intelligentsia and is not fascinated by the false solutions. He has written eight plays in Kannada and translated four of them into English. The English plays are *Tughlaq*, *Hayavadana*, *Naga-Mandala* and *Tale-Danda*. He borrows his themes from history in *Tughlaq* and *Tale-Danda*, from myth in *Hayavadana* and from folklore in *Naga-Mandala*. He makes use of *Yakshagana bayalata*, a Kannada folk-theatre, in *Hayavadana*.

Tughlaq received acclamation and Karnad was recognized as a promising playwright. The play was translated into other Indian languages. It presents Muhammad-bin-Tughlaq, the eponymous and enigmatic character, who keeps on changing his roles. He thinks that he alone can rule his kingdom ideally. So he gets his father and brother assassinated in a contrived accident and inherits the kingdom. He is a great scholar and visionary. He is caught in the game of power. He plays the role of Rescuer in order to feel powerful. Though his favourite role is the Rescuer, he shifts to the other roles of the Drama Triangle, Persecutor and Victim. He effects several reforms that, he thinks, will benefit his people. He announces equality of justice on the second anniversary of his coronation. Aziz takes advantage of it and, in the guise of a Brahmin named Vishnu Prasad, files a suit against the government after buying a confiscated land from a Brahmin with a back date. He is offered five hundred silver dinars and also a post in the Civil Service as a compensation for the loss of his land. Tughlaq feels overwhelmed about his success in implementing his ideal. He addresses his people and says:

> My beloved people, you have heard the judgement of Kazi and seen for yourselves how justice works in my kingdom—without any consideration of might or weakness, religion or creed. May this moment burn bright and light up our path towards greater justice, equality, progress and peace—not just peace but a more purposeful life. And to achieve this end I am taking a new step in which I hope I shall have your support and cooperation. Later this year the capital of my empire will be moved from Delhi to Daulatabad.[1]

He is thus blind to how some people like Aziz exploit his reforms which therefore fail to reach the intended people. And people are not happy at all about his rule. A Hindu, for example, does not commend his removal of jiziya tax and condemns him for hypocrisy:

> We didn't want an exemption! Look, when a Sultan licks me in the teeth and says, 'Pay up, Hindu dog,' I'm happy. I know I'm safe. But the moment a man comes along and says, 'I know you are a Hindu, but you are also a human being'—well, that makes me nervous. (2)

Thus Muhammad does not mind becoming the Victim of his own ideals or the people. Perhaps for this reason, he forgives Aziz at the end when he comes to know all his crimes of misusing the reforms for his gross selfish needs. He prefers the misuse of his reforms to the objection of them. He shifts to the role of the Persecutor when anybody tries to oppose or abort his reforms. When the Amirs of Delhi try to abort his attempt to shift the capital from Delhi to Daulatabad, he gets them killed. He who once gave an option to the people to leave for Daulatabad now makes it compulsory. He says to Najib:

> Najib, I want Delhi vacated immediately. Every living soul in Delhi will leave for Daulatabad within a fortnight. I was too soft, I can see that now. They'll only understand the whip. Everyone must leave. Not a light should be seen in the windows of Delhi. Not a wisp of smoke should rise from its chimneys. Nothing but an empty graveyard will satisfy me now. (44)

This shift from the Rescuer to the Persecutor in him repeats on such occasions. In the end, he is horrified by his own violence. He feels helpless and hopeless. He finds himself straying away from his ideals. As a Victim, while praying, he appeals to God, the Supreme Rescuer to free him from this turmoil:

> God, God in Heaven, please help me. Please don't let go my hand. My skin drips with blood and I don't know how much of it is mine and how much of others. I started in Your path, Lord, why am I wandering naked in this desert now? I started in search of You. Why am I become a pig rolling in this gory of mud? Raise me. Clean me. Cover me with Your Infinite Mercy. I can only clutch at the hem of Your cloak with my bloody fingers and plead. I can only beg—have pity on me. I have no one but You now. Only You. Only You . . . You . . . You . . . You. (67)

Muhammad's condition evokes pity in us. We sympathize with his ideals and identify with him though we denounce his violence.

There is something archetypal about the roles that Muhammad played. In Hindu mythology, there are several examples of these roles. For instance, Lord Shiva rescues Bhasmasura, his demon devotee, granting his wish that the person on whom he places his hand may be burnt. Then Bhasmasura runs after his God to test the power of his boon on him. Lord Vishnu in the guise of Mohini, a charming nymph, rescues Shiva from Bhasmasura by making him burn himself. Similar instances can be found in the mythologies and legends of other religions. Jesus Christ sheds his own blood for the sins of the other people and thus tries to rescue them from damnation of Satan. This archetype of Rescuer is engraved in the collective unconscious of Indians. So, history repeats itself. Karnad finds a parallel to the great failure of Nehru's idealism in the reign of

Muhammad-bin-Tughlaq.

Aparna Dharwadkar aptly points out, "Tughlaq's madness and tyranny—the only qualities his subjects attribute to him—are thus forms of powerlessness posing as power."[2] And M.K. Naik compares Karnad's *Tughlaq* with Camus's *Caligula* and finds the fiasco of power in both of them. *Tughlaq* can also be compared with Tendulkar's plays, especially with *Ghasiram Kotwal* where power game is very intense. Muhammad plays the Rescuer while Ghasiram becomes the Persecuter to exercise power. Steiner says, while explaining how and why people play these roles, "Having been in powerless position, we make ourselves feel better by taking, and assuming power over others as Rescuers or Persecutors."[3]

This history of Muhammad reflects that of mankind. Man thinks, he is superior to animals—other kings in the case of Muhammad—on account of his education and civilization. In his quest to prove his superiority, he alienates himself from Nature and forgets that he is a living organism himself. He wants to be different from and superior to animals. In endeavouring to be ideal, he dehumanizes himself and intensifies his alienation. In doing so, he prefers his mind to body. This shapes his culture and civilization. Its strong impact can be seen both in the society and individual. In the Hindu society, Brahmins, the caste of education and priesthood working with mind, has been accepted as superior to Shudras, the castes of physical labour till today. And in the individual, the head has been considered the supreme organ for ages. The sixth story of *Vetala Panchavimsati* tries to prove this. Girish Karnad borrows his theme for *Hayavadana* from this through Thomas Mann's *The Transposed Heads*.

The problem of alienation is brilliantly delineated by Norman O. Brown, a psychoanalyst, in his *Life against Death*.[4] He states that Apollo and Dionysus stand for self-alienation and self-unification respectively. Once man enjoyed Dionysian ego but he lost it in the process of civilization in his great endeavour to prove to himself that he is superior to all the other beings in Nature. And his mind started working independent of his body. This led to the emergence of Apollonian ego where the feelings of his mind do not spread through his body and where the sensations of his body do not reach his mind. This makes his personality and his life incomplete. Then he strives to overcome this and feels frustrated at his failure. *Hayavadana* illustrates this crisis of mankind very effectively. And

Karnad exploits *yakshagana*, the folk theatre of Karnataka, very cleverly to bring out this theme.

The play starts with the ceremonial worship of Lord Ganesha. The Bhagavata sings the hymn to Him and comments:

> An elephant's head on a human body, a broken tusk and a cracked belly—whichever way you look at him he seems the embodiment of imperfection, of incompleteness. How indeed can one fathom the mystery that this very Vakratunda-Mahakaya, with his crooked face and distorted body, is Lord and Master of Success and Perfection?[5]

Thus the invocation itself hints at the theme. As the Bhagavata starts introducing the story and the characters, the eponymous character, Hayavadana comes on the stage to the fright of Actor I. He has a human body and a horse's head. This intensifies the intended effect. It shows the alienation of the head from the body. Hayavadana narrates to the Bhagavata all his vain attempts to attain completeness. He is then advised to seek the blessings of Goddess Kali on Mount Chitrakoot. As he leaves, the play continues.

Devadatta and Kapila are very good friends in Dharmapuri. Devadatta is a Brahmin, a great scholar and poet and very fair in complexion. Kapila is an ironsmith, a good athlete and craftsman and dark in complexion. Their friendship is based on the fact that each depends on the other for what each lacks. Both of them suffer from self-alienation. In addition to that Devadatta has a brilliant mind and a weak body while Kapila has a strong body and a dull mind. Devadatta falls in love fifteen times and now his sixteenth love also seems to be a fiasco to him. Kapila easily arranges his marriage with Padmini. But he does not fall in love so easily. And he knows his love for her very late. Padmini, however, feels fascinated by his manly body. Devadatta is overwhelmed by his intense jealousy for this. All this leads them to Goddess Kali where both the men behead themselves while Padmini tries to revive them. In her haste, she transposes their heads and Kali revives them on her request. Devadatta's body gets Kapila's head and Kapila's body gets Devadatta's head. Devadatta argues that he is the rightful husband since the head is the supreme organ. This is endorsed by a sage. Padmini happily leaves with Devadatta for the town as her unconscious wish for a strong body and a brilliant mind is fulfilled in him. Kapila remains unhappily in the forest.

Devadatta and Padmini enjoy marital life much more than before. He goes to the gymnasium and takes part in wrestling and other sports to the astonishment of his friends. She is very happy about it. But he gradually loses interest in athletics and discontinues his physical exercises. He now resumes his customary duty of reading and writing and consequently loses his physical vigour. Padmini is not very happy about this change and asks him why he discontinues his physical exercises. He says: "It was fun the first few days because it was new. All that muscle and strength. But how long can one go on like that? I have the family tradition to maintain—the daily reading, writing and studies." (46) Padmini's conscious wish for the virile body finds expression in her dreams. She sends him to the Ujjain Fair to bring new dolls for their son. When he leaves for Ujjain, she takes her son and leaves for the forest in search of Kapila. She finds him without much difficulty. He says how he has retained his strong body by doing physical exercises regularly. After some time, Devadatta arrives with a doll and a sword in each hand. They exchange their experiences after the transposition of their heads. Kapila admits that he also loves Padmini. Then he suggests that they all should live together like the five Pandava princes and their common wife Draupadi in the *Mahabharata*. Since Padmini does not consent to this, they fight a duel and kill each other. Then she conveys to the Bhagavata her oral will that her son should be brought up by the hunters in the forest as the son of Kapila for five years and then by Vidyasagara, her father-in-law, as the son of Devadatta. She then commits *sati* on the pyre of Devadatta and Kapila.

After five years, Padmini's son is like Kapila. He is as morose as he. But he starts laughing for the first time in his life when Hayavadana who is now a complete horse except his human voice talks and laughs like a human being. The horse gives him a ride while the boy sings a nursery rhyme. He now loses his human voice and starts neighing. Thus they free each other from their incompleteness.

There remain certain questions to be answered: why does Hayavadana's mother feel happy about being cursed to become a mare by her husband? Why does Kali make Hayavadana a complete horse instead of a complete man? Why does the juxtaposition of a brilliant head and a strong body by Padmini fail to achieve the unification? Why does the head always win over the body? These can be answered by using the hypothesis of alienation. Animals are free from self-alienation and enjoy life fully. So the mother of Hayavadana feels very happy about her becoming a mare. Kali grants the wish of Hayavadana to become complete and he becomes a complete horse because it is not possible for men with Apollonian ego to be free from self-alienation. Padmini's juxtaposition of Kapila's strong body and Devadatta's brilliant head miserably fails to achieve unification because their heads carry Apollonian ego in themselves. For the same reason, Devadatta and Kapila become their old selves again. When Padmini realizes this, she says to Kapila:

> Your body bathed in a river, swam and danced in it. Shouldn't your head know what river it was, what swim? Your head too must submerge in that river—the flow must rumple your hair, run its tongue in your ears and press your head to its bosom. Until that's done, you'll continue to be incomplete. (58)

But Padmini does not give up her aim of achieving unification and tries to achieve it through her son posthumously as her oral will testifies it.

The division of labour has brought about both social and gender disparities. Alienation has invaded our society in two planes: class or caste and gender. Gender and caste are actually socio-cultural constructs but not biological realities. They are against the progress of a society and welfare of a person as they cause not only alienation but also antagonism among people. *Naga-Mandala* and *Tale-Danda* deal with these gender and social inequalities respectively.

Karnad wrote *Naga-Mandala* after a very long gap. He borrows the theme from two Kannada folk tales that he has heard from A.K. Ramanujan, his friend and guru. The play mocks at and questions the unjust values of our patriarchal society. It is about Rani, representing a typical Hindu wife. Apanna, a wealthy village youth, marries her and brings her to his house when she attains womanhood. He has a bath and lunch, locks her in and goes to his concubine. He does not care for her feelings and considers her a subhuman slave who is to serve him with absolute loyalty. He treats her with the contempt of a typical male chauvinist. She feels lonely, frightened and miserable. When she expresses her fear and loneliness, he mercilessly disregards her feelings. He says to her: "Look, I don't like idle chatter. Don't question me. Do as you are told and you won't be punished."[6] She is literally imprisoned in the house and it is almost a solitary confinement for her as he orders, "She won't talk to anyone. And no one need talk to her." (14) She is deprived of the affection of her fellow human beings and the knowledge of the outer world. So her personality remains underdeveloped. She is just a child mentally. She daydreams that she is taken by an eagle to her parents who caress her affectionately. She moans in her sleep for her parents. When she gets up, she weeps over her miserable life. According to Karnad, her being locked in the empty house symbolizes the apathy of her in-laws.[7] This also reminds us of the chastity belt of medieval ages.

Kurudavva, the friend of Appanna's mother, visits Rani and learns about her pathetic condition. She sympathizes with her and consoles her when Rani bursts into tears. She then gives her two pieces of aphrodisian root and advises her to administer a piece with his food to him. Appanna sees blind Kurudavva at his house. He does not want anybody to visit his house and so fetches a dog. Rani prepares a curry and mixes the paste of the root. But it gives out sinister fumes and she fears that it may harm her husband. So she throws the curry on the anthill. Appanna slaps her so hard for going out that she falls onto the floor. Here Rani's care not to cause any harm to her husband and his punishing her hard for her impeccable behaviour are juxtaposed to bring out the gross injustice meted out to women in our patriarchal society.

Naga, a king cobra living in the anthill, consumes the curry and at once falls in love with Rani. At night, he enters her home and assumes Appanna's form. He is very kind and affectionate to her. She feels elated but cannot believe it since Appanna cannot be so humane. So she asks, "You talk so nicely at night. But during the day I only have to open my mouth and you hiss like a . . . stupid snake." (22). After a little argument, he orders: "I am afraid that is how it is going to be. Like *that* during the day. Like *this* at night. Don't ask me why." (23) So, she willingly suspends her disbelief and enjoys his love. Rajinder Paul points out, "It is a play where a cobra plays the lover and proves to be better behaved than his human counterpart who is as insensitive as a husband as we read about in bad tales."[8] It can also be that Appanna and Naga represent the two unconnected roles of a husband—"as a stranger during the day and as lover at night," as Karnad rightly observes.[9]

Rani feels very happy when she becomes pregnant because she is now sure that her nocturnal joy is real. But Naga is shocked to hear it as it will reveal his identity. He asks her to keep it secret as long as possible even from him by which he means that Appanna should not be told about it. But Rani is totally confused as she still thinks that it is Appanna who visits her at night. As it dawns, Appanna comes and finds his wife pregnant. He, being enraged at it, curses her cruelly: "Aren't you ashamed to admit it, you harlot? I locked you in, and yet you managed to find a lover! Tell me who it is. Who did you go with your sari off?" (33) He drags her out and lifts a boulder to kill her but throws it at the cobra which comes out to save her. At once, she runs in and bolts the door. He curses her and goes out to arrange the village court. Naga again comes that night and advises her to take the snake ordeal and promises to fulfill all her wishes.

The village Elders sit in judgement the next day. Appanna accuses her of adultery and Rani pleads innocence. They ask her to prove her innocence by taking the red-hot iron ordeal. But she requests them to let her take the snake ordeal. As they consent to her request, she puts her hand into the anthill and takes out the cobra. While holding the cobra, she says that she has not touched anybody except her husband and that cobra. Then the snake goes up and spreads its hood above her head like an umbrella. This rare spectacle awes everybody there and all prostrate in front of her with reverence. Even Appanna cannot comprehend the situation. His concubine repents for her sins and becomes Rani's servant-maid. Appanna becomes a docile and devoted husband. Rani bears a son. Thus she gets everything that Naga has promised her.

Rani commits adultery without knowing it since Naga always visits her in the guise of Appanna whereas Appanna openly commits adultery with his concubine. Yet the Village Court tries the case of Rani only. This juxtaposition of male and female culprits at the Village Court which ignores the crime of Appanna highlights the gender biased justice. A similar juxtaposition can be found in Tendulkar's *Silence! The Court is in Session*, which is taken from a real life incident. In the name of a mock-trial, a troupe of amateur actors inhumanly torture Leela Benare mentally by accusing her of fornication while excluding the male culprit from the trial.

Tale-Danda is historical, like *Tughlaq.* It throws light on the inhuman system of caste that has prevailed for ages in the Hindu society. According to the Hindu tradition, there are four varnas: Brahmins, Kshatriyas, Vaishyas and Shudras. Their functions are priesthood and education, administration and war, trade, and productive work. Brahmins are the most privileged of all. And the last class which is not considered a *varna* is that of *Panchamas*, untouchables. Ambedkar points out, "Caste system is not merely a division of labourers—which is quite different from division of labour—it is an hierarchy in which the divisions of labourers are graded one above the other."[10] Eight centuries ago, in the court of Bijjala, the king of North Karnataka, there were great scholars and poets who rebelled against the inhuman traditions of Brahminical culture under the leadership of Basavanna, the king's officer and the great poet-philosopher. They shed their caste and became *sharanas*, devotees of Lord Shiva. Their noble movement ended in a disaster when the marriage of a Brahmin girl to a Dalit boy led to the fateful war between the orthodox people and *sharanas*. *Tale-Danda* dramatizes this.

Bijjala is a Shudra, a barber by caste. But his forefathers were very rich and bribed the Brahmins enormously for branding the caste of Kshatriya on their heads. Thus they acquired the eligibility to rule a kingdom. Yet he is looked down upon by the orthodox Hindus. However, he receives due respect from *sharanas* and is grateful to them. He also likes them because they work hard and help his city prosper. They also reciprocate his good will for them.

Bijjala marries a royal princess, Rambhavati who bears him a son, Sovideva. He loves Sovideva but detests his unprincely behaviour. So he does not favour him while he makes the sons of his other wives local lords. Sovideva resents this and also his father's association with Basavanna. He therefore waits for a chance to make Basavanna unpopular and thus to gain his father's favour. He enters the royal treasury to steal coffers and then accuse Basavanna of spending royal revenue on *sharanas* when Basavanna is away. But Jagadeva, a *sharana*, knows it in time and, with the help of thousands of *sharanas*, prevents Sovideva from stealing coffers. Basavanna later arrives and releases Sovideva after finding the treasury intact. Sovideva loses the confidence of his father and becomes more resentful than before.

One day, *sharanas* assemble at Basavanna's house and propose the marriage between Kalavati, a Brahmin girl and Sheelavanta, a

Dalit boy. Their parents invite Basavanna to the betrothal. There, he expresses his apprehension about its dire consequences: "It's a question of life and death for these children. From tomorrow the wrath of the bigoted will pursue them like a swarm of snakes, to strike as they pause to put up a roof or light an oven. Who will protect them?"[11] Overwhelmed by the fervour of performing this casteless marriage, they misunderstand him and question, "So how many more generations have to roll by before a cobbler marries a Brahmin?" (44) Thus, being urged, he finally agrees with them and they leave happily.

Bijjala requests Basavanna to stop the inter-caste marriage as it leads to lethal communal riots. Basavanna says that he does not make decisions for *sharanas* and adds that he will sit with them if he tries to stop it. Bijjala has no choice but to use his army to avert the communal violence during the marriage. This enrages the orthodox people and they rebel against the king with the help of Sovideva and royal priests. They first kill Bijjala's loyal servants and then imprison him in his own palace. Later, they begin butchering thousands of *sharanas* and ravaging their property. Sovideva leaves for his father-in-law's house to save himself from the wrath of *sharanas*. Other *sharanas* then become furious at their massacre and attack the palace under the leadership of Jagadeva. They do not find their enemies and feel frustrated. Jagadeva then kills Bijjala and commits suicide in utter disappointment.

The persecution of *sharanas* continues and they flee into the forest. Being informed of this, Sovideva says to his army:

> Pursue them. Don't let them escape. Men, women, children—cut them all down. Set the hounds after them. Search each wood, each bush. Burn the houses that give them shelter. Burn their books. Yes, the books! Tear them into shreds and consign them to the wells. Their voices shall be stilled for ever. . . . From this moment all *sharanas*, foreigners, and free thinkers are expelled from this land on pain of death. Women and the lower orders shall live within the norms prescribed by our ancient tradition, or else they'll suffer like dogs. Each citizen shall consider himself a soldier ready to lay down his life for the King. For the King is God incarnate! (90)

The crowning ceremony of Sovideva goes on when the city of Kalyan is ablaze. The pathetic screams of the victims, and the eulogies of Sovideva by Brahmins are heard simultaneously. Manchanna predictably says to Sovideva, "The *sharanas* have lost their drive and in course of time are bound to revert to caste for sheer survival." (79) It did happen and the fled *sharanas* later became the caste of Lingayats. So Karnad remarks, "You perceive deep irony, because, after all the martyrdom of the *sharanas*, when they re-emerged after three centuries of underground survival as lingayats, they were totally caste-ridden." (76) Commenting on the relevance of the play in the present age, he points out, "When people all around us are slaughtered in the name of a temple, I hear echoes from those times long past." And adds, "It seems 800 years have solved no problems. We are back exactly where we started." (76)

Karnad deals with the power game of the eponymous character and his role-shifting in *Tughlaq*, the problems of self-alienation in *Hayavadana*, gender inequality in *Naga-Mandala* and social inequality and the failure of Basavanna's reforms in eradicating it in *Tale-Danda*. These illustrate how the conventional solutions invariably fail. The protagonists in these plays strive very hard and sacrifice everything to solve the problems. Their noble struggle meets with a fiasco on account of the mighty antagonism of our morbid culture and their wrong perception of the problems. Muhammad endeavours to build for his people a heavenly kingdom of equality and communal harmony but ends up causing monstrous suffering to them. Padmini attempts to obtain the perfect man without self-alienation, through the boon of Goddess Kali but her juxtaposition of a brilliant head and a strong body is easily undone by the hegemony of Apollonian culture carried in the head. Kurudavva fails to bring about marital harmony between Rani and Appanna with her aphrodisiac root and even Naga's divine intervention cannot remove the gender inequality but reverses the gender relations only in a family. And Basavanna's indefatigable endeavour o eradicate the caste system and social disparities of the Hindu society ends up with his *sharanas* emerging as a caste, Lingayats, three centuries later. Thus Karnad makes use of myth, folk tale, legend and history. He also exploits the elements of *Yakshagana bayalata* and folk theatre in *Hayavadana*. Though he does not want to use this folk theatre anymore, he cannot give it up completely. So in his *Naga-Mandala*, the Story plays the role of the Bhagavata while the Man and the Flames are very much like the Hayavadana and the Dolls of *Hayavadana*.

NOTES

1. Girish Karnad, *Tughlaq* (Delhi: O.U.P., 1987), p. 3.
2. Aparna Dharwadker, "Historical Fictions and Postcolonial Representation: Reading Girish Karnad's *Tughlaq*," *PMLA*, Vol. 110, No. 1, Jan. 1995, p. 52.
3. Claude M. Steiner, *Scripts People Live* (New York: Bantam, 1980), p. 182.
4. Norman O. Brown, "Apollo and Dionysus," *Life against Death* (London: Routledge and Kegan Paul, 1959), pp. 155-76.
5. Girish Karnad, *Hayavadana* (Delhi : O.U.P., 1988), p. 1.
6. Girish Karnad, *Naga-Mandala* (Delhi: O.U.P., 1990), p. 7.
7. Girish Karnad, "Author's Introduction," *Three Plays* (Delhi: O.U.P., 1993), p. 17.
8. Rajinder Paul, "Karnad Plays with a Cobra," *The Book Review*, July-Aug. 1990, p. 31.
9. Girish Karnad, "Author's Introduction," p. 19.
10. *Dr. Babasaheb Ambedkar: Writings and Speeches* (Bombay: Government of Maharashtra, 1987), p. 67.
11. Girish Karnad, *Tale-Danda* (Delhi: Ravi Dayal, 1993), p. 38.

Metamorphosis as Metaphor: Shape Shifting in Girish Karnad's Plays

MAKARAND R. PARANJAPE

On the right is a slightly raised alcove which is the book lined study of a writer-academic.
On the left is a seminar table at the head of which the SUTRADHAR speaks.

SUTRADHAR, stepping into the spotlight: A strange thing has happened, esteemed colleagues, which forces me to dispense with the usual invocations, salutations and introductions. To come to the point directly, an academic paper which I was supposed to write, suddenly turned into a play. What is more, the subject of this paper, I mean play, is the theme of metamorphosis or shape shifting in Karnad's plays. If the idea is to explore the importance of shape shifting in Karnad's plays, what better way of doing it than through the transformation of an academic paper into a play? So what I now present to you is actually a play on a play.

Enter, a harassed academic, the real author of the paper. He stands at his desk and questions the SUTRADHAR.

AUTHOR: But how are you going to go about this? There's so little time, you know. And what's new about *that*—every paper is a last minute exercise. In this case, the task is even more daunting. What does one do about setting, characters, conflict, all of which are essential to drama?
SUTRADHAR: As you can see, our author is a worried man. He doesn't know how to go about his task. If I were him, I would straightaway start a conflict by introducing a villain.
AUTHOR: A villain? The most logical villain would be one who exposed my own weaknesses.

Enter WRITERS' BLOCK, a character dressed in black: I am the villain of this play, as you will have very well guessed by my dress. What's my name? Call me writers' block. I hate my author's attempts to overcome me. I keep reminding him of his unworthiness and inadequacies. For instance, I've been telling him that he's simply not qualified to write on drama, let alone write a drama. Moreover, if he wishes to write on Karnad, he should study the Kannada plays, which he hasn't done. What's the point of reading only the English translations of a couple of plays. I tell you, this author is an imposter. . .

Author falls into a swoon, felled by these strictures.
Lights dim. From a trap door in the floor beneath the stage, several shadowy figures emerge, whispering indistinctly. There's a hubbub in which nothing is clear at first.

SUTRADHAR: Ladies and gentlemen, if you've been wondering who these shady chaps are, let me tell you. They're the hazy ideas which go into the making of any paper. Let's call them paragraphs because that's the way they'll finally appear in this play of a paper.
PARAGRAPH 1: Our poor author is asleep. The tension of writing a paper has totally overpowered him.
PARAGRAPH 2: Yes, but when the conscious mind, dominated by the intellect sleeps, a lot goes on in the unconscious. That's when we come into our own, we, the disjointed thoughts and ideas that are being churned over and over in our author's mind.
PARAGRAPH 3: Look, enough of this palaver. Our audience hasn't got three hours to listen to us, but just thirty minutes. What's it that we are supposed to do?
PARAGRAPH 1: We are the various paragraphs of the author's paper. We should organize ourselves to convey the main points of his argument. I, for instance, as the host of the "thesis statement," was supposed to introduce the topic of shape shifting in Karnad's plays and to, generally, act as the discussant.
PARAGRAPH 2: I to discuss shape shifting in *Hayavadana*.
PARAGRAPH 3: I in *Tughlaq*.
PARAGRAPH 4: And I in *Naga-Mandala*. And, being the wisest of you all, to do most of the answering.
PARAGRAPH 1: But isn't there a grave illogic in this scheme? How, For instance, can we paragraphs retain our identities and numbers when we reappear? Wouldn't we become different paragraphs then?

PARAGRAPH 4: Haven't you heard of theatrical illusion, suspension of disbelief; and so on? Moreover, why should you be so literal minded? As paragraphs we increase in numbers in chronological order, but as *characters*, we retain our original numbers. OK?

PARAGRAPH 1: You won't convince most of our audience, you know. But don't you think we need to define, first of all, what shape shifting is.

PARAGRAPH 4: Shape shifting is the term cultural anthropologists and folklorists use to describe the transformations that are so common in the myths and folklore of most cultures. You know, like when a plant becomes an animal or when a woman becomes a bird, or when a statue becomes a man, or when a dead person becomes alive, or when person becomes someone else by changing shape or form in any way.

PARAGRAPH 1: That's very common. You know how the prince became a frog and then became a prince again when he was kissed by the princess. Or the story of the beauty and the beast. Or how Cinderella's fairy godmother made a fine carriage out of a pumpkin, or the legend of the werewolf. . . .

PARAGRAPH 4: Our own epics, *puranas*, and folk tales are also full of examples of shape shifting. No wonder, Karnad draws upon such resources in his plays. *Hayavadana*, as we know, is based on a story from the *Vetal Panchavimshati* and Somdeva's *Brihatkatha Saritsagar*, which were also used by Thomas Mann in a story. And *Naga-Mandala*, is based on a couple of folk tales which A.K. Ramanujan told Karnad.

PARAGRAPH 1: Is shape shifting the same across cultures or is it different?

PARAGRAPH 4: That's a tough one to handle. Earlier, our observations hinted at a universal cultural tendency to shape shift. But on closer thinking, we find that in shape shifting, to use a Judeo-Christian terminology, is something distinctly pagan, even unChristian. In traditional Christian belief, only the Devil had this power and therefore shape shifters were usually evil, like werewolfs, witches, or vampires. Abrahamic religious traditions, it would appear, were pretty literal minded, allergic to metaphor. Legitimate and "good" shape shifting was, of course, reserved only for Christ, who became a man though he was the Son of God, and who later came back to life after being crucified. We Hindus, though, have no such difficulties or squeamishness about shape shifting.

PARAGRAPH 1: But what does shape shifting represent? What does it mean? What are its functions?
PARAGRAPH 4: We have seen that shape shifting is a universal motif which does not, however, have a uniform significance. In other words, its meanings and functions change depending on the context.
PARAGRAPH 1: But surely there must be an underlying purpose.
PARAGRAPH 4: It seems to me that shape shifting is a way of exploring similarity and difference.
PARAGRAPH 1: But we need to go further than that.
PARAGRAPH 4: Well, in a sense, it proves the underlying similarity and interchangeability of all life, vegetal or animal or human. That is, all life is of the same substance and can therefore be transformed from one to the other.
PARAGRAPH 1: What a far-reaching idea. You mean that we are all the same, all of us, plants, animals, humans?
PARAGRAPH 4: We are essentially similar. We are made up of the same building blocks, which as science tells us are cells.
PARAGRAPH 1: But science totally disallows shape shifting, does it not?
PARAGRAPH 4: Depends on how you look at it. What about evolution? Doesn't it assume that one form of life gradually evolves into another through natural selection and mutation? Today don't we have organ transplantation, gene splicing and patenting of life forms?
PARAGRAPH 1: But all of that is much slower and quite less dramatic than a jilted lover turning into a *harsingar* tree or a tiger turning into a man as we have in our stories!
PARAGRAPH 4: Obviously. Literature and myth merely dramatize, heighten, and highlight what is theoretically possible in nature and science.
PARAGRAPH 1: By changing from one thing to another, what purpose is served?
PARAGRAPH 4: Well, it's like an equation or a theorem. Something is posited through a hypothesis, and then worked out in the body of the play. Shape shifting, at least in Karnad's plays, is a means to work out some ideas.
PARAGRAPH 1: Therefore, the playwright forces us to think by introducing such thought situations through the artifice of shape shifting.

PARAGRAPH 4: Yes, but remember that shape shifting is very deeply imbued in the spirit of drama itself. In any play, an actor playing a character pretends to be someone else. Drama itself depends on shape shifting. A mask, which is the central metaphor of theatre, is after all, symbolic of shape shifting.
PARAGRAPH 1: Hmm! So shape shifting, which enables us to be someone else, however temporarily, seems to be so important to all entertainment.
PARAGRAPH 4: That's why the real word for entertainment is recreation. Real entertainment doesn't just refresh you or titillate you, but it recreates you. It makes you anew.
PARAGRAPH 1: So shape shifting in Karnad is not merely a central structural strategy but a means of reviving the ancient and sacred function of drama as ritual.
PARAGRAPH 4: Yes.
PARAGRAPH 1: So far we've only considered the meanings and implications of shape shifting, but what about its necessary preconditions and consequences?
PARAGRAPH 4: You were right to raise this question. Shape shifting, after all, isn't a *normal*, ordinary, routine occurrence, no matter how prevalent it is in folklore and myth. Remember that it's common only in a certain kind of literature.
PARAGRAPH 1: You mean you won't find it in the so-called "realistic" or "naturalistic" mode?
PARAGRAPH 4: Precisely. Shape shifting only takes place in non-realistic fantasies, fables, myths, or folk tales. It is, moreover, associated with the supernatural. The crossing of boundaries, after all, is a dangerous, even magical event. It needs special powers and might have unpleasant consequences.
PARAGRAPH 1: That's why, in Karnad's plays, shape shifting often has disastrous consequences. It might end in death, destruction, or unhappiness. It's as if he who transgresses must pay the price, like Naga in *Naga-Mandala* who must die once his shape shifting is found out.
PARAGRAPH 4: Yes, shape shifting only takes place under unusual circumstances and at the behest of a powerful person or spell. In *Hayavadana*, Padmini seeks a boon from the Goddess in order to transpose the heads. In *Tughlaq*, the Emperor uses the incredible concentration of power in his hands to effect a change in the capital. And in *Naga-Mandala* the shape occurs only after Naga has been

affected by the old woman's magic potion. And in each of these cases, there is an unforeseen, unfortunate, even tragic outcome of the shape shifting.

PARAGRAPH 1: That, I think, is modern aspect of Karnad's plays. The artifice of shape shifting is traditional, ritualistic, mythical, but the outcome is tragic in a modern sense. It reveals the characters' loneliness, isolation, frustration, or self-knowledge—all achieved at a very heavy price.

PARAGRAPH 4: Some critics have accused Karnad of being a revivalist or a purveyor of gimmicks. They allege that the audience he has in mind is Western. Only will *they* be charmed by his use of myth and ritual, the argument goes. But I think we have seen that the use of myth is not merely a gimmick or a ritual or even merely a structural device. It is a means of exploring a modern outcome of a traditional situation. Thus, Karnad's plays too work out the dialectical relationship between tradition and modernity, which is a central theme in contemporary Indian society and literature.

PARAGRAPH 1: Shape shifting, in other words, is instrumental to some illumination in Karnad's characters.

PARAGRAPH 2: After having looked at the concept in general, let's take a quick look at how it works in the plays. Take *Hayavadana*. The question is of completion. What is a complete human being? Also, is the head more powerful than the body? The answer in the end is, yes, the head is more powerful than the body—if you have the head of a horse, you'll end up as a horse. Instead of a constant tension between a man and horse, it's better to be just a horse, perhaps. But also that there's no perfect being possible. For a human being, that is, it's better to live with a constant and opposing tension rather than try to resolve it through some impossible hankering after perfection. Kapila's head on Devadatta's body, therefore, results not in perfection, but in failure in the end.

PARAGRAPH 3: In *Tughlaq* the major example of shape shifting is the attempt to change the capital to Daulatabad. What's being tried is to turn Daulatabad into Delhi. The attempt, of course, fails. Why? Because there's a fundamental difference between illusion and transformation. In the former, one thing pretends to be another; in the latter, one thing becomes another. *Tughlaq* is a play full of dissimulations, illusions and lies. In fact, the whole play is about lies and hypocrisies. This is the dominant theme, illustrating the moral decline of a polity, so apt in our own times. No wonder, the play abounds in metaphors from theatre as some critics have pointed out at great length. Tughlaq himself is a great role player; in Aziz he finds his double. No wonder, Aziz kills Ghias-ud-din and pretends to be him. Daulatabad cannot succeed in being Delhi because it is blessed not by a holy man but by a murderer masquerading as a holy man. In *Tughlaq*, then, shape shifting does not really take place; instead, there is merely "acting," dissimulation, pretence and betrayal.

PARAGRAPH 4: Before I come to my task of talking about shape shifting in *Naga-Mandala*, I'd like us to remember that it is the central motif also in *Yayati* (1961), Karnad's first play, and in *Hittina Hunja* (The Cock of Flour, 1980).

Naga-Mandala (1986) has several examples of shape shifting. The main one, of course, is the cobra assuming the form of Appanna to make love to Rani. But earlier, the flames take on human shapes to gossip at the temple after they've been "put out" in the houses. In the New Flame's story of the old woman who knew a story and a song, the story becomes a young woman and the song, a sari. Wearing the sari, the story walks out of the old woman's house. The point is that stories mustn't be stingily confined to oneself as the old woman did, but shared. As Flame 1 puts it, "So if you try to gag one story, another happens." And later, the woman Rani, after her cobra ordeal, is apotheosized into a living goddess, an extraordinary woman.

PARAGRAPH 1: Please explain the significance of the shape shifting in this play.

PARAGRAPH 4: The way I see it, this play is about narrativity, or the truth of fictions. The union of Rani and Naga is fruitful, though the latter is not a man. Why? Because reality (Appanna) is harsh, unkind, and cruel, but fantasy, art, love (Naga) is more fulfilling, satisfying, and energizing. In this case, the recreation is literal—Rani and Naga have a child but not Rani and Appanna.

PARAGRAPH 1: But in your scheme, what does Rani represent?

PARAGRAPH 4: Rani stands for the creative mind, a mind which is innocent, open to imagination and to love. Appanna is the anti-creative principle—propriety, social restraint and philistinism. He keeps Rani locked up inside the house and consorts with a prostitute. But Rani finds a genuine lover in Naga. Later, Appanna is forced to submit to Rani when she is transformed by the power of the imagination into her full potential. The creative principle triumphs over social propriety.

Just then a loud noise is heard on stage. The lights come on to reveal the villain, WRITERS' BLOCK, storming onto centrestage. All the PARAGRAPHS cower in the harsh light.

WRITERS' BLOCK: Stop this nonsense. This is no play, neither is it an academic paper. It's an absurd farce. How can you call these jokers characters? They all sound alike.

The AUTHOR who has been lying supine so far, has been gradually stirring to consciousness during this interruption. Now he suddenly stands up and squares up to WRITERS' BLOCK

AUTHOR: Oh, so it's you! Terrorizing my poor paragraphs when I was asleep. What do you mean they all sound alike! Why shouldn't they? They're not characters, they're only paragraphs. Written by the same author. Me! Now, if you'll excuse all of us, including the audience, we have work to do. My sleep has been refreshing. I think my paper is done. There's no room for you anymore in this play. Kindly leave.

WRITERS' BLOCK has been gradually engulfed by darkness during this dialogue. Now he's completely invisible, like a shadow which has dissolved.

AUTHOR: There! We've banished him from this paper. That was easier than I had imagined.

He gestures to his paragraphs. They straighten themselves, and begin to arrange themselves into a nice formation.

AUTHOR: Now my essay is complete. Look at all these paragraphs. How neatly they've fallen into line. Yet, something is missing. Perhaps, all I now need is a conclusion.
Voice from off stage: That shouldn't be very difficult.

Enter GIRISH KARNAD, the playwright.

KARNAD: When we met, you didn't tell me you were planning to write a *play*! I must say your exercise caught me by surprise; even I hadn't thought of making paragraphs into characters!
AUTHOR: Sorry, I'm embarrassed. I must thank you, though, for

talking to me. You remember how you told me that shape shifting was like mathematics to you: hold one thing constant, change another. Then see what happens. Where does it take you? Keep pushing the idea to its logical conclusions.
KARNAD: That's what you seem to have done. Make an academic paper into a play; then see what happens.
AUTHOR: I hope you don't mind the outcome; it's my "humble tribute," as the cliche goes, to a dramatist I hugely admire. But I don't know how my "real" audience will take this exercise.
KARNAD: It's tough; you only find out on the opening night!
AUTHOR:To tell you the truth, I'm somewhat perplexed by the whole thing: I never intended to do this, even in jest.
KARNAD: It's an example of shape shifting. You know, don't you, that I never intended to be a playwright either. I wanted to be a poet, and that too in English.
AUTHOR: Luckily, for us, you changed shapes.

Enter, SUTRADHAR again.

SUTRADHAR: Learned ladies and gentlemen! Thank you for indulging this presentation of an academic paper in the shape of a play. A play, moreover, in the manner of Girish Karnad. That is, a play not in the derivative Ibsen-Shaw tradition of naturalistic drama which goes by the name of social theatre in India, but a play redolent with myth and mystery, with masks and music, in a word, a play as a ritual.

If we've confused you, we beg your pardon. Let me make your task a little easier by reiterating the main points:

Shape shifting is a central metaphor in Girish Karnad's plays.

It is both a structural and a thematic device.

It is structural in it that reflects the kind of drama that he practises. It also echoes, copies, and re-enacts within the play one of the primary functions of drama itself, which is allowing a person to be someone else for a short while in order to provide recreation to both audience and performer.

Shape shifting, then, appeals to our deepest instincts for freedom and flexibility, giving vent to our urge to escape the limiting confines of our physical and psychological beings.

Shape shifting is thematic in that Karnad uses it to work out certain theses and antitheses. It is the chief vehicle of his ideas in the plays.

Shape shifting is a convenient method of exploring differences and similarities between characters, situations, and ideas. It proves an underlying unity in the substratum of life while allowing multitudinous diversity on the surface.

Shape shifting, however, is a kind of transgression. And transgressions always have a heavy price tag. Usually, there is death or destruction. Hence, though as a device it is traditional, the consequences of shape shifting in Karnad's plays are always modern. In the end, shape shifting in Karnad's plays is a means to illumination and self-knowledge, not only for the characters, but for the audience.

NOTE

For the most detailed treatment of the subject, see the monumental *Motif-Index of Folk Literature* by Stith Thompson (Bloomington, Indiana: Univ. Press, 1955-1958). A briefer, informative essay on shape shifting can be found in *The Encyclopedia of Religion*, ed. Mircea Eliade (New York: Macmillan, 1987). There are entries in other reference works such as *Encyclopedia of Religion and Ethics*, ed. James Hastings (1915; rpt. Edinburgh: Clark, 1958) and *Encyclopedia Britannica* under "Metamorphosis" and "Animals and Plants in Myth and Legend," respectively. Shape shifting is also known as lycanthorpy.

A brief but illuminating interview of Girish Karnad by Rajinder Paul was published in *Enact*, 54 (1971). The playwright's "Meet the Author" address on 16 November 1989 was subsequently published in *Indian Literature* under the title "Acrobating between the traditional and the modern."

The Play of Power-Politics: A Study of *Tughlaq*, *Hayavadana* and *Tale-Danda*

GEETA KUMAR

Ronald V. Samson in *The Psychology of Power* brilliantly analyses how power corrupts basic human relationships. If politics is taken as power-structured relationships or arrangements whereby one group of persons is controlled by another and since the essence of politics is power, the play of power-politics would work towards domination and imposing of one's will on others.

Girish Karnad's play *Tughlaq*, a superb classic in pan-Indian literature, is incomparable in depth and range. Based on historical facts, it is not just a political allegory but a tightly-knit drama about the failure of an idealistic but megalomaniac ruler of the fourteenth century who combined in himself so many qualities such as patriotism, liberalism, scientific temper and studious nature, innovative and original ideas which achieve nothing but chaos at personal and state level.

The play of power-politics is expertly handled by the crafty ruler, Muhammad-bin-Tughlaq ruling in Delhi in 1327. Despite his various commendable qualities, he turns out to be a tyrant who causes untold sufferings not just to the people surrounding him but also his subjects. The symbiotic relationship between the titanic ruler and his cringing courtiers wanting to curry favour with him to climb the ladder of political power is always uneasy and shaky.

Throughout the play, Tughlaq does not have a single moment of peace and rest as he is always suspicious of the motives of the people close to him. How many imposters, betrayers, rebels and treacherous people prowled around him and yet basked in his misplaced patronage. Merely mouthing platitudes, they never lent him any real support. The country's maladies which needed the solid support of not only the Amirs but also the popular pyramid was never there. The people thought him mad and the Amirs termed him tyrannical.

Tughlaq however is a formidable ruler who would not let anything or anybody come in his way of the pursuit of power. His answer to resistance is his sword. His unpopular schemes such as moving the capital from Delhi to Daulatabad and making copper coins the acceptable currency create many foes for him. He calls these no "mad whims of a tyrant" but gives solid reasons such as Delhi being too near the border and Daulatabad being a city of Hindus turning into a bond between Hindus and Muslims. But this cuts no ice with either the people or the Amirs.

Tughlaq is an usurper, having come to the throne after getting his father and brother murdered during prayer time, and has blood on his hands at such a young age. The murky path to political power has been traversed by this power-politicker, having committed heinous crimes of parricide and fratricide. Such questions are irrelevant for this ruthless man and sharing of power is out of question. Dissent of course would be blasphemous in his kingdom. He would prefer to have only fawning sycophants around him.

To have the reins of power firmly in his hands, all formidable foes are silenced one by one. A discriminating study of power-politics in *Tughlaq* would make it amply clear that to survive in the game of snakes and ladders, the merely competent like Shihab-ud-din, the upright saint like Sheikh Imam-ud-din and later the slightly independent stepmother have to be weeded out ruthlessly.

The play of power-politics works in a fascinating way when Tughlaq invites Sheikh Imam-ud-din, his worst critic, to address a meeting of the people in the yard in front of the big mosque. The Sheikh has been reported to have said that Muhammad has forfeited the right to rule by murdering his father and brother during prayer-time, thereby polluting the prayer. Kanpur, where he addressed meetings, witnessed riots. Muhammad arranges things in such a way that not a single person turns up for the meeting. Imam-ud-din is disappointed but points out 'scores of transgressions' on Muhammad's part and accuses him of having put the best of Ulemas and Sayyids behind bars in the name of justice. Muhammad's answer is: "They tried to indulge in politics. I couldn't allow that."[2] Imam-ud-din accuses Muhammad of trying to become God: "Beware Sultan, you are trying to become another god. It's a sin worse than parricide. . . . Religion! Politics! Take heed Sultan, one day such verbal distinctions will rip you into two." (21)

Muhammad's master stroke in power-politics is yet to come. He persuades Sheikh Sahib to go as his envoy to meet Ain-ul-Mulk to dissuade him from marching to Delhi. The bait is that such a saintly person would not like to see Muslims slaughtered at the hands of fellow Muslims. The Sheikh who resembles Tughlaq is given royal robes and is put on the royal elephant. The meeting is set near the plains of Kannauj. The enemy thinks it is Tughlaq coming for peace talks. Tughlaq's soldiers start the attack, hiding behind the hills. Sheikh Sahib is killed and Ain-ul-Mulk's army rushes in the trap set by Tughlaq. Superb statecraftsmanship is evident as two birds are killed with one stone. Both adversaries crushed—one is literally turned into a gory human porcupine because of arrows—the other Ain-ul-Mulk crushed with the generosity of pardon because he is able to detect a flaw in the solution found by Muhammad to the famous chess-problem set by Al-Adli. As for the common soldiers, it was the 'bloodiest massacre' ever seen, says Ratan Singh, an eyewitness and 'a front ranker' in the platoon of Sheikh Sahib.

Shihab-ud-din and some Amirs of Delhi who hatch a conspiracy against Tughlaq are called ostensibly for consultations and discussions. A "long rope" is given to them in the form of asking for suggestions and being told about future plans. Muhammad kneels before them and asks them to take an oath on Koran to support him in his new measures. There is not an inkling about what the master strategist is planning to do. Undoubtedly it is Ratan Singh who has betrayed all of them. The Amirs are arrested and taken away. Muhammad himself stabs Shihab-ud-din repeatedly as if in a frenzy, orders all involved to be beheaded, their bodies stuffed with straw to be sent around his kingdom for all to see. But the smart power-politicker that Tughlaq is, he knows how to turn the volatile situation which would follow to his advantage. He says: "Make a public announcement that there was a rebellion in the palace and that the nobles of the court tried to assassinate the Sultan during prayer. Say that the Sultan was saved by Shihab-ud-din who died a martyr's death defending him. The funeral will be held in Delhi and will be a grand affair. Invite his father to it and see that he is treated with the respect due to the father of a loyal nobleman." To this, Barani replies, "Oh God! Aren't even the dead free from your politics?" (43-44)

Subsequently Muhammad becomes even more cruel. Prayers are banned throughout the kingdom till Ghiyas-ud-din, the descendent of the Khalif would visit the kingdom. He orders Delhi to be vacated immediately. "Nothing but an empty graveyard of Delhi will satisfy me now," he says.

It remains for Aziz, a Muslim Dhobi who is masquerading as Vishnu Prasad, to gain wealth and position to comment on power-politics working at other levels in Delhi as it has been, before Tughlaq's order: "Look at me. Only a few months in Delhi and I have discovered a whole new world—Politics! My dear fellow that's where our future is—politics! It's a beautiful world—wealth, success, position, power—and yet it is full of brainless people, people with not an idea in their head." (50)

Yet this power-politics has led the protagonist of the play to nothing but loneliness, insomnia, a honey-comb of diseases, uprisings and revolts in Bengal, Deccan, Doab as also the consequent frustration. Barani the historian advises Muhammad: "You are a learned man. Your majesty, you are known the world over for your knowledge of philosophy and poetry. History is not made only in statecraft, its lasting results are produced in the ranks of learned men. That's where you belong, your Majesty, in the company of learned men. Not in the market of corpses." (55)

The stepmother in her own selfish pursuit of power, wants to control Muhammad. Not just satisfied with the incestuous relationship with him, she has the Vizier Najib poisoned. But Muhammad's mad lust for power, which he wouldn't allow anyone to share, makes him sentence her to stoning to death in public. His conscience, however, does not let him rest and nagging questions sting him like mad. "My skin drips with blood," he says again and again, "why am I become a pig rolling in the gory mud?. . . . I am teetering on the brink of madness." (67-68)

Seven years have passed since Delhi was forced to shift to Daulatabad. The meandering road to Daulatabad is littered with corpses, people have no food and instead eat burnt strips of skin and skins of dead horses, riots have broken out and in an ironic twist of circumstances, it is Aziz, the masquerader, the murderer and the villain who is sent to be appointed as an army officer in Deccan by Muhammad because he claims to be a true disciple of his. Is it power-politics, diplomacy or face-saving on Tughlaq's part because he had publicly fallen at the feet of Aziz masquerading as Ghiyas-ud-din, welcomed him as a saint and called him a saviour?

In a final 'mad' decision, Tughlaq decides to shift the capital back to Delhi. Would this decision assure him of peace of mind and security and approbation he had been looking for? Or has the play of power-politics taken its toll as he is haunted by memories and has only frustration and disillusionment to look forward to? There are no answers because the play ends with Muhammad looking around dazed and frightened as though he can't comprehend where he is.

II

Power-politics in *Hayavadana* is of a totally different kind. Not Kate Millettian but Freudian. Psychoanalytically speaking, the unknown forces and drives in the mental structure of Devadatta [his unconscious] were always aware of the fatal attraction between his wife and his best friend Kapila. In *Hayavadana*, there are no realms to be won over, no kingdoms to be fought over. Rather it is the heart of a young maiden Padmini, "the Shyama Nayika—born of Kalidasa's description."

But power-politics is certainly there. It is a psychological warfare. If Devadatta seems to have won in the beginning, his victory is only illusory. And Kapila never stops trying. He has only to set eyes on Padmini before he goes weak-kneed. He thinks she needs 'a man of steel,' which of course, he qualifies to be. He runs errands for her, looks at her with 'dog's eyes,' is totally devoted and all in the presence of her husband and his best friend, Devadatta. He may call her sister-in-law but his eyes and his gestures betray that his heart is at variance with his tongue. For him she is "Yakshini, Shakuntala, Urvashi, Indumati, all rolled into one."[3] Not only that, she is "fast as lightning" and as sharp. He is so besotted with her that Devadatta can see through him easily and says in an aside: "He only has to see her and he begins to wag his tail. Sits up on his hind legs as though he were afraid to let her words fall to the ground." (22)

The plot of *Hayavadana* is from *Katha Saritasagara*, an ancient collection of stories in Sanskrit. Girish Karnad has, however, borrowed from Thomas Mann's retelling of the story in "The Transposed Heads." Both Girish Karnad and Thomas Mann seem to be pointing out that head is not superior to the body, as in the original story. In fact there can be no differentiation between body and the 'Uttam Anga,' the head.

According to the Bhagavata in Karnad's play, the two friends with "one mind and one heart" fall for the same woman—"They saw a girl and forgot themselves." (11) Devadatta tries to cancel the Ujjain trip with Kapila in tow because he does not want Padmini to be drooling over Kapila the whole day, "twittering, Kapila, Kapila, every minute." (21) Kapila feels crestfallen "as though the whole world has been wiped out for a whole week." (23)

The war of nerves is stopped temporarily because Padmini suddenly decides to go on with the trip. It is Devadatta's turn now to feel defeated and the Bhagavata puts it beautifully: "Why do you tremble, heart? Why do you cringe like a touch-me-not bush through which a snake has passed?" (24)

Kapila is totally under Padmini's spell throughout the trip, over-eager to please her; and runs off to get the fortunate lady's flower, climbing a tree and swinging up its branch, brings a heap of flowers for her. Devadatta has noticed "the pleading in his eyes, stretching out its arms and asking for a favour." (26)

Devadatta, on finding the first suitable opportunity, sensing imminent psychological defeat, goes up to the Kali temple [the other two have gone to the Rudra temple] but instead of offering his arms, as he had earlier promised if he won over Padmini, cuts off his head as an offering to the Goddess. When Padmini and Kapila come back, Kapila goes to look for Devadatta, finds his headless body and in anguish, after giving a long speech full of protestations of love and devotion for "my brother, my father, my friend" and commenting that Devadatta had "spurned" him in this world, he too cuts off his head. It may seem at first that it's all genuine reaction to a very dear friend's death but the real reason is given by Goddess Kali:

> The rascals! They were lying to their last breaths. That fellow Devadatta—he had once promised his head to Rudra and his arms to me! Think of it—head to him and arms to me! Then because you insisted on going to the Rudra temple, he comes here and offers his head. Nobly too—wants to keep his word, he says—no other reason!
>
> Then this Kapila. Died right in front of me, but "for his friend." Mind you, didn't have the courtesy to refer to me. And what lies! says he is dying for friendship. He must have known perfectly well he would be accused of killing Devadatta for you. Do you think he wouldn't have grabbed

> you, if it hadn't been for that far? But till his last breath "Oh my friend! My dear brother!" (33)

The story however doesn't end here. On Padmini's entreaties, Goddess Kali grants her Devadatta and Kapila's lives if she would rejoin their heads to their respective bodies and press the sword on their necks. In her excitement, however, she mixes up the heads so that Devadatta gets Kapila's body and vice versa. Both are highly amused and have a good laugh over their becoming 'blood-relations.'

The politicking for the power to possess Padmini's heart starts in right earnest when the question arises as to with whom Padmini will go. Kapila now thinks he is on a safe wicket and so demands that Padmini must come home with him. His logic is unbeatable but is not accepted by Padmini and Devadatta who consider the head to be "the sign of a man." Kapila says: "This is the hand that accepted her at the wedding. This the body, she's lived with all these months. And the child she's carrying is the seed of this body." (87)

When Devadatta tries to convince him quoting the sacred texts, he snaps back: "Don't tell me about your sacred texts. You can always twist them to suit your needs." Arguments, bodily stepping between the husband and the wife, prepared to "kick up a row in the streets" and the final ultimatum: "You will have to kill me before you really escape me."

This is indeed a new Kapila, confident, aggressive and could even be violent if straightforward politicking fails him. The urge to possess Padmini is powerful enough to make him go to any length. Forcefully asserting his right to have what he thinks is rightfully his, he would stop at nothing.

However fates will otherwise. The "three unfortunate beings" whose entire future hangs in balance, go to a great Rishi who rules in Devadatta's favour by saying: "As the heavenly Kalpa Vriksha is supreme among trees so is the head among human limbs. Therefore the man with Devadatta's head is indeed Devadatta and he is the rightful husband of Padmini." (40)

Kapila, broken-hearted, drags his feet away but it is only a diplomatic withdrawal. He knows Padmini will come back to him and sooner rather than later. He has a kind of consolation as Padmini in an aside says to him: "It's my duty to go with Devadatta. But remember I'm going with your body. Let that cheer you up." (41)

Very soon, she tires of the fabulous body, fabulous brain of fabulous Devadatta and remembers with fondness "the unwashed sweaty smell of Kapila." She starts dreaming and fantasizing about him and their past life. One fine day when Devadatta has gone to Ujjain on the pretext of showing her child the witching fair of the dark forest, goes to meet Kapila asking the villagers, the pilgrims, the hunters, the tribesmen, the way to the forest. She meets Kapila and shows him the son claiming it was his son, "begotten of that body with the mole on the shoulder." Kapila resists first but this is what he has been hankering after. Kapila's head is also to know what his body—[previously Devadatta's]—has already known. As Padmini puts it:

> Your body bathed in a river, swam and danced in it. Shouldn't your head know what river it was? What swim? Your head too must submerge in that river—the flow must rumple your hair—run its tongue in your ears and press your head to its bosom. Until that's done you will continue to be incomplete. . . . My Kapila, my poor, poor Kapila! How needlessly, you've tortured yourself. (58)

The politicking has won for Kapila what it wanted. It is triumphant, albeit temporarily, but it is bliss as long as it lasts. When Devadatta finds them after "four or five days," there has to be a fight to the finish. Living like "Pandavas and Draupadi" is impossible and so there is a bloody duel and it is understood by both that they have to die. Girish Karnad uses animal imagery when Devadatta says: "No grounds for friendship now. No question of mercy. We must fight like lions and kill like cobras." (60) The Bhagavata refers to it as a fight of "cocks in a pit."

Padmini commits sati leaving her son to the care of the tribesmen giving them the impression that it is Kapila's son. She tells the Bhagavata that the son is to be taken to Revered Brahmin Vidyasagara of Dharmapura when he is five and to be told that it is Devadatta's son.

Power-politics in *Hayavadana* comes to an end with all the three major characters being dead but Padmini has the last word:

> They burned, lived, fought, embraced and died. I stood silent. If I'd said, "Yes, I will live with you both" perhaps they

> would have been alive yet. But I couldn't say it. . . . You would have had to share not only me but your bodies as well. . . . You could have only lived ripping each other to pieces. I had to drive you to death. (62)

III

The play of power-politics in *Tale-Danda* is fascinating although it is based on a historical incident which took place in the twelfth century but the issues it raises are extremely relevant in contemporary society.

Unlike *Tughlaq*, here it is a group of people, the upper-caste Brahmins and the ruling class nobility which along with King Bijjala's son Sovideva play power-politics first deftly and when it fails, ruthlessly to suppress and kill all opposition. There is terrible bloodshed at the end of the play in Kalyan [where the play is set] so that the whole city is drowned in a sea of blood. The Hindi translation of *Tale-Danda* is appropriately called *Rakt Kalyan*. Probably the stakes are higher in this play. In view of the defenders of the system, on stake is not just one kingdom but a whole set of two thousand-year-old values supporting the caste system. As the caste in India is derived from birth alone, it is a closed system. The caste cannot be transferred from one class to another class or be gained as a reward for the highest merit or bestowed as an honorary title by even the most powerful monarch. The essential features of the caste system such as hierarchy, restrictions on marriage and food and hereditary occupation are challenged and flouted by Basavanna, and his followers in *Tale-Danda*. This is just not acceptable to the conservative elements of the society and the confrontation can only lead to disaster.

Basavanna, a poet and social reformer, is King Bijjala's treasurer. Through his path-breaking ideal, he has been able to gather round him, a number of people—*sharanas* [these include Brahmins too, as Jayadeva and Madhuvarsa are] as they are called who believe in his ideal of a casteless and classless society. This movement exhorts people to believe in the idea of 'work is worship.' Basavanna has the king's support too as King Bijjala himself is a 'Kalchoori'—a barber. The difference is that since five generations back, this family has been messengers and through marriages in royal families and grabbing power have got some semblance of respectability. King Bijjala himself has married into a Kshatriya Royal family of Hoysalas. Bijjala is quite conscious of his caste and says only *sharanas* are not bothered about his low caste. He says:

> A man's caste is like the skin on his body. You can peel off the skin but whenever the new skin appears, people recognize the skin—the same old skin—same old caste—Kshatriyas, Rajputs. Untouchables, herdsmen—This is the special trait of this earth—special trait of the water here. . . . I am sixty-two. In all these years, the only people whose eyes did not have a shadow of my caste are *sharanas*, Basavanna and his people.[4]

Basavanna has agreed to be the treasurer of the Royal treasure as, according to him, the king is only a keeper of the people's money. But he quits when doubts are raised by Sovideva, the king's son, about his honesty. On Sovideva's opening of the lock of the Royal Treasure, ten thousand *sharanas* surround the treasury to make sure, no conspiracy is hatched to involve Basavanna.

Bijjala's play of power-politics is ironically inspired by Basavanna's ideals. He says:

> Some fifteen years back I was a feudal lord in Mangalwad with Chalukyas. I thought being a feudal lord, my life was blessed. Then I met Basavanna. He was hardly twenty then but his life-philosophy was ready—King is not by birth but by merit, by authority. Suddenly I thought this is absolutely right. I can rule a kingdom very ably. The fool that rules Kalyan, I can rule better than him. So I finished him off and became the king. Without Basavanna, I would have never thought of such a thing. (29-30)

Bijjala has already ruled for fifteen years but finally it is power-politics of the troika of Damodar Bhatt (Queen Rambhavati's priest), Manchanna Kramita (Advisor to the King) and Prince Sovideva (who is being denied the right to be called heir-apparent by his father) which succeeds in its evil design of dethroning the king and grabbing power. Not only that, they succeed in destroying the momentum of a new reformist movement with progressive ideas which rejected idol-worship, rituals, class-distinctions, casteism, superstitions, profiteering and other obscurantist ideas.

The news of the marriage-celebrations between a boy and a girl from *sharana* families proves to be the last straw as tempers are already running high in certain sections of the society. The boy belongs to the erstwhile untouchable community and the girl to a Brahmin family but both families are converts to the new *sharana* faith. The old system has been challenged and the Brahmin ghettos witness some unrest.

Damodar Bhatta's politicking starts with convincing Sovideva to rise in revolt against his father because the King has failed to stop the marriage and has instead tried to protect *sharanas*. According to him: "This marriage is a blow to our Vedic civilization. It takes centuries to create a new civilization breaking a chain of beliefs but one blow can destroy a whole civilization. . . . Inequality is in nature itself. Struggle, competition and violence are all part of Mother Nature. The varnashrama follows this." (64)

King Bijjala is dethroned but not killed by Damodar Bhatt, Manchanna Kramita and Prince Sovideva to save their own skins. It is left to Jagdev, a brahmin-turned-*sharana* who enters the palace through a secret passage and kills Bijjala by enticing him to come out of the Siva temple. The Queen had died earlier and the king is half-mad when he is killed.

Basavanna leaves Kalyan with about 770 *sharanas*. But there are still over a lakh of *sharanas* in Kalyan. The politics players can certainly not afford to allow them to live in peace or even escape. The three of them have a crucial meeting to decide what is to be done. Manchanna Kramita is emphatic about the decimation of the *sharanas*: "Maharaj, the Kashmir Emperor Mihirbala destroyed 1600 Buddha Viharas to stop the Buddhists. You know yourself that our neighbour, Tamil Emperor Pandeya got 8000 Jain Munis crushed. Why should we be so contemplative? Why such cowardice? . . . The king is God Incarnate." (85)

As a result of the power-politickers' decisions, the fathers of the bride and groom are caught, their eyes are gouged out. Tied to an elephant's feet, they are dragged through the streets of Kalyan. The whole city burns. There are widespread riots, stampedes, fires, murders, rapes and looting. Damodar Bhatt is also killed by a soldier but Sovideva is still not satisfied. He wants total annihilation of the *sharanas*: "These *sharanas* are after me. They are snakes, destroy them. Don't let them run, pursue them and kill them. Men, women and children—Don't spare anyone—set the hunting dogs on them. Bushes, forests, houses, whatever protects the *sharanas*, burn it—Burn their holy books—I will have to kill my brothers too—All tongues and hands against the king will be cut—*sharanas*, atheists, foreigners and free thinkers will not be allowed to enter our kingdom. Women and men of lower castes will have to live within their limits as has been the practice in the past or their fate will be worse than those of dogs—the king is the incarnation of God on this earth." (94-95)

The whole city of Kalyan is bathed in the blood of innocent people because the power-hungry rulers and the obscurantist nobility would not accept change. Their pathological hatred of the lower castes has led them to behave bestially. For the manipulators of the political system, men and women are merely pawns to be sacrificed at will for self-interest and grabbing of power.

NOTES

1. (New York: Random House, 1968).
2. Girish Karnad, *Three Modern Indian Plays* (New Delhi: OUP, 1989), p. 20.
3. Girish Karnad, *Hayavadana* (New Delhi: OUP), p. 16.
4. Girish Karnad, *Rakt Kalyan*, trans. into Hindi by Ramgopal Bajaj (Delhi: Radhakrishan Prakashan, 1994), p. 24.

Karnad's *Yayati* Reconsidered

SEEMA SUNEEL

Indian drama written during the recent decades manifests a significant influence of the west. Several playwrights writing during this period show their indebtedness not only to Sartre, Camus, Pinter, Beckett, Ionesco but also to Pirandello and Brecht. Girish Karnad, P. Lankesh, Chandrasekhara Kambar and Chandrashekara Patil, conscious of the western norms as also of the Indian tradition, have enriched the contemporary Indian drama immensely.

Karnad is regarded as one of the three great writers of the contemporary Indian drama, the other two being Vijay Tendulkar and Badal Sircar. Whileas Badal Sircar and Vijay Tendulkar deal with the problems of the middle-class, Girish Karnad takes refuge in the Indian myths and legends and makes them a vehicle of a new vision. By using these myths, he tries to show the absurdity of life with all its elemental passions and conflicts, and man's eternal struggle to achieve perfection.

II

Girish Karnad, popular playwright, script writer, is a significant name on the Indian literary scene. He is an actor, director and a film-maker. Son of Raghunath and Kasibai, he was born in Maharashtra though his mother tongue is Kannada. Before joining the celluloid world he undertook several assignments. He worked as Manager of Oxford University Press, Madras (1963-70); was Director of Film and Television Institute, Pune (1974-75). Also he had a number of academic assignments in foreign countries, and wrote extensively on art, literature and culture. Currently, he is the Chairman of the Sangeet Natak Akademi, New Delhi.

Karnad's significant plays include *Yayati, Tughlaq, Hittina Hunja, Hayavadana* and *Naga-Mandala*. He was given a state award for *Yayati*. In 1972, he received the prestigious Sangeet Natak Akademi award. He was honoured by the Bharatiya Natya Sangha for his play *Hayavadana*.

In plays like *Yayati* and *Hayavadana*, Karnad has taken traditional puranic themes but has given a fresh interpretation to these. His plays have pioneered a style which unites the elements of traditional Indian theatre, such as 'Yakshagana' and strikingly modern sensibility for contemporary socio-political realities.

III

Girish Karnad's *Yayati* retells the age-old story of the mythological king who in his longing for eternal youth sought to borrow the vitality of his own son. Karnad has borrowed the myth from the *Mahabharata* and other puranas. The *Mahabharata* story runs thus: Yayati was one of the six sons of king Nahusha. Devayani, whose love for Kacha remained unrequited, marries Yayati to spite Sharmishtha for whom she nurses childhood jealousy. Sharmishtha is deeply in love with Yayati and subjects herself to a lot of physical and mental torture for love. A son is born to her out of her clandestine liaison with Yayati. Yayati, blinded by his insatiable thirst for sensual pleasures, dreads old age. Puru, Sharmishtha's son, offers to exchange his youth for the age of his father. Enlightened now, Yayati gives up the throne and retires to forest to lead a life of renunciation with Devayani and Sharmishtha.

Girish Karnad has given this traditional tale a new meaning and significance highly relevant in the context of life today. The symbolic theme of Yayati's attachment to life and its pleasures as also his final renunciation are retained.

Karnad's originality lies in working out the motivations behind Yayati's ultimate choice. In the *Mahabharata*, Yayati recognizes the nature of desire itself and realizes that fulfilment does not diminish or finish desire. In Karnad's play, however, Yayati recognizes the horror of his own life and assumes his moral responsibility after a series of symbolic encounters.

V.S. Khandekar, the eminent Marathi novelist, also used the Yayati myth in his novel *Yayati*. Published in 1959, the novel received several awards such as State Government Award, the Sahitya Akademi Award (1960) and the Jnanpith Award (1964). In his novel, Khandekar made Yayati a representative of modern common man who in spite of receiving much happiness in life remains restless and discontented. The mythical Yayati ran after sensual pleasures but Khandekar's Yayati runs after all kinds of materialistic pleasures—cars, bungalows, fat bank accounts, beautiful clothes, dance, music. Though the tale is taken from the puranas, Khandekar's Yayati is a modern man.

The existentialists like Sartre and Camus put a great stress on choice and responsibility. In an interview, Karnad says: "I was excited by the story of Yayati, this exchange of ages between the father and the son, which seemed to me terribly powerful and terribly modern. At the same time, I was reading a lot of Sartre and the Existentialists. This consistent harping on responsibility which the Existentialists indulge in suddenly seemed to link up with the story of Yayati."[1]

The purpose and theme of the play are revealed through the character of the Sutradhara. As the play opens, the Sutradhara informs the audience that it is a mythical play—a page from the history of the unknown past. The characters, the incidents and circumstances are related to the old times. However, the reality depicted in the play is applicable to modern times as well.

The Sutradhara says that neither a scholar nor an ordinary person can escape the burden of responsibility wherein lies the joy of life. Whether it is an old man in search of lost youth or a saint lost in the darkness or the mute actress following him—everyone carries a tree of responsibility all along one's life journey and finally hangs from it. The Sutradhara brings forth the theme of responsibility:

> Sometimes when we are walking along a path we see two paths in front of us. We can take only one road and feel that we are fulfilling our life's purpose. However, we are always conscious of the inaudible voice which says: What would have happened if we had walked on the other road. . . . Yet let the untrodden road be untrodden and let its secret remain buried. Let us stick to the morals of the grandmother's stories that we heard in our childhood. This is the sad story of our life.[2]

The play starts on a quiet note, with Swaranlata complaining to Devayani against Sharmishtha. Though Devayani defends Sharmishtha we soon learn of the on-going conflict between the two. Sharmishtha does not accord proper respect to Devayani because she knows too well that Yayati married the latter as she was the daughter of Shukracharya who could bless him with immortality. When Sharmishtha and Devayani have an argument Sharmishtha tells Devayani:

> Yayati hopes for only one thing: nectar to be immortal. (14) Who does not want to be immortal? He accepted you in the hope of immortality. As soon as he came to know that you were Devayani, he had an urge to conquer death. (15)

When Devayani insists that Yayati did not know her identity when he married her, Sharmishtha sarcastically comments:

> Yayati asked your name only after your marriage? Even a prostitute's name is asked beforehand! If you were not Shukracharya's daughter he would have left you there. Without bothering about your virginity, he would have passed you by. (16)

Sharmishtha brings a turmoil in the life of Yayati. It is because of her that Devayani falls into the well and Yayati appears on the scene and saves her. That is what Yayati intends when he says: "You pushed Devayani into the well, and hence this crisis. I saved her but am caught in the crisis. Didn't you have an atom of humaneness when you did this?" (21)

Yayati knows that his problems are due to Sharmishtha's presence in the palace but he doesn't have the heart to tell Sharmishtha to go away. Even Devayani does not do so and Yayati is conscious of this. He tells Sharmishtha: "Sharmishtha, no one is as mad as Devayani. She is playing with fire." (26)

The crisis in the life of Yayati is precipitated by his refusal to part with Sharmishtha. Devayani doesn't want Sharmishtha in the palace and bluntly asks her to leave the palace. But Yayati does not agree to this. He says in a decisive voice:

> If it concerned somebody else, I would have agreed. . . . I have been winning over the hearts of various girls by my talks and my handsomeness. But today Sharmishtha has taken me by surprise. She has defeated me not with her looks or with her beauty but only with her talks. Should Bharata family be defeated like this? If I want to have peace, I will have to win

> her over. . . . I was feeling old. Sharmishtha has enthused me and returned my youth to me. I cannot leave her. (35)

Despite the on-going conflict between Devayani and Sharmishtha, Devayani does not order the latter to go away from the palace. Thus she is the one who is responsible for Sharmishtha's presence in the palace. When the crisis in the life of Yayati comes, instead of owning up her responsibility, Devayani leaves the palace. She refuses to yield and the result is the curse of premature old age on Yayati.

When Yayati learns that Shukracharya has cursed him with old age, he does not accept the responsibility of what he has done. He accuses Sharmishtha for this: "Old age . . . Old age! Old age before the nightfall? And what more later? Sharmishtha, Fiend, only you are the cause of this. . . . This circumstance has arisen because you led me into it." (48-49)

The curse demoralizes Yayati. He refuses to believe that his son, Puru, would be of any help in saving him from the curse: "On seeing me even my son spits fire. Would he try to save me from the curse? No, I myself should go. I should go and meet Shukracharya." (49)

Yayati loses control on himself and does not know how to handle the situation. When Sharmishtha asks him to keep calm, he protests: "Calm. . . . This calmness. . . . This calmness is like the one a person experiences before falling into a bottomless well, Sharmishtha. Speed without any inspiration, baseless stability, what can be more dangerous than this?" (49)

Sharmishtha tries to pacify Yayati by asking him to accept what has come his way: "Do not be angry. Nobody can escape old age. You have unnecessarily invited it prematurely. There is no hindrance. Now please accept the life of a hermit. I will also accompany you. I do not know the depth of your sorrow, but I can imagine." (49) Yayati gets violent and refuses to accept old age. He remains adamant: "If I have to retain my identity then I should retain my youth, Sharmi. I should remain young." (50) Sitting on his bed he looks here and there like a mad man and looks for something on the bed. He says:

> I am trying to hold back my past. I cannot believe that it was here that I used to have fun with my queens. I competed with

> time. . . . I enjoyed day and night the happiness and sadness of numberless queens. I found greater pleasure in their crying than in their laughing. That is why I intentionally irritated them. (50)

He goes to the extent of saying that Puru must be celebrating the occasion for it gives him an opportunity to assume the mantle of the King immediately. "Now he [Puru] must be dancing with joy. . . . He wanted this. . . . He hates me. . . . He must be dreaming about becoming a king." (50-51)

Karnad's Yayati speaks a lot against Puru in the presence of Sharmishtha. He can do this because in Karnad's play, Puru is not Sharmishtha's son as in the *Mahabharata* but son of another wife of Yayati.

When Puru comes back and informs that Yayati's curse can be redeemed if some young person accepted his old age, Yayati is jubilant. He fails to understand the seriousness of his actions and accuses Sharmishtha and Puru of not being happy in his happiness: "Why are you two silent? Why aren't you two happy? I have crossed burning fire, aren't you happy at this? Why don't you speak?" (53)

When Puru informs Yayati that nobody is ready to accept his old age, the latter does not believe it. Yayati thinks that all his subjects would come forward and readily accept his old age. It is Sharmishtha who brings him to his senses:

> Why should they accept the result of your actions? Sins and good deeds are not money which can be given and taken back. . . . Do not beg any insane person or a hermit to transfer your curse to him. Let us quietly go to the forest. (53)

Yayati cannot believe his ears and protests: "What do you mean? Should I kick this opportunity to seek redressal and again jump into the firepot. What kind of love is this? What kind of sympathy?" (53-54) Yayati dreads old age and the decrepitude it brings. He feels very hurt when nobody comes forward to take upon himself the curse of old age. He is ready to give whatever one wants in return. He even proposes to take back his old age after five or six years. Everybody is at his wit's end to make Yayati accept the responsibility for his action. Puru also asks Yayati to accept his old age and go to the forest. At this, Yayati requests him:

> Puru, do not ridicule me. I beg of you. Do not talk like this. It seems you can't imagine the extent of my suffering. Do not laugh inhumanly. If old age had come to me in its normal course of time I would have had the patience to bear it. . . . This is a curse. . . . If somebody accepts my curse I would free him in five or six years. . . . He should not feel disheartened for that. If I accept this curse, think. . . . Puru, I would be left with just one thing. . . . To go on and on. To return from such a path would be impossible. It is possible to take a path that is without light, Puru, but how to go on a dreamless path? (57)

Yayati cries bitterly and with folded hands looks at Puru. Puru decides to accept the curse of senility inflicted on his father. When Puru proposes that the curse given to Yayati should be transferred to him, Sharmishtha tries to dissuade him, saying: "Remember, the pride of sacrifice is also a kind of poison." (60) Sharmishtha then reminds him of his responsibility towards his wife. But Puru doesn't desist from his decision: "Don't remind me of her [Chitralekha]. I am like an infant standing at the threshold of a new life. Don't push me back with this one word [the name of Chitralekha]." (60)

Puru offers to accept the curse even though he tells Sharmishtha that Yayati is not worthy of her self-sacrificing love. Puru feels that he is not making a sacrifice: "Not pride but joy. I want to know the inner meaning of that. I want to know what the power was that gave birth to my ancestors." (60) Suddenly Puru starts feeling weak and is about to fali when Sharmishtha helps him. When asked by Sharmishtha what has happened, Puru replies: "It is the curse, mother. It is the sorrow of new life." (60)

Thus Yayati succeeds in transferring his old age and his sins to Puru, but in the process he experiences shattering disillusionment and loss of faith. The argument that he puts forward is that his people need him as a king and therefore he is doing this. But to his own self, it is clear that this is not truth.

The final recognition of the horror of the situation comes to Yayati through Chitralekha, Puru's young wife, who finds reality too much to bear and kills herself. She poisons herself in order to be relieved from the miserable condition in which she has been living.

When Swaranlata gives Chitralekha the news that Puru has accepted his father's old age, she is absolutely stunned but takes courage to say:

> Why should I cry, Swaran, rather I should laugh. Do you know I have been unjust to my husband! I took him to be a weak person. Thinking of him being a coward, I cursed my luck for it. But I am a lucky person, Swaran! Which other lady has been honoured thus. Why should I shed tears for this? (66)

She adds that old age as a curse has come to him at the right time, otherwise she would have cursed her husband and her luck like a mad person. Now she can curse her foolishness. When Puru asks for forgiveness, Chitralekha replies: "Do not talk like this. The fault was mine. I did not know about your greatness. I had never thought that I would get such reward." (68)

Puru wants her support for the responsibility he has undertaken. Chitralekha gladly extends her support. But when she sees the face of old Puru, she realizes what has befallen her. She gets frightened and tells him: "Don't come near me. . . . Go away from here. . . . Do not touch me." (69) She curses herself for not being as great as her husband, for turning her husband out. She requests Puru to reconsider his decision but to no avail. Even Yayati tries to console Chitralekha by saying "You are sensible. Get up, don't cry." (72)

He advises Chitralekha to behave in a way as behoves the daughter-in-law of the Bharata family. He tries to console her by assuring her that he would soon take back the curse on himself: "I promise you Chitralekha! I shall not keep Puru's youth for many years. I will return it as soon as my goal is achieved." (72) He asks her to accept the 'old' Puru happily for which sacrifice the Bharata family will always feel obliged to her. When Chitralekha refuses, he exercises his authority as her father-in-law and as a king, and orders her to obey him. When Chitralekha offers to leave the kingdom, he scolds her: "Why did you marry? You have forgotten the pledges that you took having Fire-god as a witness? You should follow him [Puru] whether it is home or forest." (73) Chitralekha adds ironically: "You have forgotten one thing. I should follow him to his pyre also." This annoys Yayati and he rebukes Chitralekha for wishing death for her husband. Chitralekha then accuses him for her plight:

> You are the one who are taking him close to his pyre, not I: and then you advise me? Without understanding my grief, you are lecturing me thus? What have you done? You got a foolish son. *After transferring the burden of your sins on him*, you are advising me how to conduct like a woman? (73-74, italics mine)

Chitralekha holds Yayati responsible for pushing Puru towards death. Yayati tries to idealize Chitralekha's sacrifice: "On one side is your [Chitralekha's] life, and on the other side is the bright future of the whole country." (75) He asks Chitralekha to rise above petty considerations and be a great woman. But Chitralekha does not yield to his argument: "Cowards and liars will always argue. With your arguments, you have woven a net around me." (76)

To come out of this net, Chitralekha puts a proposal before Yayati. She would like Yayati to take the place of Puru in her life so that she can bear a child of the family:

> When I accepted Puru as my husband I did not know him. I had chosen his youth. . . . The qualities that I had chosen in him are not present in him any longer but . . . but you still possess all those qualities. (75)

When Chitralekha offers herself to Yayati, the latter is shocked. He accuses Chitralekha of harbouring such low thoughts. But Chitralekha cannot see any light in her future life. She tells Yayati: "Neither will you return Puru's youth nor will you accept me!" (79) Finding herself in such a sad plight, Chitralekha muses: "You [Yayati] have youth, Puru has got the sense of sacrifice. What am I to do here." (79) Chitralekha can think of only one solution to this problem. Suicide. However, after taking poison, Chitralekha is not willing to die. She behaves in an irresponsible manner: "Save me, Don't let me die, Swaran, save me, . . . Save me. Swaran. . . . Swaran." (80)

Sharmishtha accuses Yayati of forcing Chitralekha to end her life:

> You have destroyed her life. You didn't listen to me. You had the desire to be young. . . . This is the foundation of your future life. One woman [Chitralekha] became a ghost, the sec-

> ond [Devayani] a mad person and the third [Sharmishtha] a fallen woman. (80)

When Yayati sees the dead body of Chitralekha he repents but says: "Daughter-in-law, even the fire of poison has not finished my desire to live?" (81) Sharmishtha sarcastically calls Chitralekha's death as "the first victory of Yayati's new life!"

In Khandekar's novel, Puru's sacrifice brings a new, liberating awareness to Yayati. *Kama* blinds Yayati temporarily but his *dharma* brings him to his senses. In Karnad's play, it is Chitralekha's suicide that brings Yayati to his senses and he owns up responsibility for his actions:

> The fear of sacrifice led me to sexual pleasures but this unnatural youth could not obtain that. Puru, take back your youth. Be a good king. There could be no better lesson than Chitralekha's death. (82)

He proposes to Sharmishtha to accompany him to the forest before the nightfall: "We should wash our sins by doing penance in the forest. I have spent my youth in this city but will spend my old age in the forest." (82-83)

When Chitralekha dies, Puru is stunned but does not cry. It is only when he regains his youth that he repents for what he has done:

> It seems we had called you here just to die. But you never belonged to us, you taught us the lesson as if to repay some debts of your previous births. We will never understand the true meaning of your suicide.
>
> What is the meaning of all this. O God, what is the meaning of all this? (83)

NOTES

1. Rajinder Paul, "Girish Karnad Interviewed," *Enact*, No. 54 (June 1971), n.p.
2. Girish Karnad, *Yayati*, trans. into Hindi by B.R. Narayana (Delhi: Saraswati Vihar, 1979), p. 9. English rendering mine.

Karnad's Tughlaq as an Alienated Protagonist

CHRISTINE GOMEZ

Girish Karnad's play *Tughlaq*[1] works out its protagonist's progressive alienation with existential overtones. This paper is an attempt to interpret the play in the light of certain concepts of alienation. Like Camus's *Caligula,*[2] *Tughlaq* also may be seen as a play which deals with an alienated Outsider figure, estranged at various levels, from society and the individuals around him, from traditional religion, from existence and the human predicament in this world and from himself. This paper aims at studying the various levels of alienation in Tughlaq.

From the opening scene, Tughlaq is seen as a man estranged from his society, primarily because he is a man ahead of his age. He is not understood by the society around him because his ideas and ideals are far above the comprehension of his contemporaries. In an age of religious fanaticism and hostility between Hindus and Muslims, his broadminded religious tolerance seems foolish to the Muslims and cunning to the Hindus who suspect his motives (scene one). He wants to win the confidence of his subjects and build an ideal empire together with them but fails to carry his people with him. Since society is held together by its traditions, any attempt to undermine them meets with a violent reaction. Hence arises the perennial dialectic between the Outsider and society. The changes proposed by Tughlaq pose a threat to the time-honoured conventions and beliefs of society and so he meets with stiff opposition from all classes of people. His plans regarding the change of capital and the introduction of a token copper currency are sound and reasonable but fail to convince his subjects. His frustration at their non-comprehension is understandable. "But how can I spread my branches in the stars while the roots have yet to find their hold in the earth?" (10) He realizes here that his idealistic dreams can never reach the stars unless they are rooted in the firm support of his people. But despite all his efforts he is unable to win the confidence of his subjects—both the aristocrats and the commoners. He fully realizes the tragedy of his predicament. 'But how can I explain tomorrow to those who haven't even opened their eyes to the light of today?' (39) It is the alienation of Tughlaq from his people which is responsible for the failure of his grandiose schemes. If they failed to understand his reasons for proposing these schemes, he too fails to foresee their reactions to them. He does not take into account the emotional attachment of people to their native soil when he proposes a change of capital involving not only the shift in the administrative machinery but also of the people, lock, stock and barrel. Neither does he foresee and take precautions against the possibility of counterfeiting when he introduces token copper coins. The repeated failure of Tughlaq to win the confidence of his people paves the way for his gradual disillusionment and fall from his ideals, which ultimately ends in a state of existential alienation, as it will be seen later.

Not only is Tughlaq alienated from the society in which he lives, he is also estranged at the interpersonal level from the individuals around him. His interpersonal alienation manifests itself in two ways. First of all he is shown to manipulate people for his own purposes, treating them as objects and not persons. Secondly he is unable to establish meaningful communication with others and is seen to be play-acting continually.

Erich Fromm[3] has defined as a form of alienation the relationships among men who see each other not as human beings but as objects which can be used to achieve their own goals. In scene 3 Tughlaq is seen as an ace schemer who manipulates Sheikh Imam-ud-din to act exactly according to his own pre-arranged plans. By a diabolically clever strategy he gets rid of both his enemies—Sheikh Imam-ud-din and Ain-ul-Mulk at one stroke. Tughlaq sees others through an alienated vision—not as persons but as pawns in a political game of chess, objects to be used and discarded.

In Tughlaq's relationship with others there is very little genuine communication. Most of the time he seems to be play-acting, thus revealing his alienation from others at the interpersonal level. He seems to be giving a performance all the time, striking a series of histrionic stances and poses. In the very first scene Tughlaq tries his best to impress his people by playing the role of a just and impartial ruler. (3) At the end of the episode the Guard dismisses the crowd, saying, 'What are you waiting for? *The Show's over*! Go home.' These words suggest that the Guard has almost seen through the theatricality of the entire performance which had been staged by Tughlaq to win popular support. Not only in public does Tughlaq indulge in role-play. Even in private conversation with his step-mother he seems to be acting, though he says that she is one of the three people in whom he can confide. When she asks him why he does not sleep at night, he launches into a long piece of inflated rhetoric. (10) It is so obviously theatrical that the stepmother bursts into laughter with the amused comment, "I can't ask a simple question without your giving a royal performance." (10-11) According to Erving Goffman, "To the degree that the individual maintains a show before others . . . he can come to experience a special kind of alienation from self."[4]

Though at first Tughlaq distances himself from others by adopting a role, later the inability to communicate becomes a matter of anguish for him. In scene viii when Tughlaq unburdens his soul to the young guard at Daulatabad, he meets with gross incomprehension. "I don't understand what your majesty is saying" (54) responds the Guard. This infuriates Tughlaq who rages at him, 'You don't understand! You don't understand! Why do you live? Why do you corrupt the air with your diseased breath?" (54) His angry outburst resembles that of Leonido at Tizon in *The Bond Honoured*[5] by John Osborne. It is the alienated Outsider's rage at the insider's lassitude and drifting through life without thinking. But anger is followed by a philosophical acceptance of the fact that the listener cannot help his incomprehension. "I'm sorry. It's my turn to apologize. It isn't your fault. You are also one of them." (54)

Alienated from society and the individuals around him, Tughlaq is also estranged from the religion followed by those around him. Tughlaq's alienation from traditional religion arises primarily from the fact that he is an existentialist in his religion and therefore inevitably comes into conflict with the orthodox believers and fundamentalists in religion. This conflict is vividly presented in scene three in the debate between Sheikh Imam-ud-din and Tughlaq. The Sheikh believes that the Koran is the only guide and that "if one fails to understand what the Koran says one must ask the Sayyids and the Ulema." (20) Tughlaq asserts his allegiance to the Koran as the Word of God—"I have never denied the word of God, Sheikhsahib, because it's my bread and drink," (20) but he refuses to depend only on God and prayer and believes in his own strength and resources. "But why should I call on God to clean the dirt deposited by men?" (20) He believes that "no one can go far on his knees," that is through prayer alone. To the Sheikh this sounds like blasphemy and a desire to reject the Koran and God, setting oneself up as God. "Beware Sultan, you are trying to become another God" (21) says the Sheikh to the Sultan. The Sheikh sees Tughlaq as one who aspires to omnipotence and godhead, usurping God's power and position. The fact that Tughlaq is an existentialist in religion is seen from his refusal to accept the Koran as the *Sole* receptacle of truth. He cannot reject Greek philosophy and the truth contained in other religions like that of Zarathustra or the Buddha. A fundamental principle in existentialism is that "existence precedes essence,"[6] that a man's experiential knowledge drawn from existence is superior to any principle or philosophy in its theoretical essence. From his own experience, Tughlaq finds it impossible, to deny or kill that part of him which had appreciated the Greeks. He finds the Koran and Islam too narrow to hold his comprehensive spirit. He therefore experiences fragmentation, torn between his allegiance to the Koran and his appreciation for other forms of truth. Islam requires that he should kill that part of him which had responded to the Greeks. Tughlaq speaks ecstatically of the charm that Greek philosophy and literature had held for him. He had felt the thrill of a brave new world opening before him.

> I can still feel the thrill with which I found a new world, a world I had not found in the Arabs or even the Koran. They tore me into shreds. And to be whole now, I shall have to kill the part of me which sang to them. And my kingdom too is what I am—torn into pieces by visions whose validity I can't deny. You are asking me to make myself complete by killing the Greek in me and you propose to unify my people by denying the visions which led Zarathustra or the Buddha. (21)

The microcosm within the king is reflected in the macrocosm of his kingdom.

Tughlaq is not alienated from human existence right from the beginning of the play. The first scene reveals him as an idealistic reformer who hopes to lead his people into a utopia. It is only when the idealist becomes disillusioned, on seeing the unbridgeable gulf between aspiration and reality, that he moves towards existential alienation. Though all the innovative measures of Tughlaq like giving equal rights to Hindus, change of capital and introduction of copper currency are excellent in principle, they fail because of two main reasons—his inability to win the people's confidence and his failure to foresee the flaws in his schemes. His social alienation from the people thus paves the way for his existential alienation. Scene two reveals Tughlaq's longing to be accepted by his people as their saviour-monarch. "Come, my people, I'm waiting for you." (10) He also realizes the helplessness of the individual and the brevity of human life. "I have only one life, one body and my hopes, my people, my God are all fighting for it." (10) In scene three, there are brief intimations of the beginning of existential alienation in Tughlaq. This is seen when he tells Sheikh Imam-ud-din about the "surrounding void" which sometimes pushes itself into his soul and starts "putting out every light burning there." (20)

The turning point in Tughlaq's life, 'the boundary situation'[7] of existential philosophy, which sends him hurtling down the abyss of existential alienation, comes in scene six. The treachery of Shihab-ud-din, whom Tughlaq genuinely liked and trusted, turns Tughlaq against the world. His anguish at not being understood by his people, at being betrayed by those whom he loved and trusted, is revealed in his tortured question to Barani: "Why must this happen Barani? Are all those I trust condemned to go down in history as traitors? . . . Will my reign be nothing more than a tortured scream which will stab the night and melt away in the silence?" (43) This reveals an intense awareness of the fertility and absurdity of human existence, similar to that of Macbeth who sees human life as "a tale told by an idiot, full of/Sound and fury signifying nothing."[8]

In Camus's *Myth of Sisyphus*,[9] the absurd is seen as the relationship between the individual and the world of existence. The absurd is the encounter between the individual's longing for order and rational explanations and the absolute chaos and irrationality seen by him in the universe. Tughlaq just cannot find a rational explanation for the treachery of Shihab and his courtiers' incomprehension of his idealistic measures. The absurdity of human existence impresses itself upon him in this totally unreasonable (according to him) act of treachery. He thus has a vision of the absurd, the meaninglessness and chaos of existence.

Like Caligula in Camus's play, Tughlaq also tries "to control and release his metaphysical anguish by an exercise of tyrannical power."[10] His cruelty in the play arises from his anguish. Anguish, in existential philosophy, is the reaction of the man who has had a vision of the absurd and realizes the nothingness, the void that is at the centre of all existence.[11] The repeated frenzied stabbing of Shihab even after he is dead, the order that the bodies of the conspirators should be stuffed with straw and exhibited throughout the kingdom and the insistence on the immediate vacating of Delhi are acts of cruelty and tyranny arising from his existential anguish. He decides to give up the method of rational explanation and persuasion which he had hitherto tried with his people. Instead he is now determined to rule them with an iron hand. "I was too soft, I can see that now. They'll only understand the whip." (44) In his movement from idealist to tyrant, Tughlaq resembles Camus's protagonist Caligula, whose existential alienation drove him to a deliberate choice of tyranny.

Tughlaq's existential alienation is made all the more poignant by juxtaposing it with his earlier idealism. Karnad uses the flashback technique to give us glimpses of the youthful idealism of Tughlaq. In an idyllic scene on the ramparts of Daulatabad, Tughlaq shares his youthful aspirations with a young guard. (53) He also recaptures a magical moment from his youth when he felt fully in harmony with the world around him. It was a moment of total communion with nature, the elements and man's works, a 'beautiful fusion with the things of this world.'[12] Tughlaq recalls nostalgically,

> One night I was standing on the ramparts of the old fort here. There was a torch near me flapping its wild wings and scattering golden feathers on everything in sight. There was a half-built gate nearby, trying to contain the sky within its cleft. Suddenly something happened—as though someone had cast a spell. The torch, the gate, the fort and the sky—all melted and merged and flowed in my bloodstream with the darkness of the night. . . . I was the earth, was the grass, was the smoke, was the sky. (53)

Tughlaq had been trying to recover that experience throughout his life, but in vain. Instead he found himself wandering aimlessly in existential alienation as an Outsider, searching for the end of estrangement from the universe around. The hopelessness of his search for that lost moment of communion is also revealed. "I have searched for that moment since then and here I am still searching for it. But in the last four years, I have seen only the woods clinging to the earth, heard only the howl of wild wolves and the answering bay of street dogs." (54) The despair and agony felt by him are brought out in the images of discord—the howl of wild wolves and the bay of street dogs. The speech reveals an Outsider estranged from the universe, totally out of harmony with it.

Towards the end of the same scene (scene eight), there is yet another juxtaposition of Tughlaq's earlier idealism and present degeneration. Such a contrast becomes an important structural device and is repeated once more in scene ten. At the end of scene eight, it is Barani who eloquently evokes Tughlaq's idealistic past and appeals to him to recapture the ideals once again, eschewing tyranny and cruelty. Barani tells Tughlaq: "Your majesty, there was a time when you believed in love, in peace, in God. What has happened to those ideals? . . . why this bloodshed? Please stop it." (56) Barani pinpoints the disease and diagnoses it as arising from a rejection of God and fellowmen by Tughlaq. He suggests that Tughlaq should renew his bonds of relationship with God and neighbour. But if Tughlaq were to accept this prescription, it would mean acknowledging that he was wrong all these years, which he is not prepared to do. "But for that, I'll have to admit I've been wrong all these years. And I know I haven't. I have something to give, something to teach, which may open the eyes of history, but I have to do it within this life. I've got to make them listen to me before I lose even that." (56) Here, as in *Caligula*, we see the fanatic zeal of a man who has a mission to accomplish, a lesson to teach.[13] If tyranny is the only means of forcing that lesson on people, he will continue to adopt it. If people respond only to cruelty and violence, then he will use only those means to reach his end.

Again and again in the play, Tughlaq is made to realize the vast gulf between aspiration and fulfilment, ideals and reality. As Cruickshank puts it, 'Intellectual awareness of the absurd is the experience of a person who has expected a rationally ordered cosmos, but finds instead a chaos impervious to reason.'[14] Tughlaq is forced to admit that his innovative measures like the change of capital and the introduction of a token copper currency have proved themselves to be hopeless failures. The rose garden which he had envisaged as a visible symbol of visionary hopes to create a utopia, becomes a rubbish dump where useless copper coins are piled up. This degeneration symbolises the reduction of his kingdom to 'a market of corpses' instead of becoming a Utopia. In scene ten, in the conversation with the stepmother on the rose garden, there is again the juxtaposition of the past idealism with the present corruption. The stepmother tells Tughlaq: "It's only seven years ago that you came to the throne. How glorious you were then, how idealistic, how full of hopes. Look at your kingdom now. It's become a kitchen of death." (65) When his stepmother taunts him with killing his father, brother and Sheikh Imam-ud-din, Tughlaq claims to have killed them for an ideal, perhaps the ideal of building a Utopian empire, which he considered to be his life's mission. "I killed them—yes—but I killed them for an ideal." (65) In this conversation, Tughlaq confesses that eschewing violence is no longer under his control. Once he has tasted the exhilarating power of killing, it has become a compulsion. He traces the turning point to Shihab's murder. Further he has found that the most powerful argument lay not in words, but in the sword, in cruelty, violence and murder. He has therefore adopted tyranny as a way of life, a means to an end, a vehicle to fulfil his mission in life.

> I couldn't [i.e. hold back the sword]. Now now. Remember Shihab-ud-din of Sampanshahr? He was the first man I killed with my own hands. And I had a glimmer then of what now I know only too well. Not words but the sword—that's all I have to keep my faith in my mission. (66)

Soon after this, Tughlaq insists that none of the deaths which he had brought about were futile. "No, they were not futile. They gave me what I wanted—power, strength to shape my thoughts, strength to act, strength to recognize myself." (66) This speech reveals a startling attitude to murder. Murder is seen as a definitive act which leads to self-recognition and self-identity. Murder has given him power and self-realization through independent thinking and action. Cruelty and tyranny are seen almost as vehicles to help him to overcome existential alienation and a sense of the absurdity of human existence. This is close to the Nazi mentality exposed by Camus in *Caligula.*[15]

Self-alienation has been defined in philosophy as 'alienation of a self from itself through itself.'[16] It is state of a division of self into conflicting parts which become alien to each other. When the self-division becomes extreme, the person suffers from various psychological disorders and may even be driven beyond the border of sanity into the total self-estrangement of madness. In scene ten, soon after condemning his stepmother to death, we find Tughlaq experiencing intense self-estrangement. Left alone, he falls to his knees, clutches his hands to his breast and desperately pleads with God to help him. "God, God in Heaven, please help me. Please don't let go of my hand. . . . I started in your path, Lord, why am I wandering naked in this desert now?" (67) The tone of despair, helplessness and bewildered incomprehension are unmistakable in this prayer. Yet when Barani enters, he jests at his own praying gesture in self-mockery. But a note of anguish is recognizable at the end. "I was trying to pray! Think of that—no one in my kingdom is allowed to pray and I was praying. Against my own orders! But what else could I do Barani? My legs could not hold me up any longer." (68)

One can almost hear the break in the voice when he says, 'But what else could I do Barani?' He now realizes that his own strength is not enough to sustain him and so he needs to kneel and pray. Though his prayer sounds genuinely desperate, he says that it was merely from the lips and memory and not from the heart. "I was trying to pray but I could only find words learnt by rote which left no echo in the heart." (68) He realizes his own self-alienation and knows that he has reached the extreme edge of self-estrangement, which is madness. "I am teetering on the brink of madness, Barani, but the madness of God still eludes me." (68)

In scene eleven, Tughlaq again indulges in play-acting and self-dramatization. He strikes a pose of humility and dramatically falls at the feet of Aziz Ghiyas-ud-din. This histrionic gesture has its effect on the crowd which gasps and kneels down. In scene twelve, Aazam reports the nocturnal vigil of the Sultan in his proposed rose garden-turned-rubbish-dump. (75) Aazam calls it madness, while Aziz puts it down to insomnia. But to Tughlaq, it is an expression of his anguish at the trick played on him by life—it had promised him a rose garden and gave him a rubbish dump. He wanted to rule a Utopia but ended up ruling a 'kitchen of death' as the 'lord of skins.' This contrast between man's expectation and the harsh reality of existence is indeed the experience of the absurd.

At the end of the play as Barani passes out of his life, Tughlaq reaches a dead end in complete exhaustion.

> Barani, all I need now is myself and my madness—madness to prance in a field eaten bare by the scarecrow violence. But I am not alone, Barani. Thank heaven! For once I am not alone. I have a companion to share my madness now—the omnipotent God! (Tired). (85)

Tughlaq claims that his madness is a divine frenzy, dancing in a world torn by violence, a kind of *Rudra Tandava*. But it has left the man exhausted and he falls asleep just as prayer is restored in his kingdom after a ban of five years. As far as the theme of alienation is concerned, the play is open-ended and inconclusive.

Many of the other characters in the play serve as foils to the protagonist. Najib, Barani, Aazam and Aziz highlight certain elements in the character of Tughlaq seen as an alienated existential Outsider. In a moment of self-revelation, Najib reveals himself as a former idealist, who has not become an existentialist, grasping the present moment as it is. He had given up Hinduism because it spoke only of the salvation of the individual soul and not of society. The social consciousness of Islam therefore attracted him and so he became a Muslim, hoping to bring the kingdom of Heaven on earth through Islam. But his youthful idealism met with disillusionment when he realized that schemes to bring in a golden age do not work out practically. So finally Najib concluded that all that matters is the present moment of existence, which must be grasped firmly and utilised fully, "I became a Muslim. Islam worried about this world, I said it'll bring the kingdom of Heaven on earth. But I know now—it won't work. There's only the present moment and we must grasp it firmly." (14) Thus an experiential encounter with life had transformed Najib also from being an idealist to becoming an existentialist.

Barani is a close confidant of Tughlaq who frankly and fearlessly points out the Sultan's degeneration from idealist to tyrant. But in the last scene of the play, Barani pays a tribute to Tughlaq that though he is in the midst of violence, he is not drawn into it. Barani, the gentlest and mildest of men, imagines with relish the most tortuous deaths to be meted out to Aziz. But Tughlaq stops him with a mild rebuke which brings Barani to a shocked self-realization of his fall from grace. He says, "I am a weak man your majesty. I don't have your strength to play with violence and yet not be sucked in by it. Your Majesty warned me when I slipped and I am grateful for that. I ask your Majesty's permission to go while I'm still safe." (85) This speech of Barani throws light on Tughlaq's detached use of violence for a specific purpose—to fulfil a mission in life. Though he is in the whirlpool of violence and bloodshed, he is able to maintain his objectivity and is not sucked into the vortex.

Aazam and Aziz, the comic pair derived from the Akara-Makara tradition[17] in Kannada drama and reminiscent of Vladimir and Estragon in Beckett's *Waiting for Godot*, present an interesting parallel to Tughlaq's existential alienation in a lighter vein. In scene nine, Aazam assumes a worldweary mood which is almost a parody of Tughlaq's existential alienation and experience of futility and meaninglessness in the previous scene. "It's so hot—I'm fed up, I'm fed up of life, I'm fed up of the whole bloody world," (57) says Aazam. But Aziz is totally unsympathetic and does not encourage him in his self-pity. Aziz asks dispassionately, "Why don't you just go and commit suicide?" (57) Actually this flippant suggestion is one of the ways in which the alienated individual may strive to escape from the problem of the absurd. Camus in *The Myth of Sisyphus* speaks of "physical suicide"[18] as one of the ways out of the absurd impasse. Since the absurd is a relationship between the individual and the world, suicide tries to negate the absurd by destroying the individual.

Aziz reveals some startling similarities to Tughlaq. He too had a moment of revelation when the futility of human life was revealed to him in an existential vision. This is revealed in flashback in the last scene. Aziz recalls his career as a servant of officers, when he was engaged in stuffing corpses with straw for exhibition.

> Such famous kings, warriors and leaders of men passed through our hands then! Beautiful strong bodies and bodies eaten up by corruption—all, all were stuffed with straw and went to the top of poles. . . . One day, suddenly I had a revelation. This was all human life was worth, I said. This was the real meaning of the mystery of death—straw and skin! With that enlightenment I found peace. (82)

Thus Aziz had his encounter with the absurd in the market of corpses—an existential vision of the futility and meaninglessness of life. Soon after that Aziz had run away to the hills and started his career as a highway robber. It is remarkable that in Aziz too, as in Tughlaq and Caligula, the absurd vision of life is followed by a plunge into violence and cruelty. In scene nine, Aziz speaks of crime as an assertion of power, as a means to acquire power: "What's the point in raping for sheer lust? That's a mug's game. First one must have power—the authority to rape! Then everything takes on meaning." (57) This speech suggests that the acquisition of power, expressed through acts of violence and cruelty, imparts meaning to life. The attitude is similar to that of Tughlaq who had said that murder gave him "power, strength to shape my thoughts, strength to act, strength to recognize myself." (66) Both of them believe in the necessity of crime to assert one's identity.

The game of chess and the rose garden are two important recurring images which are part of the inner structure of the play. Both are metaphors of alienation and may be related to Tughlaq's alienation. Chess symbolizes Tughlaq's game-approach to life wherein he regards other people as pawns to be manipulated for his own advantage. In his political game he is checkmated by Aziz. The rose garden which becomes a rubbish dump is a perfect objective correlative of Tughlaq's idealistic aspirations meeting with defeat, frustration and disillusionment. It becomes an image of the absurd, the unbridgeable gulf between man's expectations of orderliness and the chaos and irrationality which confront him in the universe.

Thus, in Karnad's play, Tughlaq is presented as an alienated protagonist who experiences interpersonal and social alienation, existential alienation and self-estrangement. Many of the other characters in the play are also seen to experience alienation, which serves to highlight Tughlaq's predicament. The recurring images of chess and the rose-garden also reinforce this theme of alienation at a subliminal level.

NOTES

1. Girish Karnad, *Tughlaq* (Delhi: Oxford University Press, 1972).
2. Albert Camus, *Caligula*, trans. Stuart Gilbert (London: Hamish Hamilton, 1947).

3. Erich Fromm, *The Sane Society* (London: Routledge and Kegan Paul, 1956), pp. 126-27.
4. Erving Goffman, *The Presentation of Self in Everyday Life* (New York: Doubleday Anchor, 1959), p. 236.
5. John Osborne, *A Bond Honoured* (London: Faber and Faber, 1966), p. 16. Leonido, the protagonist, is intensely alive and rails at the somnolent existence of others around him, especially his servant Tizon.
6. Jean-Paul Sartre, *Existentialism and Humanism*, trans. P. Mairet (London: Methuen, 1948), p. 26.
7. A concept in the philosophy of Karl Jaspers, cf. E. Latzel, "The Concept of Ultimate Situation in Jaspers' Philosophy," *The Philosophy of Karl Jaspers*, ed. P.P. Schilp (La Salle, Illinois: Open Court Publishing Company, 1957), pp. 177-208.
8. William Shakespeare, *Macbeth*, ed. D. Wilson (Cambridge: University Press, 1947), V.v. ll. 26-28.
9. Albert Camus, *The Myth of Sisyphus*, trans. Justin O'Brien (London: Hamish Hamilton, 1955), pp. 24-31.
10. Cf. my paper "The Tyrant as Outsider in Shakespeare's *Macbeth* and Camus' *Caligula*," *Indian Journal of Shakespeare Studies*, Vol. II (1986), p. 38.
11. Maurice Cranston, *Sartre* (Edinburgh and London: Oliver and Boyd, 1962), p. 49. 'Anguish is the natural feeling that comes from confronting the absolute openness of our own future, the nothingness in the centre of which we live.'
12. Sylvia Plath's phrase, cited by George Slade, "Afterword" in Nancy Hunter Steiner, *A Closer Look at Ariel* (London: Faber and Faber, 1974), p. 70.
13. *Caligula*, p. 15. "They are without understanding and they need a teacher."
14. John Cruickshank, *Albert Camus and the Literature of Revolt* (New York: Oxford University Press, 1960), pp. 49-53.
15. Germaine Bree, *Camus and Sartre: Crisis and Commitment* (London: Caldar and Boyars, 1974), p. 147. In Caligula 'Camus was marking his distance from all doctrinarians and from the neo-Nietzscheanism of the Nazis in their attempt to revitalize society through violence.'
16. Gajo Petrovice, "Alienation," *The Encyclopaedia of Philosophy*, ed. Paul Edwards (New York: Macmillan and Free Press, 1967), Vol. I, pp. 76-80.
17. U.R. Anantha Murthy, Introduction, *Tughlaq*, p. vii.
18. *The Myth of Sisyphus*, pp. 47-49.

A Reassessment of the Character of Karnad's Tughlaq

K.K. JOHN

Muhammad Tughlaq is a well-known king in the Indian history—known more for his wickedness and insane policies than for anything else. Girish Karnad has immortalized this character in his play titled *Tughlaq*, the English version of which was published in 1970. The character of Tughlaq deserves a re-appraisal since he has been portrayed in poor light both by historians and critics. Thus a Karnad reader is likely to approach the character of Muhammad Tughlaq with a slightly prejudiced mind. Needless to say, a character drawn from history and projected in fiction ceases to be a historical figure. He is merely a character in fiction and needs to be treated as such. This is essential to appreciate the play in its proper perspective.

Admittedly, Karnad's play *Tughlaq* is an excellent work of art, with an intricate plot, subtle irony, copious satire, delicate symbolism. But over the years scholars have been over-emphasizing its value as a political satire. No doubt, a work of art is open to more than one interpretation. However, the glorification of the play as a political satire and nothing more seems to be a rather under-estimation of the work, and thereby doing injustice to the author. The play, *inter alia,* offers an excellent psychological study of the character of Muhammad Tughlaq—his motives, his vision, his efforts to assert himself as the ruler of the people, as also how he takes his own failure. This paper aims at throwing some light on certain aspects of Tughlaq's character, espsecially that teen-aged monarch of the early part of the play, where he is mostly at the 'receiving end,' as he is misunderstood and opposed by a large section of the people in the country.

History has it that Muhammad Tughlaq had killed his father and brother in order to become the Sultan of Delhi. The charge of murder may or may not be true, for history draws heavily on conjectures. However, the playwright only casts a shadow of doubt of parricide on Tughlaq. Admitting that it was a pre-planned murder, the question arises how the elephant went amok exactly when prayers were offered, and dashed against the wooden pandal resulting in its collapse and the instant death of the reigning Sultan? There is room for doubt in that allegation. Be that as it may.

Tughlaq's struggle begins with his assumption of power as the Sultan of Delhi. His enemies are on the wing to swoop down on their prey. The chieftains of Delhi, the Amirs, Sheik Imam-ud-din, Ain-ul-Mulk and all such powerful personalities had started a proxy war against the young Sultan. And, whatever Tughlaq does against them, he does in self-defence. He has to preserve his self, his ideals, his visions and dreams. In fact it is his opponents who begin the offence and thereby force him to take up the cudgels.

Muhammad Tughlaq's opponents are all men of vested interests. Ain-ul-Mulk's aim is to capture the throne of Delhi. Imam-ud-din and the chieftains of Delhi are seeking to enhance their power and influence by making the State subservient to Islam. As against this background, the Sultan, young as he is, has his own visions of a secular India where Hindus and Muslims would live in perpetual amity and brotherhood. This is indeed a noble vision especially for a monarch of the fourteenth century India. He places humanism above religion. To him religion seems to be only a means to achieve an end—and the end in this case is to bring about a fusion of all his subjects as citizens of a secular state. On the other hand, the Sultan's opponents are fanatics and selfish men.

The cardinal question before Muhammad Tughlaq is: Is man meant for religion, or *vice versa*? In his view, religion should play a positive role in human life, to enhance the progress and happiness of the people. This is the bone of contention between the Sultan and his opponents. So, clearly, at least in the initial stage of the play, the conflict is between two ideologies, two attitudes. The theme turns tragic only when the young Sultan refuses to dance to their tunes, and decides to defend his ideals and visions.

This is not, in any way, to applaud all the deeds of Tughlaq. He did commit many unpardonable crimes and blunders. He is responsible for bloodshed and murder. He brought untold misery and agony to the people so much so that even those who are very close to him doubt his sanity. But this is altogether a different issue. In the beginning of the play, he is neither insane nor cruel. Circumstances have probably forced him to take harsh decisions. His initial attempts are to remain faithful to Islam, and at the same time to rule his people as a secular and liberal monarch committed to fair play and justice. To him religion is apparently a pesonal matter. Two instances will prove the above point. During his conversation with Sheikh Imam-ud-din, Tughlaq says: "I have never consciously tried to go against the tenets of Islam." When the Sheikh accuses Tughlaq for putting religious men behind prison bars, he bluntly tells him: "They tried to indulge in politics—I couldn't allow that." (20) He further says: "My kingdom has millions—Muslims, Hindus, Jains." (20)

So, here is a monarch who treats all his subjects as one people, irrespective of their caste or creed. It is doubtful whether any other Muslim monarch, except perhaps Akbar the Great, had ever had such a noble vision. But his opponents apparently believe that religion should have a hand in the affairs of the State. They seem to hold the notion that politics (State) is an organ to achieve the ends of religion. In short, Tughlaq's detractors are desperately trying to have a foot-hold in the affairs of the State but the Sultan would not allow it. He has a clear vision before him. He says to Sheikh Imam-ud-din: "you propose to unify my people by denying the visions which led Zarathustra or the Buddha. . . . I'm sorry. But it can't be done." (21)

In the initial stage of the play, Tughlaq struggles hard to keep his ideals intact. And he struggles alone against overwhelming odds. It would be worthwhile to remember that the theme of the play and the characters belong to the early fourteenth century when Europe had hardly come out of the tunnels of the Dark Age. And what harm the Church had done to the European culture by combining the State and religion is now hisotry. The Muslim Chieftains of Delhi were also trying to create a similar situation by trying to intimidate the Sultan. But Tughlaq boldly refuses to become another Charlemagne.

The first part of the play portrays Tughlaq as a highly intelligent and enlightened ruler. Of course, he deals ruthlessly with his enemies, but only after he is convinced of their conspiracy against him. Had he not done so, he might have become another Hamlet in the annnals of Indian history. He kills two birds with one stone when he gets rid of Sheikh Imam-ud-din and turns the rebel Ain-ul-

Mulk into his ally. He achieves this twin victory with a simple trick. Moralists may raise eyebrows on Tughlaq's cunningness, but the fact is that had he not done so, his very existence would have been in peril. Again, in the sixth scene, during the Durbar-i-Khas he traps the Amirs and Shihab-ud-din who had come to the palace fully armed to murder the Sultan during the prayer. He smartly outmanoeuvres his enemies. It is a paradox that the very elements that accused the Sultan of parricide are here plotting a regicide—that too during the prayer. The entire episode exposes the hypocrisy of the Chieftains. If we study the character of Muhammad Tughlaq from this standpoint, we will see that the Sultan is victim-turned-sinner.

NOTE

1. Girish Karnad, *Tughlaq* (Madras: Oxford University Press, 1993), p. 20.

The Rescue Triangle in *Tughlaq*

M. SARAT BABU

The concept of the Rescue Triangle is borrowed from 'Transactional Analysis,' a neo-Freudian school of psychology, originated by Dr. Eric Berne. It is developed by Stephen Karpman and hence it is also known as Karpman Drama Triangle. According to it, there will be three roles in the Drama Triangle: the Rescuer, the Persecutor and the Victim (Capital letters begin these words to be differentiated from a real rescuer who helps a real victim who shows gratitude to the rescuer). Since most of us suffer from various psychological problems without knowing the intensity of their damage to our life, we tend to act in one of these roles, instead of living our lives naturally and spontaneously. Each of us has his own favourite role, depending on his favourite feelings. These feelings accumulate to form a racket as we are urged to suppress or repress them by our culture. A racket of guilty feelings makes one play the Rescuer, a racket of angry feelings makes one play the Persecutor; and a racket of helpless feelings makes one play the Victim. It is rather difficult for a person to be aware of his playing a role while others perceive in it something unnatural and something dramatic. That is why, "There is a close parallel between life and theatre and quite often life is theatre-like and vice versa"[1] as P. Ramamoorthy says.

The Rescuer feels that he is superior to the Victim and that the latter is helpless and hopeless without his rescuing him. He conveniently ignores the inherent ability of everyone to help himself. He internally feels 'not OK' about himself and feels 'OK' only in rescuing a Victim; other guilty feelings obsess his mind and make him restless. So he sacrifices his own interests and comforts for the sake of rescuing a Victim which usually proves to be a failure. He is never thanked for his rescuing; moreover he finds himself exploited and thus persecuted by his Victim. This naturally enrages him and the racket of angry feelings turns him into a Persecutor; but he whose favourite role is the Rescuer returns to his role of rescuing soon after his angry feelings are spent and he starts feeling guilty for having persecuted his Victims. A typical Rescuer chooses such a profession as allows him to play his role; so he usually becomes a teacher, a social worker, a preacher or a leader.

The Persecutor also feels that he is superior to the Victim and that the latter is hopeless and mean. He feels he is 'OK' and the Victim is not 'OK'. His favourite feeling is anger. As his angry feelings gather to form a racket, he looks for his Victim who of course behaves complimentarily by doing something wrong in the presence of his Persecutor who punishes him verbally or physically. This repeats several times. Then the Persecutor is likely to feel guilty and so shifts to the role of the Rescuer. And he connives at his being exploited by his Victim, only to justify his role of persecuting later. It is also likely that the Persecutor is persecuted by his Victim and thus there can be a temporary reversal of roles. A typical Persecutor opts for such a profession as enables him to play his role; so he generally becomes a strict officer, a police officer, a public prosecutor, a jailor or a military officer.

The Victim feels that he is not 'OK'. He feels helpless. He looks pliant and lets others take advantage of him and exploit him, or victimize him. He then sends non-verbal or verbal signals to the Rescuer to rescue him. He does not try to help himself but enjoys being rescued by the Rescuer. Yet he resents being belittled by the Rescuer whom he never thanks for the help he receives from him. Moreover he pushes his Rescuer down to the role of Victim by exploiting his rescuing and even by persecuting him. On the other hand, he also appears to be flaccid and easily succumbs to doing mean or immoral things or to committing mistakes repeatedly. Thus he invites the attention of his Persecutor to persecute him and his mean behaviour triggers the racket of angry feelings in the Persecutor. Then the Victim receives the punishment, he unconsciously craved for, from his persecutor. A typical Victim selects such a profession as lets him play his role; he naturally becomes an attender, a peon, a clerk, a watchman or a servant.

The Rescuer, the Persecutor and the Victim form the Drama Triangle as shown in the diagram. Though a person plays mostly only one role which is his favourite, he often shifts to the other roles temporarily as the situation urges him. The Rescuer, after rescuing for long, finds himself being unduly exploited by his Victim who never bothers to thank his Rescuer; then he becomes angry and as his anger mounts up to form a racket, he becomes the Persecutor and punishes his Victim. This makes him feel guilty and the guilty feelings urge him to return to his original role. In the same way, after a long persecution of his Victim, the Persecutor feels guilty and takes pity on his Victim. He then assumes the role of the Rescuer and soon finds that his rescuing is exploited by his ungrateful Victim and feels enraged only to return to his original role. Similarly the Victim resents his being undervalued and rises to the role of Persecutor and punishes his Rescuer or Persecutor who go down to the role of Victim. After a little persecution, the Victim feels guilty and takes up the role of Rescuer.

DRAMA TRIANGLE

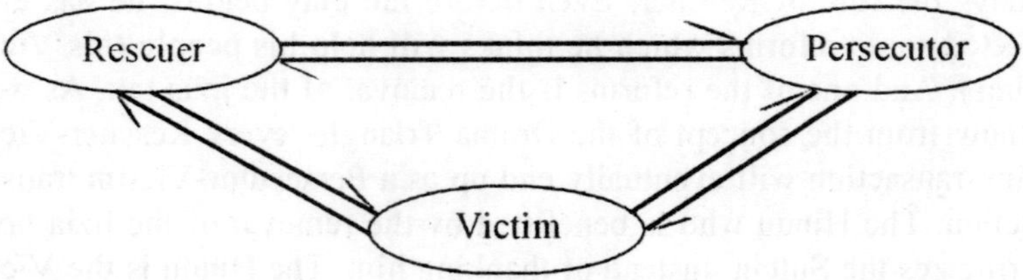

Soon he finds himself inadequate in rescuing and resumes his favourite role of Victim. All this is a psychological game which we play in order to steal away the attention, the affection and the recognition which we need for our survival and which we fail to get in a normal and a natural way. And each one desperately tries to feel fine and powerful hence a kind of power play can be seen in the relationship of the roles.

In a typical family, Father plays the Persecutor, Mother plays the Rescuer; and their children play the Victim. The roles can change according to the situation. When Father hurts children, Mother rescues them. Then Father becomes her Victim as she persecutes him for hurting children. Later she becomes the Victim of her children who exploit her kindness; and they rescue Mother when Father hurts her. When children grow up, they rescue their parents who are helpless. They also persecute their parents for being victimized by them for long. Thus we find a person shifting from one role to another and usually "Every Rescuer-Victim transaction will eventually result in a Persecutor Victim transaction"[2] and it can also be vice versa.

The concept of Drama Triangle betters our understanding of Karnad's play, *Tughlaq*.[3] Almost every character seems to be involved in the Drama Triangle. Even in the beginning, we find the old Muslim persecuting Muhammad verbally and the young Muslim rescuing the Sultan.

Old Man:	God, what's this country coming to!
Young Man:	What are you worried about, grandfather? The country's in perfectly safe hands—safer than any you've seen before. (Scene I, p. 1)

The dialogue runs into five pages in this way. The central and eponymous character in the play, Muhammad-bin-Tughlaq himself plays the role of Rescuer. Even before the play begins, he has effected some reforms which he thinks will help his people (his Victims). And one of the reforms is the removal of the jizia tax. As we know from the concept of the Drama Triangle, every Rescuer-Victim transaction will eventually end up as a Persecutor-Victim transaction. The Hindu who is benefitted by the removal of the jizia tax criticizes the Sultan, instead of thanking him. The Hindu is the Victim who is rescued by Muhammad. But the Hindu ungratefully persecutes his Rescuer. The young man calls him "ungrateful wretch." Muhammad is an archetypel Rescuer. His subjects (people) are his Victims. They are helpless and without his rescuing them, they, he thinks, are miserable. He feels that he alone can do it and that other kings could not do it.

Muhammad:	No, really. Suppose I die in the battle. What of it? Why should I waste my last few days worrying? I am not worried about my enemies. I'm only worried about my people.
Stepmother:	Pompous ass! As though other kings didn't do that.
Muhammad:	No, they didn't. (Scene 2, p. 11)

Like a typical Rescuer, Muhammad foregoes his own physical comforts such as sleep and marital bliss, and even his mental peace, in order to rescue his people. He wants to build an 'ideal' kingdom for his people. He says:

> Then again I want to climb up, up to the top of the tallest tree in the world and call out to my people: 'Come, my people, I am waiting for you. Confide in me your worries. Let me share your joys. Let's laugh and cry together and then, let's pray. . . . History is ours to play with—ours now! Let's be the light and cover the earth with greenery. Let's be darkness and cover up the boundaries of nations. Come! I am waiting to embrace. You all! . . . I wish I could believe in recurring births like the Hindu but I have only one life, one body, and my hopes, my people, my God are all fighting for it. Tell me, how dare I waste my time by sleeping? and don't tell me to go and get married and breed a family because I won't sleep. (Scene 2, p. 10)

Even his stepmother says "and he works so hard for the people. He doesn't even go to bed these days." (Scene 2, p. 17)

The favourite feeling of the Rescuer is guilty feeling. Muhammad seems to like guilty feelings. He feels inadequate about himself and guilty about his shortcomings and crimes.

> Barani: It's as your Majesty said. . . . He says the Sultan is a disgrace to Islam.
>
> Muhammad: That's all? I could find worse faults in me. What else? (Scene 2, p. 13)

Ratansingh also comments: "He murders a man calmly and then actually, enjoys the feeling of guilt." As a racket of guilty feelings develops, it urges him to rescue somebody. Therefore Muhammad tries to do what he thinks good for his people without their asking for it. Since his rescuing is not realistic, he fails miserably and his people exploit his reforms and remain ungrateful to him. This repeats throughout the play.

The Sultan announces equality of justice to all on the second anniversary of his coronation. He further says that people may file a suit against the Sultan himself for the misbehaviour of his officers. Aziz tells Aazam, his friend how he exploited this:

Aziz: There's no future in being a dhobi these days. So I did a bit of thinking. There's a Brahmin called Vishnu Prasad whose land had been confiscated recently. I shaved my head and went to him. I said I would buy the land.

Aazam: The land was confiscated, wasn't it?

Aziz: Exactly, that's what he said too. But I said, 'Never mind about that.' So he sold me the land back-dating the contract. And I filed my suit. Well, here I am. Five hundred dinars for nothing, and a job in His Merciful Majesty's own Civil Service.

(Scene 1, pp. 7-8)

Aziz is ever ready to exploit every reform of Muhammad. He plans to exploit the people on their way to Daulatabad for small concessions as he is an officer. He tells his friend: "There's money here and I will make a pile by the time we reach Daulatabad." (Scene 1, p. 8)

When Aziz knows that the 'Sultan is going to introduce copper coins,' he readily decides to 'make counterfeit coins.' (Scene 7, p. 50) Later every Hindu home becomes a domestic mint making counterfeit coins. It is clear that not only Aziz but other people also victimize Muhammad by taking advantage of his rescuing. That is, Muhammad is shifted to the Victim from the Rescuer while the people, his Victims, become his Persecutors. As he becomes a helpless Victim, he looks at the Supreme Rescuer, God for help. He prays: "Good God in Heaven, please help me. . . . I have no one but you. Only you." (Scene 10, p. 67)

As the Rescuer finds that he is exploited by his ungrateful Victims, he becomes angry. And as his angry feelings form a racket, he turns into a Persecutor and persecutes his Victims. Muhammad announces that the capital is shifted from Delhi to Daulatabad and leaves an option to the people that those who desire to leave Delhi, may go to Daulatabad. When he learns that the Amirs of Delhi and Shibab-ud-din, unwilling to leave Delhi, hatched a plot to murder him at prayer, he gets the Amirs killed by the Hindu soldiers and after the prayer he stabs Shihab-ud-din mercilessly. This shift from the Rescuer to the Persecutor is expressed by Muhammad himself.

Najib, I want Delhi vacated immediately. Every living soul in

> Delhi will leave for Daulatabad within a fortnight. I was too soft, I can see that now. They'll only understand the whip. Every one must leave. (Scene 6, p. 44)

Similarly Imam-ud-din and his stepmother also become his victims whom he gets killed.

As his angry feelings are spent, Muhammad again feels guilty for his persecuting the Victims more than necessary. As the racket of guilty feelings forms, he resumes his original role, the Rescuer. So after getting Imam-ud-din killed, he excuses Ain-ul-Mulk who rebelled against him. "I didn't just set him free, Najib, I gave him back the kingdom of Avadh, and I promised not to send him to the Deccan." (Scene 4, p. 27) He then says that Ain-ul-Mulk solved a chess problem easily and quickly for him and so he forgave him. Similarly he excuses Aziz the worst perjurer and scoundrel who exploited all the Sultan's reforms and who came in the guise of Ghiyas-ud-din after killing him. Aziz says that he did all these things only to act according to the Sultan's edicts. (Scene 13, p. 82) Then Muhammad asks him what punishment he should give him for his crimes. Aziz asks him to make him an officer of his state and Muhammad agrees to make him an officer in the Deccan army. (Scene 13, p. 83) Thus "Muhammad keeps changing roles," says P. Ramamoorthy.[4]

The roles of other characters in the play can also be seen in the same way. Muhammad's own mother seems to have understood his morbid mentality and keeps herself away from the psychological game of the Drama Triangle. But his stepmother takes pity on him and offers to be his Rescuer. She also takes active interest in politics, she thinks that Najib is misleading her step-son and she feels that she ought to rescue Muhammad from the bad influence of Najib, so she gets him poisoned. She expresses her feelings to him. "I want nothing for myself. You are my life, Muhammad." Muhammad cannot forgive her, his Rescuer, though he forgives his Persecutors Ain-ul-Mulk and Aziz. He orders her to be stoned to death mercilessly.

Imam-ud-din is also a Rescuer. He wants to rescue the people from the Sultan who he thinks goes against Islam. So he criticizes the Sultan severely in public. But he agrees to rescue the Sultan, his own enemy, by going to Ain-ul-Mulk as his envoy. Thus Imam-ud-din, who was once Muhammad's Persecutor, becomes his Rescuer. And Muhammad gets Imam-ud-din killed by guile. As Ratansingh reports to Shihab-ud-din, the Sheik (Imam-ud-djn) stood up on the royal elephant to say something when the Sultan's army, according to his secret orders, charged and Ain-ul-Mulk, mistaking the Sheik for the Sultan, killed him. (Scene 4, p. 29)

Shihab-ud-din is another Rescuer in the play. He looks after Delhi in the absence of Muhammad. He agrees to join the Amirs in their plot to murder Muhammad after being convinced by Ratansingh that the Sultan is evil and crooked. Ratansingh whom he believed betrayed him and Muhammad stabbed him mercilessly.

Najib and Barani are also rescuers. Najib rescues Muhammad politically while Barani helps him spiritually. Therefore Muhammad takes the help of Najib whenever he faces critical political problems (Scenes 2 & 4) and seeks Barani's company in spiritual crisis (Scenes 8, 10 & 13). Najib, though a shrewd politician, fails to suspect Muhammad's stepmother and pays the price of death for his connivance of her hatred of him. But Barani smells the danger and quits Muhammad in the last scene.

Ain-ul-Mulk is a friend of Muhammad and on his orders he goes to Avadh and suppresses the rebellion. But when he is ordered to go to the Deccan to contain the turmoil, he resents it. He develops anger against Muhammad and rebels against him. Muhammad excuses him though he became his Persecutor.

Aziz is the anti-thesis of Muhammad. He is the Persecutor as much as Muhammad is the Rescuer in the play. As a typical Persecutor, Aziz thinks that the people are helpless, bad, base and mean. And so he feels they deserve his persecution. His ill feelings towards the people can be exemplified from his own words to his friend Aazam.

> No, truly, listen. If you remain virtuous throughout your life no one will say a good thing about you because they won't need to. But start stealing—and they'll say: 'what a nice boy he was! But he's ruined now. . . .' Then kill and they will beat their breasts and say: 'Heavens! He was only a petty thief all those days. Never hurt anyone. But alas!' Then rape a woman and the chorus will go into hallelujahs: 'He was a saint, a real saint and look at him now.' . . . One should be able to rob a man and then stay there to punish him for getting robbed.
>
> (Scene 9, pp. 57-58)

So he unscrupulously exploits everybody—the king, the saint and the pauper. In spite of the grave crimes he commits, he escapes unpunished as Muhammad, his Rescuer, not only forgives him but also concedes to his request to make him an officer.

Thus, in *Tughlaq*, we find, every Rescuer-Victim transaction eventually becomes Persecutor-Victim transaction. This can be read in the comment of U.R. Anantha Murthy in his introduction to the play: "Both Muhammad and his enemies initially appear to be idealists; yet in the pursuit of the ideal, they perpetuate its opposite. The whole play is structured on these opposites: the ideal and the real; the divine aspiration and the deft intrigue." The idealism and the divine aspiration are the reflections of the rescuing; and the realism and the deft intrigue are the angry reaction of the Rescuer or the victim who become the persecutor of the other.

This is what we see in the characters of Muhammad, Imam-ud-din, Shihab-ud-din and others. This analysis can be useful in understanding such situations in a piece of fiction or drama or in life and we may prevent such painful situations in our lives.

NOTES

1. P. Ramamoorthy, "He That Playeth the Sultan: A Study of *Tughlaq*," p. 156 in this book.
2. Claude M. Steiner, *Scripts People Live* (New York: Grove Press, 1974), p. 184.
3. Girish Karnad, *Tughlaq* (Delhi: Oxford University Press, 1977).
4. P. Ramamoorthy, p. 157 in this book.

The Betrayal Motif in Karnad's *Tughlaq*

K. RATNA SHIELA MANI

Girish Karnad's play *Tughlaq* has been much acclaimed by critics for its depth and range. It contains within itself the suggestiveness and richness of a work of art which lends itself to various interpretations of its thematic concerns at different levels.

The historical theme in *Tughlaq* is quite obvious as Karnad explores the paradox of Muhammad Tughlaq, the idealistic Sultan of Delhi, whose reign is considered to be one of the most spectacular failures of Indian history. But *Tughlaq* is not an ordinary chronicle play but a very imaginative reconstruction of some of the most significant events in the life of a great king. *Tughlaq* has been compared to Camus's *Caligula,* for both the plays present a tyrant using his power absolutely, indulging in wanton and senseless cruelty. Yet, neither play can be called historical drama because liberties have been taken with regard to historical fact in both of them.[1] The theme of the play is from Indian history, yet the treatment is not historical but highly political.[2]

Attention has been paid to the political theme of the play as it reflects the political mood of disillusionment in the sixties. In Karnad's own words, what struck him "absolutely about Tughlaq's history was that it was contemporary."[3] But *Tughlaq* is not merely a political allegory.

The greater part of the fascination and appeal of the play surely arises out of the complex personality of Tughlaq who has been realized in great psychological depth. The ambiguities in Tughlaq's character come from the fact that he is at the same time the most idealistic and the most intelligent ruler ever to have come on the throne of Delhi. Several characters in the play attest to the fact that Tughlaq has power, learning, intelligence and talent; yet he is cruel and crafty. He is an idealist, but is also impulsive and cannot tolerate opposition. M.K. Naik feels that *Tughlaq* is basically concerned with the tragedy of the limits of human power in a predominantly psychological context. (138)

Again, it would perhaps be unjust to say that the play is about an 'interesting' character, for the play relates the character of Tughlaq to philosophical questions on the nature of man and destiny of a whole kingdom which a dreamer like him controls. Thus, critics have also studied the theme of alienation with existential overtones.[4]

However, the lasting interest of the play is due to the way all these themes are subtly woven together and the way each of them gains significance from the others. For example, the political theme in this play is ingeniously linked with people, religion and history.

Whatever the central concerns—religious, political, social, historical, psychological and interpersonal—one motif which is evident throughout the play and which unites the action in the thirteen scenes is that of betrayal. Betrayal may be physical and emotional and takes different forms in this play—betrayal of ideals, of trust, of friendship and so on. Revolving round the theme of Power as it does, the play is replete with lies, intrigue, dissimulation, hypocrisy and treachery. Underlying the different sorts of betrayal is irony, from whence the play acquires much of its significance, allowing a multiplicity of meanings to be read into the play. Betrayal also is a prime factor leading to the disillusionment and despair of the protagonist. This results in the alienation of the protagonist from traditional religion, society and from individuals around him. Tughlaq's subsequent acts of cruelty and tyranny arise from his anguish at the incomprehension he meets all around him and betrayal by those he has trusted.

Quite early in his reign, Tughlaq has come into conflict with the orthodox believers and fundamentalists in religion. This is mainly an account of the Sultan's idealism, secularism and his aiming at Hindu-Muslim unity. The Muslim fundamentalists see him as betraying Islam by his ideals and practices. His idea of brotherhood is vehemently practised by him causing great annoyance and irritation to the Moulvis and Mullahs of the state. They call the Hindus infidels and want Muhammad to reimpose the jiziya tax on them which he had abolished earlier.

But the young find Tughlaq a true representative of Islam; he is human and a humanist. He is not an "Insult to Islam," as the older people say he is, but a king who has made a law that the Muslim have to pray five times a day. Moreover, the Koran is allowed to be read in the streets. But the fanatics as represented by Sheikh Imam-ud-din believe that the Sultan is going against the Islamic tenets: "If one fails to understand what the Koran says one must ask the Sayyids and the Ulema." (20) Tughlaq asserts his allegiance to the Koran: "I have never denied the word of God, Sheikhsahib, because it's my bread and drink." (20)

But Muhammad refuses to depend only on God and prayer and believes in his own strength and resources. "No one can go far on his knees," that is, through prayer alone. To the Sheikh this sounds like blasphemy and the desire to set oneself up as God: "Beware Sultan, you are trying to become another God." (21) In resentment the Ulemas and Sayyids take to open criticism of the Sultan, stirring up people's religious emotions by their fiery speeches, such as given by Sheikh Imam-ud-din in Kanpur. They are promptly put behind bars in the name of justice; "they tried to indulge in politics—I couldn't allow that," (20) says the Sultan. The Sheikh also pays for his alignment with politics in what can be considered a classic case of betrayal. He accepts the plea of the Sultan to serve as his envoy and dissuade Ain-ul-Mulk of Avadh from the folly of turning against the Sultan. A platoon of heavily armed soldiers follow him when he goes as an emissary of peace. The Sultan manages to have the Imam (who bears a physical resemblance to the Sultan) killed in such a way that nobody will suspect him.

Betrayal of religion is also evident in the way "prayer" is treated by the Sultan as well as his detractors, the "upholders of Islam." Prayer, which is deeply related to religion, is used for murder in the play. It is widely criticized that Muhammad had his father and brother killed during prayer time. And yet, those same priests, along with the Amirs, hatch a plot to murder Muhammad while at prayer.

Although the Amirs' revolt is shrewdly forestalled and crushed, it is nevertheless a shattering blow to Tughlaq's pride. He also feels betrayed: "I had wanted every act in my kingdom to become a prayer, every prayer a further step in knowledge, every step to lead us nearer to God, But our prayers too are ridden with disease and must be exiled." (44)

He summarily decrees that "there will be no more praying in the kingdom. . . . Anyone caught praying will be severely punished." (44) This severely wounds the religious susceptibilities of his subjects, making his alienation from them complete; it further makes him guilty of blasphemy, of a kind of revolt against God himself, as is the case of Caligula. Prayer has thus lost its efficacy and sanctity, having become merely a means to an end in the hands of both the Sultan and the religious leaders.

Not just from religion, but Tughlaq is also seen as a man estranged from society. It is an age of religious fanaticism and hostility between Hindus and Muslims. In a society where suspicion and distrust are rife, Muhammad wants justice and brotherhood. He wishes justice to work in his kingdom without any consideration of might or weakness, religion or creed. But he is not understood by the society around him because his ideals are far above the comprehension of his contemporaries. His broadminded religious tolerance seems foolish to the Muslims while his very motives are suspect to the Hindus. In other words, the people in that society appear to be constantly on the lookout for betrayal, so deep-rooted is their suspicion, as is evident from their reaction to the event of a Hindu (infidel) going to the court against the Sultan and winning his case.

Tughlaq wants to win the confidence of his subjects and build an ideal empire together with them, but fails to carry his people with him. The changes proposed by him pose a threat to the time-honoured conventions and beliefs of society and so he meets with stiff resistance from all classes of people.

Tughlaq's plans regarding the change of capital from Delhi to Daulatabad and the introduction of token copper currency are sound and reasonable to his own mind but fail to convince his subjects. Thus he feels frustration at their non-comprehension. "But how can I spread my branches in the stars while the roots have yet to find hold in the earth?" (10) If they failed to understand his reasons for proposing these schemes, he too fails to foresee their reactions to them. He does not take into account the emotional attachment of people to their native soil when he proposes a change of capital involving not only the shift in the administrative machinery but also of the people. He did not also foresee and take precautions against the possibility of counterfeiting when he introduces token copper coins. The repeated failure of Tughlaq to win the confidence of his people paves the way for his gradual disillusionment and fall from his ideals. Thus both the parties feel aggrieved and hurt as the incomprehension is mutual; this leads to further alienation of the Sultan from his society.

Tughlaq is also alienated at the interpersonal level from the individuals around him. In order to bring about Hindu-Muslim unity, Muhammad takes the new step of transferring the capital of his empire from Delhi to Daulatabad, as Daulatabad is the city of the Hindus. But he meets with severe opposition by the Amirs and the religious priests who suspect his every move. The Amirs feel that the Sultan is taking them to Daulatabad just to weaken them, because they are strong in Delhi. So, immediately after Imam's death in the "Peace-mission," they cold-bloodedly plan to murder him during the next courtiers' meeting and the Muezzin's call to prayer is to be the signal of attack. The conspiracy being out, the Sultan orders the beheading of all those involved in it, their bodies stuffed with straw and hanged up in the palace yard. This is a monstrous betrayal and the Sultan turns a murderer causing blood to flow in the palace.

Perhaps the greatest treachery of all which has a disastrous impact on Muhammad is that of Shihab-ud-din, whom Tughlaq genuinely liked and trusted. Shihab, the prince of Shampanshahr is called by Muhammad to look after the State in the Sultan's absence, as a gesture of good will and generosity towards his powerful father. An idealist and most loyal to Muhammad though he was, Shihab is pevailed upon by his adopted brother Ratan Singh and the Amirs in the name of Islam to plan the murder of the Sultan. The scene reminds one of the persuasion scene in *Julius Caesar* where Shihab-ud-din has to be persuaded as Brutus was. One can find innumerable instances from Greek and Roman history of the trusted men who betrayed the confidence.

It is a master stroke of irony that Shihab himself becomes a victim of betrayal by his brother Ratan Singh who reveals the plot to the Sultan. Shihab's betrayal is the turning point in Tughlaq's life, which "sends him hurtling down the abyss of existential alienation"[5] and turns him against the world. His anguish at not being understood by his people, at being betrayed by those he loved and trusted, is revealed in his tortured question to Barani, the historian: "Why must this happen Barani? Are all those I trust condemned to go down in history as traitors? Will my reign be nothing more than a tortured scream which will stab the night and melt away in the silence?" (43)

Tughlaq just cannot find a rational explanation for the treachery of Shihab and his courtiers' incomprehension of his idealistic measures. His frenzied stabbing of Shihab repeatedly even after he is dead, his order that the stuffed bodies of the conspirators should be exhibited throughout the kingdom, and his insistence on the immediate vacating of Delhi are all acts of cruelty and tyranny arising from his anguish. He decides to give up the method of rational explanation and persuasion which he had hitherto tried with his people. He is now determined to rule them with an iron rod. "I was too soft, I can see that now. They'll only understand the whip." (44) In his movement from idealist to tyrant, Tughlaq resembles Caligula, Camus's protagonist, whose existential alienation drove him to a deliberate choice of tyranny.

With regard to his relationship with his mother, Tughlaq is already estranged from her, as she believes him guilty of patricide and fratricide. More significantly in scene ten comes the betrayal of his stepmother to whom he has been very close. He condemns her to death by stoning in public when she confesses to having his close adviser Najib murdered. Her reason for doing so is her resentment at the way Najib was leading Tughlaq astray and in advising him against the interests of the State and Muhammad. Subsequently, he feels intense self-alientation. Left alone, he falls to his knees and desperataly pleads with God to help him: "God in Heaven, please help me. Please don't let go of my hand. I started in your path, Lord, why am I wandering naked in this desert now?" (67)

Finally, the play shows emotional betrayal too, the betrayal of Tughlaq's earlier youthful ideals. The first scene reveals him as an idealistic reformer who hopes to lead his people into a utopia. We learn that Tughlaq is a king who "isn't afraid to be human." (1) He is a devout Muslim and yet is not fanatic, for in his kingdom, the Hindus are treated on perfectly equal terms with Muslims, something hitherto unknown. In the second scene, Tughlaq himself says that he does not want to "waste any time by sleeping" (10) at night, because he has only one life to live and so much to do in it; so he looks at the stars instead, becomes poetic, and is full of ideas of charity for all his people; he wants to climb up, upto the top of the tallest tree in the world, and call out to his people, "confide in me your worries. Let me share your joys. . . . History is ours to play with. . . . Come! I am waiting to embrace you all." (10) But he meets only with non-comprehension from his people resulting in his alienation. This is the prime cause for the falling apart of his grandiose schemes. It is also possible to see his failure as supporting the view that idealism does not pay in politics. It is bound to fail, specially when the idealist is impulsive.[6]

Another facet of Tughlaq's character is revealed in the third scene. As a young man he has read the Greek philosophers and "found a new world, a world I had not found in the Arabs or even the Koran." (21) He finds it impossible to deny or kill that part of him which had appreciated the Greeks. He therefore experiences fragmentation,[7] is torn between his allegiance to the Koran and his appreciation for other forms of truth: "my kingdom too is what I am—torn into pieces by visions whose validity I can't deny. You are asking me to make myself complete by killing the Greek in me and you propose to unify my people by denying the visions which led Zarathustra or the Buddha." (21)

But at the same time he has his political "responsibilities"; in the words of U.R. Anantha Murthy, Muhammad had divine aspiration, but he was also a deft intriguer. He is a master tactician which is seen in the way he handles the two separate threats posed by Ain-ul-Mulk, the rebel governor of Avadh and Sheikh Imam-ud-din, the holy man.

Another example of the way he turns difficulties into opportunities by his cool calculation is how after killing Shihab with his own hands, he orders an announcement to be made declaring that Shihab died a martyr while trying to protect his master from assassins, thus ensuring the neutralization of the traitor's father who is a powerful man.

The series of events traced earlier on have resulted in his progressive alienation from society, religious priests, courtiers and even from people close to him. Consequently, far from being the saviour-monarch of his people as he wished to be, he becomes a tyrant. How far he has come away from his youthful idealism is manifested in the eighth scene when he talks to the young guard in the new fort in Daulatabad. He also recaptures a magical moment from his youth when he felt fully in harmony with the world around him. "Suddenly something happened—as though someone had cast a spell. The torch, the gate, the fort and the sky—all melted and merged and flowed in my blood-stream with the darkness of the night. I was the earth, was the grass, was the smoke, was the sky." (53)

Tughlaq had been trying to recover that experience throughout his life, but the hopelessness of his search for that lost moment of communion is revealed in the lines: "I have searched for that moment since then and here I am still searching for it. But in the last four years, I have seen only the woods clinging to the earth, heard only the howl of wild wolves and the answering bay of street dogs." (54)

At the end of this scene we are given another look into Tughlaq's present degeneration in Barani's appeal to Tughlaq: "Your majesty, there was a time when you believed in love, in peace, in God. What has happened to those ideals? . . . Why this bloodshed? Please stop it." (56) Barani feels that this malaise has arisen from a rejection of God and fellowmen by Tughlaq and suggests that Tughlaq should renew his relationship with God and neighbour. Tughlaq is not prepared to do so, for it would mean admitting that he had been wrong all those years. He still feels he has a mission to accomplish, a lesson to teach.

Scene ten contains another juxtaposition of his past idealism with the present corruption when his stepmother tells Tughlaq: "It's only seven years ago that you came to the throne. How glorious you were then, how idealistic, how full of hopes. Look at your kingdom now. It's become a kitchen of death." (65) Inevitably, Tughlaq is forced to admit that his innovative measures like the change of capital and the introduction of token copper currency have proved themselves to be hopeless failures. The rose garden which he had envisaged as a visible symbol of visionary hopes to create a utopia, becomes a rubbish dump where fake copper coins are piled up. He also knows people call him Mad Muhammad. But Tughlaq is not ready to eschew tyranny as a way of life, a vehicle to fulfil his mission in life. He even admits to having killed his father, brother and Sheikh Imam for an ideal; and since Shihab's murder, killing has become a compulsion for him.

Yet in scene ten, soon after condemning his stepmother to death, in an agony of despair, helplessness and bewildered incomprehension, Tughlaq tries to pray, an act forbidden by him in his kingdom. He realizes his own self-estrangement and that he has reached its extreme edge, which is madness: "I am teetering on the brink of madness, Barani, but the madness of God still eludes me." (68)

It is only in the last scene that Tughlaq sees a parody of himself and his whole career in the unmasking of the scoundrel and cheat, Aziz the Washerman. The dhobi assumes the guise of the great grandson of His Imperial Holiness Abbasid Al-Mustansir, the Khalif of Baghdad, who was invited to Daulatabad by the Sultan.

After having murdered Ghiyas-ud-din Abbasid, Aziz who had disguised himself as a Brahmin earlier, now appears in the garb of the Muslim saint and goes to the palace of Muhammad to bless and purify Daulatabad. This scene contains in itself the greatest irony of fate and situation combined together and reveals to him the futility of his entire reign.

Completely shattered in mind and body, Tughlaq announces his decision to shift the capital back to Delhi and succumbs to sleep which had eluded him for the past five years. But the play ends with his waking up with a start and looking around "dazed and frightened as though he can't comprehend where he is." (86)

Thus we see that the different stages of the action and the different fields of interaction in the play are inter-linked by the common motif of betrayal. The betrayal takes different shapes too—religious, political, social, interpersonal and emotional. The element of betrayal running throughout the play makes for a fascinating study of the complexity of human motives. Thus it is evident that *Tughlaq*'s thematic concerns have a universal significance. Betrayal, coming as it does at various significant stages in the protagonist's life, traces the course of alienation, leads to anguish giving rise to cruelty and tyranny and finally culminates in the tragic failure of one of the most idealistic kings in Indian history.

NOTES

1. M.K. Naik, "The Limits of Human Power: A Comparative Study of *Tughlaq* and *Caligula*," *Studies in Indian English Literature* (Delhi: Sterling, 1987), p. 132.
2. P. Bayapa Reddy, "The Theatrical Representation of History: Girish Karnad's *Tughlaq*," p. 149 in this book.
3. Qtd. U.R. Anantha Murthy, Introduction to *Tughlaq* (Delhi: OUP, 1972), p. viii.
4. Christine Gomez, "Karnad's Tughlaq as an Alienated Protagonist," pp. 114-26 in this book.
5. *Ibid.*, p. 118
6. H.S. Mahle, "History and Contemporary Reality," *Indo-Anglian Fiction: Some Perceptions* (Delhi: Jainsons, 1985), p. 140.
7. Christine Gomez, p. 117.

The Theatrical Representation of History: A Study of *Tughlaq*

P. BAYAPA REDDY

> True drama is created by bringing life to the theatre and the theatre to life. . . . Good drama must be equally satisfying on each level . . . as character and action and life, on the one hand, and the highly conventional art of the theatre, on the other. And unless the dramatist works like an organist playing on two keyboards at once, the audience cannot respond as it wishes to respond.[1]

Girish Karnad is a contemporary Indian playwright who has created true drama in his play *Tughlaq*[2] in the Priestleyan sense. He explores the paradox of Muhammad Tughlaq, the idealistic Sultan of Delhi whose reign is considered to be one of the most spectacular failures in Indian history. *Tughlaq* is not an ordinary chronicle play but a very imaginative reconstruction of some of the most significant events in the life of a great king who is seen not only in India but also in the contemporary world. The theme of the play is from Indian history yet the treatment of it is not historical but highly political. In this play, politics is ingeniously linked with people, religion and history.

In the very opening of the play, an old man and a young man discuss the political situation in the country. In their discussion, they bring about a sharp contrast between the present administration of Tughlaq and the administration of the past Sultans. Again in scene vii, one finds a discussion on the importance of politics in day-to-day life. Aziz, a washerman turned politician, says: "Only a few months in Delhi and I have discovered a whole new world—politics! My dear fellow, that's where our future is—politics! It's a beautiful world—wealth, success, position, power—and yet it's full of brainless people, people with not an idea in their head." (50) In scene xi too, "crowds of citizens" discuss among themselves how the rulers went to save the common men who are ridden by starvation, dirt, disease, impatience, famine and a number of other ills. One comes to know from this how politics is used to promote the self-interest of the leaders but not the welfare of people.

In this powerful play, politics is deftly linked with religion. In scene iii, one finds the Revered Sheikh Imam, aligning himself with politics. He accepts the plea of the Sultan to serve as his envoy and dissuade Ain-ul-Mulk of Avadh from the folly of turning against the Sultan. A platoon of heavily armed soldiers follows him while he is doing the job of an emissary. The Sultan has managed to kill Imam in such a way that nobody would suspect him. Here the religious leader becomes a prey to the dirty political game of Tughlaq. Prayer, which is deeply allied to religion, is used for murder in the play. Prayer halls are being polluted with these discussions on politics. Tughlaq kills his father while he offers prayers. Chieftains are worried about the deft political intrigue practised by Tughlaq on Imam. Shihab, one of the Amirs, cries out thus: "Is it so reprehensible to worry about people? Is it a crime to speak out for oneself and one's family? What politics did Sheikh Imam-ud-din indulge in? That he was open, frank and honest?" (32) He also adds how religious leaders like Haidari and Hood are in prison. These events clearly reveal to us how religion is made use of by the politicians for their selfish ends.

Besides religion, history is cleverly linked with politics in this play. Barani, a historian, is asked to give a practical remedy for "the honeycomb of diseases" (55) like the uprising of the Deccan, the declaration of independence by Habar Ehsanshah. The historian wonders why the Sultan who has faith in love, peace and God has now grown pessimistic about the future. The playwright links history with politics by making the historian align himself with the political activity of the Sultan. As U.R. Anantha Murthy observes, "The whole play is structured on these opposites of the ideal and the real, the divine aspirations and the deft intrigue." (ix) In the main plot, Tughlaq appears to be idealistic but instead he practises selfish political game. The scenes are so juxtaposed that one is not allowed to be either carried by one's hatred towards Tughlaq for his master tactics or by one's sympathy or admiration for his idealism.

Karnad displays great talent in the delineation of the character of Tughlaq. Throughout the play, one finds elements of dualism in the character of Tughlaq. As an idealist, he aims at the welfare of his people; but he practises hypocrisy by employing a Hindu officer to watch the Muslim soldiers and vice versa. As a pious Muslim, he prescribes the customs of prayer five times a day, but as a crafty politician, he indulges in deft intrigue. He kills his father, his brother and Shihab while they are at prayer. He is highly resourceful and imaginative because he can solve easily "the most famous problem" in chess which was not solved by experts like al-Adli and as-Sarakhi. Barani rightly says: "You are a learned man, your Majesty, you are known the world over for your knowledge of philosophy and poetry. History is not made only in statecraft; its lasting results are produced in the ranks of learned man." (55) In the words of his own stepmother, Tughlaq is "an intelligent boy and he works so hard for the people. He doesn't even go to bed these days." (17) The playwright has succeeded in presenting the conflict in the mind of Tughlaq.

Karnad's handling of dialogue in the play is quite effective. He has chosen English to reflect the idiom of the language of character. A Karnad sentence often performs two or three functions at once. It sheds light on the character speaking, on the character spoken about and it furthers the plot. It almost functions ironically in conveying to the audience a meaning different from that conveyed to the character. The following lines illustrate the point:

Muhammad: No one can go far on his knees. I have a long way to go. I can't afford to crawl—I have to gallop.

Imam-ud-din: And you will do it without the Koran to guide you? Beware, Sultan, you are trying to become another God. It's sin worse than parricide. (21)

This passage throws light on the aspirations of Tughlaq to the fame of becoming a universal conqueror. He would not like to crawl but would like to gallop. In the pursuit of his ambition, he may even ignore the tenets of the holy Koran. An astute politician as he is, he feels that he has not yet made considerable advance in the realm of politics. Naturally, the dialogue here gives an insight into the political theme of the play and the playwright's power to handle this theme. The dialogue furthers the theme of the political gambit of Tughlaq.

A snatch of a phrase caught in everyday conversation may mean little. Used by an actor on the stage, it can assume general and typical qualities. In the words of Styan, "the context into which it is put can make it pull more than its conversational weight, no matter how simple the words."[2] For example, Tughlaq, who has ingeniously manoeuvred to bring about the death of Imam-ud-din in the battlefield, declares a day of mourning in honour of the Sheikh and says: "When men like him die, it's a sin to be alive." (28) These words acquire theatrical vitality easily. Equally interesting and powerful is the conversation between Tughlaq and Shihab. Tughlaq says: "It's a question of confidence. A question of trust! The other day I heard that in China they have paper currency—paper, mind you—and yet it works because the people accept it." (39)

Tughlaq is notable for its poetic value. Tughlaq comes to us as a poet when he speaks of his interest in the Greeks. He says: "Don't I know it? I still remember the days when I read the Greeks—Sukrat who took poison so he could give the world the drink of gods, Aflatoon who condemned poets and wrote incomparably beautiful poetry himself—and I can still feel the thrill with which I found a new world, a world I had not found in the Arabs or even the Koran." (21) Here poetry has made the play precise not only for the actor to work with but also for the audience to react to. The poetry here expresses and defines patterns of thought and feeling otherwise inexpressible and indefinable.

Sometimes language in the play is simple, easy and precise. The language of the people from the lower strata of life, like servants and soldiers, is direct, simple and powerful. The following is a case in point:

Old Man:	God, what's this country coming to!
Young Man:	What are you worried about, grandfather? The country's in perfectly safe hands—safer than any you've seen before.
Old Man:	I don't know. I've been alive a long time, seen many Sultans, but I never thought I would live to see a thing like this. (1)

Through such careful choice of characters and situations, Karnad endeavours to make his dialogue realistic, immediate, precise and highly effective.

Silences and pauses mark a silent interplay of conscious and unconscious motivation. One is reminded of *The Dumb Waiter* of Pinter. In scene iii, in the encounter between Tughlaq and Imam-ud-din, one finds a long silence in the middle of the dialogue. (22) Tughlaq tells Imam-ud-din that people will greet him as a spy in the market place. He also praises him that as a great saint, the Sheikh has risked his life speaking out against the Sultan. The long silence there tells us that Tughlaq is a crook and is interested in killing Imam. Again, in the conversation between Tughlaq and his step-mother, (27) Tughlaq pauses for a while when he actually describes the death of Imam-ud-din. This reflects the negative side of Tughlaq. One finds similar pauses in the conversation between Sheikh and Shihab. These silences and pauses reinforce the meaning of the play.

Tughlaq is rightly considered a piece of theatre "par excellence." Karnad experiments with a variety of theatrical techniques to create visual and auditory images, thereby producing the desired dramatic effect on the stage. By employing a variety of theatrical devices—spectacle, quick shift of scenes, blackout—he tries to control the movement of the play and its impact on the audience. Spectacle refers to all the visual aspects of production, scenery, lighting, costume, make-up and the business and the movement of the actors. In the very beginning of the play, the public announcer announces the judgement of the Chief Justice in favour of Vishnu Prasad followed by a loud discussion among a large number of people. The very appearance of Tughlaq in his striking costume adds a lot to the element of spectacle in the play.

The announcement pertaining to the arrival of Sheikh Imam-ud-din enhances the visual appeal of the play. Muezzin's call for prayer, the marching of the Amirs towards the throne of Tughlaq, the announcements made by the announcer about the shifting of capital from Delhi to Daulatabad, the call for the banning of prayer and the revival of it, the play of music and the anguish expressed by the common masses during the shift of the capital, are some of the elements of spectacle in *Tughlaq* that have come to assume an organic psychological role in the theatre that reinforces the meaning of the play.

There are thirteen scenes in the play which runs into eighty-six pages. The scene of action is almost suddenly shifted from the yard in front of the Chief Court of Justice to a room in the palace, then to the yard in front of the Big Mosque, again to the palace, then to a house in Delhi and then to the palace again. It shifts to a camp on the Delhi-Daulatabad road. Suddenly it goes to the fort in Daulatabad, to a hide-out in the hills, then to the palace, and then to a plain outside the fort of Daulatabad, and back to the palace. The playwright presents the following sequences to throw light upon the complex personality of the Sultan: the affair of Aziz and Adam, Tughlaq's attempt to levy heavy taxes on the poor farmers, his orders to change the capital from Delhi to Daulatabad, the futile conspiracy of the disgruntled Amirs to kill the Sultan while at prayer, his cruel punishment of his stepmother because she was responsible for the killing of Vizier Nazib; Aziz's impersonation of the invitee—Caliph Ghiyas and its consequences; and finally the fall of the Sultan. As these episodes follow each other on the stage, they make us focus our attention on Tughlaq as a complex character. Moreover, the sudden shifting of the scenes makes the spectator move forward and backward. The audience is constantly and explicitly reminded that it is in a theatre while the play is made as accessible as possible. Karnad deftly uses a few dramatic techniques which add much to his artistry. Irony is one technique which he employs to make his play highly theatrical. It is not merely situational but also verbal. The manner in which prayer is sought to be used as an instrument of murder against the very man who has made prayers compulsory in the state, and the role played by Aziz are examples of the irony of situation. Again Aazam and his death, Ghiyasuddin's preferring "the bloody streets" to the palace are other examples of situational irony. The beautiful bodies which are eaten up by corruption are stuffed with straw and hung on the poles. Tughlaq asks Barani not to cover the dead body of Shihab because he wants his people to see the wounds.

A few instances of verbal irony. The past Sultans of Delhi could not bear the weight of their crown. They could not leave it aside. So they died senile in their youth or they were murdered. Barani, a historian, is interested in playing chess with the shadows of the dead. The prayers offered by Tughlaq are ridden with disease and his sins have become shadows that entwine round his feet. It is ironical that Tughlaq and the Sheikh look alike but they do not think alike.

Symbolism is another technique that Karnad employs to make his play powerful on the stage. One finds four major symbols in the play. They are prayer, sleep, the game of chess and the rose. At the micro level, prayer symbolizes the religious idealism of Tughlaq. At the macro level, it connects man's unconscious need for divine protection and guidance in an hour of anguish. In the beginning prayer is made compulsory but later it is banned for a few years and again it is revived. It is reduced to a mockery when the Sultan's life is threatened at the time of prayer. "Sieep" on one level represents the need for rest in man's life. At the macro level it becomes symbolic of peace which eludes man often. The rose is a symbol of the aesthetic and poetic susceptibilities of Tughlaq. It later on becomes a symbol of the withering away of all the dreams and the ideals of Tughlaq. At the macro level, the game of chess is an ordinary game which is popular in India. It also symbolizes a political game in which the most intelligent and clever politician is checkmated by an ordinary washerman. Through this symbolist technique, the playwright has succeeded in creating the right political atmosphere. Thus *Tughlaq* emerges as one of the significant plays in the Indian theatre today.

NOTES

1. J.B. Priestley, *The Art of the Dramatist* (London: Heinemann, 1957).
2. Girish Karnad, *Tughlaq* (Delhi: Oxford University Press, 1972).
3. J.L. Styan, *The Elements of Drama* (Cambridge: Cambridge University Press, 1967), p. 11.

He That Playeth the Sultan: A Study of *Tughlaq*

P. RAMAMOORTHY

Girish Karnad's *Tughlaq* deserves a close scrutiny as it highlights one of the fundamental concepts of theatre i.e. that theatre is an illusion, a fleeting shadow, a vision and a dream-like experience. There is a close parallel between life and theatre and quite often life is theatre-like and vice versa. But at no time life is theatre and theatre is life. The thin line of demarcation between good theatre and life is very often not perceived and hence the confusion and misunderstanding that both are the same or both are interchangeable. A skilful playwright, even when he is realistic, makes us conscious: Look here! You're only watching a *play*. There are several ways of bringing in this awareness into the audience. A dramatist may, like Brecht, use epic distancing or use "fantasy" as Genet does, or he might use certain images to suggest that the audience is undergoing a theatrical experience. Girish Karnad uses theatrical images in *Tughlaq* to achieve an effect that is comparable to the achievement of John Osborne in *Luther*.

There are many references to acting, theatre and performance in *Tughlaq*. Muhammad behaves and speaks like an actor. His public appearance and his private moments are like that of an actor. In the opening scene itself, there is a reference to his theatricality. He appears before the crowd properly heralded and waxes eloquent. He speaks of "justice," "peace," "purposeful life"—rather he uses cliches to describe his desires. He makes an "exhibition" of his sense of justice. When he leaves the scene, the Guard disperses the crowd shouting at them: "All right, all right. Go home! What are you waiting for? The *show's over*! Go home."[1] (Italics mine, 5)

The Sultan's public appearance, his sense of justice, his plans are all a part of the show. The crowd is the audience for the Sultan.

It looks more or less like a scene from the street theatre. Even after the actors have moved into another part of the city the audience sometimes lingers on and comments on the players and their performance. The Guard's appraisal of the situation is clear and incisive. Just as the Guard judges the situation, in Scene Two, the stepmother sees Sultan as an actor. She laughs at his performance and that is a positive sign of the acting potentiality of the Sultan as an actor. She asks a simple question: "Then what do you do all night?" (10) and the reply is a lengthy, *theatrical* monologue. Girish Karnad, in his Stage Directions, italicizes the word theatrical. The speech is poetic, stagey and full of grandiose statement:

> Then again I want to climb up, up to the top of the tallest tree in the world, and call out to my people: "Come, my people, I am waiting for you. Confide in me your worries. Let me share your joys. Let's laugh and cry together and then let's pray. Let's pray till our bodies melt and flow and our blood turns into air. History is ours to play with—ours now! Let's be the light and cover the earth with greenery. Let's be darkness and cover up the boundaries of nations. Come! I am waiting to embrace you all!" (10)

This is not an address in the Durbar, nor is it a king's message to his citizens on his birthday. The scene takes place in a room in the palace. The only person listening to him is the stepmother. So, no wonder, she laughs and tells him: "I can't ask a simple question without your giving a *royal performance*." (Italics mine, 10-11)

The gestures and speech behaviour of Muhammad are theatrical. He plays a "role" now, then changes costumes, and plays another "role." Before Sheik Imam-ud-Din, he plays the role of a true ruler interested in establishing a "new world." He plays it so well that Imam-ud-Din tells him: "You know, Sultan, I'm just beginning to understand why they saw you are the cleverest man in the world." (24) Scene Six opens with silence. "Muhammad is restless and paces up and down. When the Amirs enter, the restlessness is gone. He welcomes them "with *obvious* warmth." Every emotion is to be shown. It is an actor's responsibility to make things obvious for the audience, either directly or indirectly. The pensive, restless mood is replaced by an imposed cordiality. Like a skilful actor, Muhammad keeps changing roles. Where there is an opportunity, he becomes theatrical in his action also. In Scene Four, when Shihab-ud-Din perceives Muhammad with a mere bow, Muhammad brings in the actor's touch: "That's no way to welcome, Shihab. Come— They *embrace.*" (Italics mine, 26)

In Scene Six, when he pleads with Amirs to support him in his plans, much to the surprise and embarrassment of the Amirs, he kneels before them. "The Amirs *almost recoil at this sudden gesture.*" (40) They are taken aback by his theatricality. Like an actor winning applause of the audience by an unexpected gesture, Muhammad outsmarts them. We must remember that Muhammad is aware of the conspiracy of the Amirs at this moment. We are told of his knowledge of the conspiracy only later in the play. So, here is a Sultan, who knows that Amirs have come to kill him and yet stage-manages a "play" before them. He could have easily arrested them in the beginning of the scene itself, but he likes to enjoy the climax of the play, and he would love to exhibit before his audience how he plays the climax. So he allows the call to prayer. When the Amirs step forward to attack him, the Hindu soldiers overpower them. "*While all this is going on, MUHAMMAD goes on praying unconcerned. Only after finishing the prayer does he step down from the throne.*" (41-42) In Scene Eight, Muhammad is given a long poetic monologue which unravels the anguish of a visionary whose vision has fled. He makes the speech dramatic.

Muhammad is an actor-type. In Michael Anderson's words, an actor is "a kind of embossed essence of human being. When he is on stage he steps into one role after another and must be on intimate terms with the entire range of human emotions, when he takes off the grease paint he lacks the protective personality that most of us carry around to shield our true nature from the prying eyes of the world; but the need to display and communicate passion which is his stock in trade is not something that can be left behind in the dressing-room along with the wings and the make-up. The actor type is always in search of an audience: all in all he can prove an enthralling but wholly demanding companion, supremely arrogant and yet supremely vulnerable."[2] In Scene Eight, Muhammad goes to the Fort in search of an audience. He sends for Barani and talks to him. He tells Barani: "When I came here, I felt *I needed an audience.*" (Italics mine, 54) He is a "demanding companion" to the young watchman. There is a constant desire for an audience.

Another important image that highlights the relationship between life and theatre is "role-playing." Disguise in *Tughlaq* is a symbol of role-playing. The parallel comic plot of Aziz and Aazam and the main plot converge at one point. Muhammad asks Aziz: "Who are you? How long did you hope to go on fooling us with your masquerade?" (79)

Muhammad recognizes a fellow actor in Aziz who is also a genius in "role-playing." When he forgives Aziz, Muhammad says: "I don't know why I am acting like a fool." (83) The various roles played by Aziz—that of a Brahmin, of a victim, and more significantly that of Khalif—are pointers to the fact that Aziz converts life into a stage and goes on with his role-playing. Aziz is Muhammad's "shadow," his "other." He tells Muhammad: "I insist I am your Majesty's true disciple." (80) Aziz checkmates Muhammad and sends him into "a guffaw." He recognizes the genius of Aziz, forgives him and makes him an officer of the State. What is made very obvious in the case of Aziz is made subtle in the case of Muhammad. Muhammad also wears masks and disguises himself. There is a basic dialectics in Muhammad's personality: the visionary and the politician; the idealist and the realist. The whole play is a projection of Muhammad's "divided self." U.R. Anantha Murthy rightly observes: "The whole play is structured on these opposites: the ideal and the real; the divine aspiration and the deft intrigue. Tughlaq is what he is in spite of his self. Knowledge and an intense desire for divine grace. He is aware of the irony of his life when Aziz, the only character in the play who has skilfully used all the schemes of Tughlaq for his own designs, kills Ghiyas-ud-Din and comes in his guise as a holy messenger of peace to purify the land and revive the banned prayer."[3] K.S. Ramamurthy also comments on the divided self of Tughlaq: "He is at once an idealist and crafty politician, a humanist and a tyrant, a man who has murdered sleep and yet not a Macbeth haunted by supernatural solicitations, a man who thinks and broods too much and yet not a Hamlet incapable of action or guilty of delay."[4]

The "divided self," pointed out by Anantha Murthy, has to be seen on the stage. To visualize the "divided self" in terms of "role-playing" is a popular English theatrical device. John Osborne does that in *Luther*. The man behind the revolution is a person in conflict with himself and his parents. Martin's rebellion is a mask that provides him an opportunity to suppress the familial conflict and fight it out in another ground.

In Karnad's *Tughlaq*, Muhammad is at war with himself. He is basically a visionary, a poet and not a ruler. He loves chess, a rose garden and enjoys reading Sadi's poems. He reads the Greeks. He is aware of the "Greek in me." (21) He speaks of his visions—of finding a "new world, a world I had not found in the Arabs or even the Koran." (21) He builds a Utopia in his visions. His visions are like "the visions which lead Zarathustra or the Buddha." (21) He is constantly talking about "tomorrow," "a new future." Muhammad tells the young watchman in Scene Eight:

> Nineteen. Nice age! An age when you think you can clasp the whole world in your palm like a rare diamond. I was twenty one when I came to Daulatabad first, and built this fort. I supervised the placing of every brick in it and I said to myself, one day I shall build my own history, like this, brick by brick. . . . Suddenly something happened—as though someone had cast a spell. The torch, the gate, the fort and the sky—all melted and merged and flowed in my blood-stream with the darkness of the night. The moment shed its symbols, its questions and answers, and stood naked and calm where the stars throbbed in my veins. I was the earth, was the grass, was the smoke, was the sky. (53)

Barani sees the visionary in Muhammad. He sees him behind the mask. When Muhammad wants to know the cure for the "honeycomb of diseases" Barani prescribes:

> You are a learned man, your Majesty, you are known the world over for your knowledge of philosophy and poetry. History is not made only in statecraft; its lasting results are produced in the ranks of learned men. That's where you belong, your Majesty, in the company of learned men. Not in the market of corpses. (55)

This learned man, the philosopher Muhammad speaks through symbols. To him every rose is "an image of Sadi's poems." (64) That is one of the reasons why Muhammad's language is poetic. He has a poet's vision in his heart. He cannot follow Barani's prescription because that means he must give up playing the Sultan:

> I have often thought of that myself—to give up this futile see-saw struggle and go to Mecca. Sit there by the Kaaba and search for the peace which Daulatabad hasn't given me. What bliss! But it isn't that easy. It isn't as easy as leaving the patient in the wilderness because there's no cure for his disease. (55-56)

Muhammad feels that he still has "something to give, something to teach, which may open the eyes of history." (56)

Aziz too has his moment of epiphany. He suddenly realizes that human life is just "bodies eaten-up by corruption," like the Sultan's moment of revelation in the rose-garden. Both Aziz and the Sultan suffer identity crisis. The Sultan, a visionary, deliberately dons the robes of a ruler. He kills his father, kills his conspirators and makes Sheik Imam-ud-Din a pawn in his game of holding the sceptre to his fist. He plays a tyrant but very often the role slips by and makes him a civil servant. The act of forgiveness is the real Sultan. He is a poet who has compassion and a comprehensive vision to tolerate human weakness. But when he plays the Sultan, he kills mercilessly even his close relatives—his father, his stepmother and Shihab-ud-Din. The conflict is between the visionary and the ruler and the struggle of Muhammad is to achieve a synthesis between the two. *Tughlaq* is an excellent tragedy that depicts the struggle and failure of a poet who wants to become a ruler, a visionary who desires to establish a Utopia. The struggle becomes significant as it ends in the failure to effect a synthesis between the poet and the ruler and the failure to found a "new world."

NOTES

1. Girish Karnad, *Tughlaq* (OUP, 1972).
2. Michael Anderson, *Anger and Detachment: A Study of Arden, Osborne and Pinter* (London: Pitman, 1976), p. 22.
3. U.R. Anantha Murthy, "Introduction," *Tughlaq*, p. ix.
4. K.S. Ramamurthy, "Some Aspects of Indian Drama in English with Special Reference to *Tughlaq*," *Litcrit*, 5, No. 1 (1979), p. 17.
5. For an insightful comparison with Caligula, read M.K. Naik, "The Limits of Human Power: A Comparative study of *Tughlaq* and *Caligula*," *Studies in Indian English Literature* (New Delhi: Sterling, 1987).

Voices in/of the Void: Logorrhoeic Discourse in *Tughlaq*

PRAMOD K. NAYAR

In the buginning is the woid, in the muddle is the sounddance.
James Joyce

Girish Karnad's highly acclaimed play *Tughlaq* (1971)[1] presents a tortured man. Muhammad Tughlaq is a king who wants to reform and improve his people. He is an idealist whose ideals' praxis renders him a dreamer and a fool. Tughlaq stands as a man deluded by his idealism and dreams.

In this essay I argue that Tughlaq's language reveals this dreamer personality. I intend to demonstrate that Tughlaq's logorrhoea is a verbal manifestation of his "visionary" (dreamer) and troubled self.

Logorrhoea is an aphasic problem where the victim is extremely voluble. However his/her speech may be replete with meaningless cliches and errors. S/he no longer comprehends the "meaning" of the speeches.[2]

Tughlaq's logorrhoea can be read at various levels of unmeaning, or misplaced, questionable meaning. For example, Tughlaq's speeches to his stepmother, to Aziz, to the Amirs are full of empty signifiers. He does not mean what he says. He refers to Ghiyas-ud-Din Abbasid as "Your Holiness" and offers due courtesy when he [Tughlaq] knows very well that Ghiyas-ud-Din is actually Aziz, a common criminal. Thus the epithet is devoid of any significance. (79) Or when Tughlaq is about to order his stepmother's arrest, he is simultaneously addressing her thus: "Because I love you more than I have loved anyone in my life." (66) Tughlaq's words locate him at a point where the signifier and the signified are completely divorced. This separation lies in the deed which attains supreme importance. In the above two examples, Tughlaq's denouement of Aziz's escapade and his condemnation of the stepmother, the words are merely words signifying nothing. If the character himself has not realised the void within his language, it becomes a good example of logorrhoea.

In addition to the emptiness of the words, Tughlaq's rhetoric is full of "insubstantial" images. By this I refer to his constant use of "abstract" nouns such as "belief," "hope," "dream," "ideal." This emphasis on non-concrete images lends an idyllic aura to his speeches. The imagery is either romanticised or cliched. For example we only have to look at his long speech to his stepmother:

> Come my people, I am waiting for you. Confide in me your worries. Let me share your joys. Let's laugh and cry together, and then, let's pray. Let's pray till our bodies meet and flow and our blood turns into air. . . . Let's be the light and cover the earth with greenery. Let's be darkness and cover up the boundaries of nation. . . . But then how can I spread my branches in the stars while the roots have yet to find their hold in the earth? (10)

The anaphoric speech is constituted by vague metaphors and cliched imagery. Even Tughlaq's orders are couched in terms of abstraction or negation. For example, his orders on leaving Delhi and cessation of all prayers: "Not a *light* should be seen in the windows of Delhi. Not a *wisp of smoke* should rise from its chimneys. Nothing but an *empty graveyard* of Delhi will satisfy me now." And later: "Henceforth let the moment of prayer walk my street in *silence* and leave without a *trace*." (44, emphasis mine) Such images in Tughlaq's logorrhoeic rhetoric lends an eerie air to the words. I suggest that it makes the signification insubstantial, incomplete and maybe even absent. Examples could be multiplied (20, 21, 39, 84-85).

When not cliched or overworked, Tughlaq's rhetoric is ironic. He revels in antiphrasis. Parricide is referred to as "a little thing" and prayer as "pollution." (13) When he refers to his mother with "love" or praises his follower's loyalty, he is being ironic. For, immediately after this lavish praise he orders their executions (66-67, 42-43). Yet again the deed dessicates the praise, terms of endearment or such "positive" signifiers of meaning.

Tughlaq's speech is also, in addition to being cliche-ridden or ironic, occasionally frenzied. As is typical of logorrhoeic discourse (defined as "prattling freely,") his language is abrupt and full of repeated words. Tughlaq compresses his language, especially in his sentences. This asyndetic nature of his discourse becomes increasingly apparent towards the conclusion of the play. Tughlaq's tortured ravings are an example: "Why am I become a pig rolling in this gory mud? Raise me, clean me. Cover me with your Infinite Mercy. . . . I can only beg—have pity on me. I have no one but you now. Only you." (67) And in the final scene (to Barani): "I am suddenly feeling tired. And sleepy. . . . Go, Barani. But before you go pray for us." (85) The tensed-up, bunched and broken speeches reflect a mind increasingly troubled.

Epizeuxis[3] marks Tughlaq's frenzied dialogues as the play proceeds. In scene Eight he rebukes a young man who does not comprehend his speech: "You don't understand! You don't understand!" (54) He tells his stepmother (Scene Ten): "They gave me what I wanted—power, *strength* to shape my thoughts, *strength* to act, *strength* to recognise myself." (66, emphasis mine) And in his prayer he repeats: "I have no one but you now. Only you. Only You. . . . You. . . . You. . . . You." (67) This unwarranted epizeuxis only emphasises the progress of Tughlaq's logorrhoea, and his personality's disintegration.

If logorrhoea is a feature of Tughlaq's rhetoric, it also marks a certain derangement of personality. In this context, one uses the term "hallucinatory" to describe Tughlaq's speech. The *Oxford English Dictionary* defines "hallucinations" (derived from "allucinari") as (a) to be deceived, suffer illusions or entertain false notions; (b) to talk idly, prate. Thus the term is coterminus with logorrhoea, especially when it comes to *Tughlaq*.

Tughlaq, as noted before, continually refers to ideals, visions and dreams. He dreams of a great empire, a unified people, prosperous subjects and so on. As U.R. Anantha Murthy has pointed out in his Introduction to *Tughlaq*, the play rests on the binary opposition of the "ideal and the real." (iii) The pragmatic possibility is never in evidence in Tughlaq's action. To extrapolate the arguments, Tughlaq's dreams/visions and speeches do not become feasible or turn out well. Thus the dream remains his hallucination, since it is (i) unrealisable and (ii) refuses to acknowledge human errors, practical difficulties or even ethics. Thus the dreams *articulated* by Tughlaq (10, 21, 39 and so on) are themselves discourses of hallucination: unreal, meaningless and hopelessly muddled. The dreams are therefore, logorrhoeic in themselves, a free but idle discourse.

When Tughlaq ceases to recognise his incomprehensible (to others) dreams, he adds an air of artifice to them. This brings us to the theatricality of *Tughlaq*.[4] We have already noted that Tughlaq's logorrhoea uses images of unreality. A feeling of illusion is sustained throughout. There are numerous references to "theatrical" and "performance" in the play. Like the words which form facades for nothing, i.e. which are "masks," *Tughlaq* is full of "masked" characters all playing "roles."

In a kind of Bakhtinian carnival all hierarchies are subverted: king/protector turns criminal/villain, a holy man becomes king, washerman/criminal masquerades as a saint, loyal subjects turn treacherous. The encomiums offered are, likewise, ironic and empty. For instance, Aziz praises Tughlaq as a "wise man." (80-81) The announcers who herald the king's entourage, or who publicise his orders, refer to him in glowing terms as "merciful," "just," "pious" and so on. The antiphrasis and irony is obvious, since Tughlaq is none of these. The praise adds to the theatricality and illusory nature of Tughlaq's existence.

Tughlaq's speech, logorrhoeic and hallucinatory, supplements[5] his self. Since Tughlaq lives in a world of illusions and (misplaced) ideals, his language must needs reflect, convey, even constitute this world. Hence the logorrhoea. Tughlaq's dream-world moves beyond and encroaches the hallucination onto his language, and thus into the world. The ephemerality of Tughlaq's logorrhoeic signifiers conveys to us his tragedy. The emptiness of his prolixity is the void of his hallucinatory life.

NOTES

1. Girish Karnad, *Tughlaq* in *Three Modern Indian Plays* (Delhi: Oxford UP, 1989).
2. *The New Encyclopaedia Britannica, Macropaedia*, 1977, Vol. 17. p. 489. The disorder's relation to the other language related illness aphasia is detailed here.
3. Epizeuxis is a rhetorical figure where a word may be repeated with no intervening words. In this case, Tughlaq repeats more than one

word in a swift, breathless epizeuxis. On the whole the iteration emphasises his precarious mental state and his chaotic location within his own language. The epizeuxis may thus be for himself, a reassuring move.

4. For a superb discussion of theatricality and the theme of "performance" in *Tughlaq,* see P. Ramamoorthy, "He That Playeth the Sultan: A Study of *Tughlaq,*" pp. 156-61 in this book. P. Bayapa Reddy has also written of this element in Karnad's play: "The Theatrical Representation of History: Girish Karnad's *Tughlaq,*" pp. 149-55 in this book.
5. I use the term "supplement" in a Derridean sense here, as both completing and "in excess." This is to re-emphasise the mutual existence, parasistic or symbiotic, of Tughlaq's language and personality.

'To become the whole': A Study of Margaret Atwood's *The Edible Woman* and Girish Karnad's *Hayavadana*

B. INDIRA

"Our wants, fears, pleasures and pains are involved in our contact with the things of the outside world."[1] That is to say that our experiences and senses are strongly rooted in the environment we live in. Surroundings act upon us whether we are aware of them or not and the creative artist's prime concern is how to interact with his or her environs, may they be natural, cultural, social or political. "The present day concern of the modern West-oriented man starts with the assumption that we have to take care of the environment as it affects our living . . . the ancient Indian seer's or poet's concern started with the assumption that we are a part of a larger existence, in order to become the whole . . . in order to live a full life."[2]

The Upanishaḍs conceive of the human body as "A living symbol of the organic relationship of the parts to the whole."[3] Each part is related to the others and all are interdependent. The body is a macrocosm of the Universe wherein Fire becomes Speech, Wind becomes Breath, the Sun becomes Sight, the Quarters become Hearing, the Animal, Herbs and Regents of the Forest become Hairs, the Moon becomes the Mind, Death becomes Vital Air and Water becomes Seed, entering the organ of regeneration.[4]

The present study tries to show how two women struggle to live a full life, taking into consideration Marian in Margaret Atwood's *The Edible Woman* which is a metaphor for Canada's fight against the American imperialism and Padmini in Girish Karnad's play *Hayavadana*, the theme of which is based on Thomas Mann's retelling of "The Transposed Heads," wherein Mann ridicules the "mechanical conception of life that draws a line between body and soul."

In a structured consumer society dominated by gender segregation, as reflected in the description of Marian's workplace in *The Edible Woman,* Marian is only a body for Peter. Peter, a typical symbol of consumerism and a prototype of the west-oriented man plays a safe custodian to that body with elan. When she visits Peter's apartment for the first time, Marian lets herself be manipulated into Peter's bedroom. But their first physical union ends in a disappointment for Marian as Peter is more bothered about sweeping away the bits and pieces of glass that gets broken in the process. Ever since Marian is dominated by an uneasy and unsettled feeling in Peter's company. In another encounter in the bathing tub—"an attempt on Peter's part to assert his youthfulness and spontaneity"[5]—a part of his personality is shockingly revealed to her—he cares mostly for 'his' physical comforts—after all his flesh is not mortified in the tub, he being on top. Marian wonders if Peter thought of her as a lavatory fixture. If Marian was ever to pronounce "rotten" about their sexual involvement, Peter, "ordinariness raised to perfection," would never believe it so. He is so sure of his physicality. Marian knows that there is not actually any life in her sexual involvement with Peter. Whenever he looked at her after the act, she would begin feeling that she was on a doctor's examination table. (149) The falsity and shallowness of the relationship puts her off to such an extent that it does not irritate her when Duncan honestly admits that she is a substitute for the laundromat for him.

Ainsley, her friend, warns Marian of Peter monopolizing her. However, caught in the conditioned body-trap, Marian evades the reality of the relationship. Marian, unable to cope with her uninvolvement in the relationship, turns into an eccentric and develops anorexia. She runs away from the middle of parties, crawls under beds to find "a private burrow." In spite of all this the body triumphs over the mind as she agrees to Peter's marriage proposal for she wants the solidity a marriage may offer. However the uncompromising mind replies to one of Ainsley's casual questions:

> "Hi going to the laundromat?" She said . . . "No," I said, "I've chapped Peter up into little bits. I'm camouflaging him as laundry . . . to bury him in the ravine." (92)

On the other hand she fantasises Duncan, who she chances to meet at one of her door-to-door campaigns and kisses him spontaneously at the end of their second meeting at the laundromat. She is herself—Marian—in Duncan's presence. And Duncan, her other self—"You sort of look like me," (144) Duncan tells Marian when she dresses herself in one of his coats. Marian's relationship with Duncan glides smoothly from "The flat hypnotic voice (of Duncan) . . . (to) the realization that he had actual flesh, a body like most other people." (144)

Caught in the cross-currents of body and mind, Marian wonders if she is a normal person. Her body assumes a different identification irrespective of her mind in the beauty parlour as she gets ready for Peter's party. She sees herself like a patient in an operation theatre, where only bodies are mended. A marriage of minds between Peter and her is now remote. When Peter asks her to pose for a photograph, her mind gets an edge over her body and all that she could manage is a frozen and rigid body incapable of any movement. Her mind by now stops getting into her smiles. She flees from the party without anybody's knowledge and her mind carries her body to Duncan's. Duncan refuses her into his bed unless she peeled all that made up junk off her face—that is, shed all those carefully nurtured pretences and be her real self. He never wants "a piece of flowered wall paper" (253) in his bed.

Towards the end, Duncan who helps Marian realise her mind-existence tells her 'you have to go now.' (265) For, he knows that Marian has now realized the strength of her mind and is ready to meet any challenge. Marian invites Peter over for tea and bakes a cake-woman for him. It's her way of telling Peter that all he wants of her is a very appetizing body which she can no longer be. Much to her relief Peter leaves Marian. Duncan too fades away from her mind. Marian no longer needs any props to put all the pieces together.

In a symbolic gesture she eats the cake limb by limb as if absorbing the body feeling into the mind. At last with a sound mind in a sound body, she gets down to clearing the apartment of its junk—the first step being defrosting the refrigerator.

Padmini's prime concern in *Hayavadana* is to live as much close to nature as possible. She "grew up running around in heat and cold and rain."[6] 'As fast as lightning and as sharp,' Padmini needs a man of steel to engage her both physically and intellectually. She, a daughter of the Goddess of Wealth, marries a son of the Goddess of Learning. Kapila, a body-man, sparks off a raging conflict in Padmini's mind. Condemned to Devadatta's intellectual world her natural instincts are frustrated time and again. Kapila's body, very close to nature in its tone is her immediate way out to live closer to nature.

Dejected by his "wife's unconcealed amorous attraction for his friend, Devadatta in a mood of sacrifice severs his head from the body at the feet of Goddess Kali. Kapila too follows suit when he comes to know his friend's gesture, confessing his lack of intelligence in understanding the intricacies of the relationship.

Left alone, the pregnant Padmini dares the dark evening in the forest and to her horror stumbles over the bodies: "How selfish you are—how unkind," (31) she wails and in order to escape blame decides to offer her head too. The Goddess intervenes and shows her a way out. In her eagerness to live closer to nature, Padmini attaches Devadatta's head to Kapila's body. Though the Goddess appreciates Padmini's desire to lead a more authentic life, she is astounded to see Padmini's action. "My dear daughter, there should be a limit even to honesty" (33) exclaims the Goddess seeing Kapila's head on Devadatta's body and that of Devadatta's on Kapila's body. Kapila's body weighs a ton on Devadatta's mind and Devadatta's head feels heavy on Kapila's body. The friends laugh merrily seeing their bodies as if they have donned themselves in a new pair of clothes. Padmini, at her wits' end, is unable to react.

Now the problem is, who should Padmini accompany? Kapila's head claims her as his present body is the father of the child. The learned Devadatta counters it by saying that "The head is the sign of man." Kapila's arguments centre around the body and those of Devadatta around the mind—"of all the human limbs the top most in position . . . is the head." (37)

They seek a sage's counsel and decide to abide by it. When the sage too pronounces that mind is what a man is, Padmini tells Devadatta's head: "Let's go quickly where the earth is soft and the green grass plays the swing. . . ." "What other canopy do I need," (41) wonders Padmini as she relaxes on Kapila's broad shoulders. The intelligent and self-willed Padmini decides to follow the better combination—Devadatta's head on Kapila's body. Devadatta realizes that "This body just doesn't wait for thought—it acts." (42)

Padmini considers the new combination—a "fabulous body—fabulous brain—fabulous Devadatta." (42) The initial joy wears away as Devadatta's present body no longer emanates "that strong, male smell." "Your body had that strong, smell before" (44) she tells Devadatta's head which is used to anointing the body with artificial sandalwood oil. Kapila's body under the influence of Devadatta's mind gets trapped in the mundane intellectual world. Devadatta confesses: "It was fun the first few days. . . . All that muscle and strength. I have the family tradition to maintain—the daily reading, writing and studies." (44)

Padmini begins to shudder at his touch. She turns pensive and dreamy, always lost in the world of Kapila. Though she assures Devadatta that she is not going to act stupid again, the other half of her wonders what Kapila might be doing, whether his body is still fair and so on.

In the absence of Devadatta, Padmini takes the first chance to reach the forest where Kapila lives. When Kapila tells her that his mind has been at war with the body, the more experienced Padmini asks, "the head always wins, doesn't it?" (55) She notices that just as Kapila's body has turned soft with Devadatta's head on its top, Devadatta's body has got toughened by Kapila's mind. If the bodies had not transformed in accordance with their heads, Padmini would not have dared the thick forest in search of Kapila. Not only that she could not tolerate the artificiality her son is condemned to. In a soliloquy, she tells the child: "My poor child, you haven't yet seen the 'whitching' fair of the dark forest. . . . There's so much. Long before the sun rises, the shadows of twigs draw 'alapanas' on the floor. The stars raise 'arati.' . . . The circus in the tree-tops. . . . The tiger-dance . . . the dance of the sun's little feet . . . then the night comes . . . right outside the fair . . . stands the tree of the Fortunate Lady . . . a close friend of ours." (53) Later she also tells Kapila: "My son had never laughed with the river or shivered in the mind or felt the thorn cut his feet. So I brought him out." (54)

Brandishing a sword in his hands Devadatta too comes to the forest searching Padmini. However, his vengeance vanishes when he sees his long lost friend who receives him endearingly. Devadatta enquires of Kapila: "Did my body bother you too ?" and Kapila replies: "It wasn't made for this life . . . it resisted . . . your body gave me feelings, new words. . . . [I] even started writing poetry." (60)

They openly confess their love for Padmini to each other. Kapila even suggests they live like the Pandavas. And very casually they decide to fight a combat with each other to claim Padmini's hand or to die at each other's hands. After a lengthy fight they stab each other to death, once again leaving Padmini alone. As Kapila wonders at the beginning of the fight—"Now whose head—whose body—suicide or murder" (61) none can really say.

Even if Padmini was prepared to live with both the friends, they "could only have lived ripping each other to pieces," (62) for intellect and instincts do not go hand in hand. The two bosom friends forgive each other—Padmini is only an intruder in their lives. "It's almost my autobiography . . . Kapila, Devadatta! Kapila with Devadatta's body! Devadatta with Kapila's Body! Four men in one life time. (56)

Padmini has the capacity for complete experience and she knows it is beyond her capacity to control the situation she is placed in. Her autobiography ends with her decision to offer 'sati,' her last wish is that her son be known as Kapila's son. And that he should be brought up in the forest till the age of five. "Your body gave him to me," she tells Kapila. "He has the same mole on his body." (55)

In a social milieu wherein men and women are unequally and differently raised and valued, Marian's immediate concern is to rise above the body—living that she has been condemned to. As she frees herself from the body trap, Marian realizes that Peter, her fiance, is incapable of refilling her emptied mind. Devadatta's head on Kapila's body throws Padmini, a woman of instincts, into a mire of problems. If Peter's responses are well tailored to measure only the bodily needs of Marian, Padmini much to her chagrin realizes that Devadatta's head has succeeded in transforming the muscular body of Kapila into a sickly soft one.

The major concern of both Marian and Padmini is how 'to become the whole.' Marian fights her way through towards growth in a highly mechanised and industrialised environment of an advanced country whereas Padmini's life ends in a tragedy as in her eagerness to live in perfect harmony with nature, she unwittingly goes against nature's course.

NOTES

1. K.S. Karanth, "Work of Art as a Product of Creative Imagination and its Milieu," *Creativity and Environment*, ed. Vidya Niwas Misra (New Delhi: Sahitya Akademi,1992), p. 75.

2. Vidya Niwas Misra, "Man, Nature and the Poet," *Ibid.*, p. 52.
3. Kapila Vatsyayan, "Indian View of Environment as a Part of an Indian Aesthetics," p. 29.
4. *Ibid.*, p. 27.
5. Margret Atwood, *The Edible Woman* (McClelland and Stewart, 1969), p. 62.
6. Girish Karnad, *Hayavadana* (New Delhi: OUP, 1981), p. 46.

The Development of Girish Karnad as a Dramatist: *Hayavadana*

SHUBHANGI S. RAYKAR

Karnad's third play *Hayavadana* was published in 1970, exactly six years after *Tughlaq*. Karnad is not a prolific writer and he is very much against writing in haste. Usually the idea of a play incubates in his mind for a long time and it is only when the total action of the play is clearly before his mind's eye that he starts writing a play. The story of *Hayavadana* comes partly from Thomas Mann's story titled "Transposed Heads," which in turn is based on one of the versions of the story in *Vetal Panchavimshati*.

A brief summary of "Transposed Heads" is as follows. Shridaman, a Brahmin by birth but Vanijya by profession, and Nanda, a cowherd and blacksmith, are very close friends. Shridaman falls in love with Sita whom he happens to see when the two friends are travelling together. Nanda laughs at the idea but agrees to act as a messenger of his friend. Sita accepts the proposal and marries Shridaman. Some months later while Shridaman, Nanda and Sita are travelling together in a cart to the house of Sita's parents they lose track, come across a temple of Kali and take a halt. Shridaman visits the temple alone and, overcome by an incredible urge, offers himself to the goddess as a sacrifice. Nanda goes in search of his friend, finds what has happened and afraid of the charge that he killed his friend because he was in love with Sita and also because he does not want to live without his friend, kills himself. Sita realizes what has happened and prepares to hang herself. The goddess Durga appears in front of her, chides her for her act and grants life to the two dead bodies. Sita, in her excitement, fixes the heads wrongly. Naturally the problem is: who is her husband? The hermit Kamdaman whose advice is sought decides in favour of Shridaman's head. Nanda's head, therefore, decides to become a hermit.

Gradually Shridaman's head begins to control Nanda's body and the body becomes refined. Sita begins to pine for Nanda, so much so that she sets out to meet him carrying Andhak, her baby boy with her. After a strenuous journey, she finds him at a pleasant spot in the forest. They spend the day and the night in heavenly bliss. Next morning Shridaman arrives on the scene. He suggests that they should kill each other in a combat and that Sita should perform sati. Sita thinks that if she lives the life of a widow Andhak's future will be doomed but if she performed sati Andhak will be a sati's son and his social image will improve. So she gives her consent and burns herself on the funeral pyre of her two husbands!

The stories in *Vetal Panchavimshati* and Somdeva's *Brihatkatha Saritsagar* are basically the same except for a few alterations in the latter, in place names and in the references to the names of the castes of characters. The story is as follows. Prince Dhavala married Madansundari, the daughter of a king named Suddhapata, through the favour of goddess Gauri, in a temple in the city of Shobhavati. Then one day Svetapata, Suddhapata's son, proceeded to his own country along with his sister and her husband. On the way he came to another temple of goddess Gauri. Dhavala went into the temple to pay homage to the goddess. Through some irresistible urge, he cut off his head with a sword which he chanced to see there, and presented it to the goddess. As Dhavala did not come even after waiting for some time Svetapata went inside. When he found out what Dhavala had done he also cut off his own head and offered it to the goddess. Then Madansundari, realizing that her husband and her brother had been away for a long time, went into the temple and saw their dead bodies lying before the goddess and, in great grief, she also began to cut off her own head. Just then the goddess Gauri appeared before her, prevented her from doing so and offered to her what she wanted. Madansundari, naturally, requested the goddess to restore her husband's and her brother's life. The goddess asked her to set their heads on their shoulders. But through excitement she joined her husband's head to her brother's body and vice versa. When they came back to life Madansundari realized her mistake. Vetala's question is "Who is Madansundari's husband?" The king answers "Of course the person with Dhavala's head on his shoulders."

Karnad's play in a characteristic way begins where the *Vetal* story ends. "How would the woman take it if it really happened and would it ultimately solve the problem for her," are the fascinating problems the artist in him faces. In all his plays Karnad takes this kind of leap from the original story and develops it further. This further development is the play of the artist's imagination and it challenges the glib solutions offered in the original stories. In the story of Yayati as it appears in the Adiparva of the *Mahabharata*, Puru's acceptance of his father's old age smoothly resolves the story. But Karnad's play *Yayati* uses this only as a starting point. If the young Puru had a wife how would she feel about Puru's extraordinary decision, becomes the starting point of his exploration of the problem raised by the mythical story. Something similar happens in his latest play *Atte Ka Kukkut* (translated from Kannada into Hindi but not translated into English so far). In the original story in the Jain Purana on which Karnad has based his play the king is a Jain but his mother is a Hindu. When he relates to her a certain dream that he dreamt, she advises him to sacrifice a cock to a goddess. He being a Jain and committed to the practice of non-violence in every sphere of life plans to sacrifice instead a cock made of dough. But in Karnad's play the cock comes to life just as it is to be sacrificed and the play develops from that point onwards. Perhaps the problem he wants to raise is, "Can something so serious as one's faith in non-violence be taken so casually? Would not the king accept the idea of violence even if he kills a cock made of dough?" The audience is thus forced to reconsider the glib solution offered in the Purana. In *Hayavadana* what Karnad wants to suggest is that for us King Vikram's solution does not solve the problem. In fact the real problem begins when it appears to be solved. That could be the reason why he dropped the version of *Vetal Panchavimshati* which had the "incest" theme at its core. At the same time he makes significant departures from Thomas Mann's story too. The sub-plot of *Hayavadana* is entirely Karnad's invention. In the play the stories of the sub-plot throughout support the main plot.

Hayavadana is an enigmatic play. Critical opinion is divided about what its main theme is. Kirtinath Kurtkoti who wrote a brief introduction to the English translation published in 1975 says: "The original play poses a moral problem while Mann uses it to ridicule the mechanical conception of life which differentiates between body and soul. He ridicules the philosophy which holds the head superior to the body. The human body, Mann argues, is a fit instrument for the fulfilment of human destiny." Karnad's play poses a different problem, that of human identity in a world of tangled relationships.

Another critic U.R. Anantha Murthy in his "A Note on Karnad's *Hayavadana*" has this to say about theme: "The play exposes the audience to a significant theme like 'incompleteness' in a comic mode." A few paragraphs later he says, "The play tries to create an illusion in us that the head determines the being of man." R.S. Sharma in a lively note says: "That completeness is a humanly impossible ideal is suggested first in the story of *Hayavadana* and later in the transposition of heads. By showing the absurdity of the ideal of completeness the play finally achieves its aesthetic goal. It implicitly asserts the value and significance of human imperfection which makes any upward movement possible."

To me, the theme of the play has two aspects, a socio-cultural aspect and a metaphysical one. At both levels it shows the conflict between two polarities (namely Appollonian and Dionysian) as the vital truth of human existence. How does one define "completeness" or "perfection"? If perfection or completeness means fusion of the two extreme polarities (at the metaphysical level), the play suggests that such fusion is not possible and this is for the simple reason that if the cycle of nature must continue, it will do so only through a dialectical relationship between Apollonian and Dionysian aspects of life. At the socio-cultural level the play suggests that the Apollonian always asserts itself and subdues the Dionysian in our socio-cultural life. So the co-existence of the two is ruled out (this point is proved later) physically as well as morally. Human society is made possible only through submission to the Apollonian principle. The collective wisdom of society flouts passion (represented in the play by the judgement of the Rishi and Padmini's passion for Kapila respectively). It will bring about the destruction of the individuals who defy order in society. Padmini's predicament is the predicament of a modern, emancipated woman in our society who is torn between two polarities, a woman who loves her husband as well as someone else for two different aspects of their personalities. A civilized Apollonian society and its moral code will not accept such a woman. The two men will not accept each other when it comes to sharing a woman and all the three will destroy themselves in the process.

Devadatta and Kapila's friendship obviously evolves out of their fascination for the aspect which each one of them lacks. They are thus complementary to each other. But the woman whom both of them love is fascinated by both of them and this creates the problem.

Anantha Murthy points out that it is significant that Kapila is a blacksmith—a lower caste in the Hindu caste system while Devadatta is a brahmin. That is why Padmini's fascination for both of them at the same time would be all the more unacceptable to the society in which they live. But this is surely an incidental complication. The real crux of the problem is that society in its present form would not accept a woman living with two men.

Devadatta, the Brahmin and husband, Padmini his wife; and Kapila the low caste, Devadatta's friend but almost like his "dasa," always willing to serve Devadatta and Padmini: this represents the social order. That is why Devadatta's accomplishments which go with the role the social order has imposed on him are so approvingly recounted by the Bhagavata.

The first is Devadatta. Comely in appearance, fair in colour, unrivalled in intelligence, Devadatta is the only son of the Revered Brahmin Vidyasagara. Having felled the mightiest pundits of the kingdom in debates on logic and love, having blinded the greatest poets of the world with his poetry and wit, Devadatta is as it were the apple of every eye in Dharamapura. The other youth is Kapila. He is the only son of the ironsmith Lohita, who is to the King's armoury what an axle is to the chariot-wheel. He is dark and plain to look at, yet in deeds which require drive and daring, in dancing, in strength and physical skills, he has no equal.

But it is clear that for Padmini who is not at all willing to play docilely the role that society imposes on her and for Kapila who also is impulsive (as can be seen from his climbing the tree the moment Padmini desires to have a flower of the fortunate lady), surely his extraordinary devotion to Devadatta and his constant fawning upon Padmini and calling her sister-in-law are but instances of introverted sublimation of his impulsive Dionysian nature, the "order" imposed by society is destructively restrictive. Devadatta and Kapila accept the restrictions and make a virtue of these restrictions and resort to platitudes such as friendship etc. to make reality bearable. Padmini, "the female principle," more bold, more frank in demanding what will fulfil her—"selfish" in the eyes of Kali—in a daring endeavour tries to get the best of both. But it is clear that Padmini's extra-marital relationship with Kapila or her accepting Kapila as a second husband will threaten the "order" in this society. That all the three die at the end shows that the Apollonian principle ("order") wins. The question that the play poses is: "Are the deaths justifiable?" If they are not justifiable (that they are not justifiable is shown through the handling of the form—comic, grotesque etc.) then obviously there is a need for change in the socio-cultural pattern. There is need of a society which will accept a woman who is in love with two men at one and the same time.

Devadatta and Kapila are close friends. Both love Padmini and yet each recoils from the obvious solution: namely they should both live with Padmini.

Devadatta:	Tell me one thing. Do you really love Padmini?
Kapila:	Yes.
Devadatta:	So do I.
Kapila:	I know. (Silence) Devadatta, could not we all three live together—like Pandavas and Draupadi?
Devadatta:	What do you think? (Silence. Padmini looks at them but does not say anything)
Kapila:	(laughs) No, it cannot be done.
Devadatta:	That is why I brought this. (shows the sword)

They, thus, yield to the Apollonian insistence on the status quo and would prefer to die and have their beloved Padmini reduced to ashes rather than obey their Dionysian impulses.

Karnad, however, wants to make his audience aware of the inadequacy, indeed futility of such a solution. This he does by making the the Bhagavata pose the question directly to the audience. "What? What indeed is the solution to this problem, which holds the entire future of these three unfortunate beings in a balance?"

But it would be worthwhile at this point to see how he has manipulated the characters in the play to prepare the audience for the response he wants from them to the the Bhagavata's question.

After the initial episode of the actor and Hayavadana (very much like the "purvaranga" in a "Kirtan" and reminiscent of the dispute over the ownership of the valley which is the opening episode in Brecht's *Caucasian Chalk Circle* which has very important implications for the story which is to unfold) the the Bhagavata begins the story of Devadatta, Padmini and Kapila.

By changing their names from the original story or the story by Thomas Mann, Karnad on the one hand makes them generic, that is to say, representative. The name of Devadatta (given by gods) reveals the Apollonian aspect whereas Kapila (dark and therefore earthy) reveals Kapila's Dionysian tendencies. Padmini, like a lotus, seeks to be a delicate bridge between the earth and the sky.

Also like a lotus she is more rooted in the earth and, therefore, has greater affinity for the Dionysian aspect of life manifest in Kapila. Their dilemma has implications for the present-day audience irrespective of their socio-cultural station in life. This device of giving his characters generic names also helps Karnad to dovetail the characters into the the Bhagavata's narration, for stories in their oral, narrative style are mostly—since they are designed to drive home a moral—about representative characters. But quite soon we realize that Karnad is intent on endowing them with striking individuality which alone could make their dilemma emotionally, that is to say aesthetically, appealing. Anantha Murthy feels dissatisfied with the play because the playwright, he feels, has not been able to "show" certain facets of the main characters, especially that of Devadatta. He, however, overlooks the facts that Karnad has used a form in which narrative "telling" is vastly more important than it is in a realistic, psychological play. Indeed in this tradition the playwright need not "show" the facts "told" by the narrator, the the Bhagavata, as they carry enough weight for the audience not to demand further "showing." But even as the the Bhagavata proceeds to "tell" the story, the characters as it were insist on coming into their own, insist, that is to say, on living their own lives, and making their own decisions. It is like the puppets in a puppet-dance suddenly insisting on dancing to their own impulses. It is in these parts of the play that Karnad succeeds in making them individuals and since his intention is just to stretch the narrative form that he is using he does not care—indeed he would seriously damage the design of his play if he did—to follow the device to the end and try to "show" the characters unfolding themselves.

Immediately after he sees Padmini, Kapila says to himself, "What she needs is a man of steel." That he is a blacksmith should make it easy for us to discern what Kapila feels about Padmini but he quickly subjugates his feelings to his more representative role; that of a loyal friend who is almost like a *dasa* to Devadatta. Later on when Devadatta decides against going to the picnic, Kapila's individual feelings surface, only to be submerged in the role that he has accepted to play:

> So it's off. What am I to do for the rest of the day? What am I to do for the rest of the week? Why should it feel as though one whole world has been wiped out for a whole week? Why this emptiness—Kapila, Kapila, get a tight hold on yourself. You are a slipping boy, control yourself. Don't lose that hold. Go now—don't come here again for a week—Devadatta's bound to get angry with you for not coming. Sister-in-law will be annoyed. But don't come back.

It is true, as Anantha Murthy points out, that Devadatta is the least "individuated" character. But this is explicable in terms of the thematic design of the play. Devadatta is the character around whom the Apollonian order is created. He, therefore, is least subject to passion and, therefore, least impulsive of the three. Even his offering his head to Kali appears to be the end product of a ratiocinative act. Before he offers himself to the goddess, Devadatta says, "Good bye Kapila, Good bye Padmini. May the Lord Rudra bless you. You are two pieces of my heart—live happily together. I shall find my happiness in that."

His generosity and selflessness professed here are forced as the audience knows from the earlier dialogue in the play. Once he realizes the nature of the relationship Padmini and Kapila are heading towards, he decides to remove himself from the scene rather than make the painful choice of sharing Padmini with Kapila.

When Kapila appears on the scene he realizes what Devadatta's "sacrifice" implies. Once again instead of obeying his impulses—which would mean going back to Padmini and taking her away with him—he chooses to do what is expected of him in his role as a "devoted friend" namely kill himself because he cannot live without a friend. He dies asserting, "No Devadatta, I can't live without you. Devadatta, my brother, my father, my friend."

The goddess—who sees and knows everything—is, however, not taken in by these platitudes. She spells out clearly what the audience might have only vaguely felt all along:

> The rascals! They were lying to their last breaths. That fellow Devadatta—he had once promised his head to Rudra and his arms to me! Then because you insisted on going to the Rudra temple he comes here and offers his head. Nobly too—wants to keep his word—No other reason!

This sarcastic statement makes it clear that Devadatta had made his promise to the goddess an "excuse," a noble and acceptable "excuse," for hiding his real motive. The goddess continues:

> This Kapila. Died right in front of me—but "for his friend." And what lies! says he is dying for friendship. He must have known perfectly well he would be accused of killing Devadatta for you. Do you think he would not have grabbed you if it had not been for that fear? No till his last breath—Oh my friend! My dear brother!

Among these three characters it is only Padmini who is courageous enough to defy order and get what she thinks will bring her fulfilment. Kapila grasps the essence of her character when immediately after he meets her he says, "She is bright like lightning and as sharp."

Unlike Devadatta and Kapila, she refuses to play the role others expect her to play. All through the play, Padmini wants to be just herself. She refuses to play the role of the bashful bride on her wedding night. Both Devadatta and Kapila express on different occasions their concern for her condition (she is expecting a baby). But on all occasions she firmly rebukes their bookish concern for her safety and insists on doing what she wants to do. Her uninhibited nature is established right at the beginning of the play through the song of the female chorus: "Why should love stick to the sap of a single body? A head for each breast. A pupil for each eye. A side for each arm. I have neither regret nor shame."

This is asserted again and again in the conversation between Padmini and Devadatta and in the conversation between the goddess and Padmini. Padmini says to the goddess, "If you'd saved either of them I would have been spared all this terror, this agony. Why did you wait so long?"

If Padmini wanted to play the role of a Pativrata (a woman devoted to her husband) she should have opted for Devadatta, suppressing her desire for Kapila. But she does not want to and says so very frankly. The goddess appreciates her frankness and says to her, "Only you spoke the truth—You spoke the truth—because you are selfish."

In fact Padmini wants them both but this would not be acceptable to society and she knows exactly what she wants from each of them. She wants Devadatta's mind and Kapila's physicality while society forces her to seek these qualities, if she can, in one man. She would like "a perfect man" who possesses both these aspects of human personality whom she, as it were, creates in her excitement by transposing the heads of Devadatta and Kapila. The goddess once again discerns her motives and says in a resigned tone, "My dear daughter, there should be a limit even to honesty" and adds "anyway so be it!"

One must choose one's course of action and then accept the consequences unflinchingly. But if understood as a deliberately chosen one Padmini's act is ultimately a consequence of the social norms imposed on her. Since she cannot have both Devadatta and Kapila she tries to get past the norms by having what she most wants from each of them. But this does not at all solve the problem.

The second act of *Hayavadana* is largely Karnad's creation for he develops it from a question that he asks himself as he arrives at the end of a traditional story. His development of the second act is based to a greater extent on the story by Thomas Mann but the conclusions offered are to be interpreted differently. The second act shows that the solution Vikram gave to the problem is inadequate in the present situation. Padmini's act of going with Devadatta's head is based on the solution of the Rishi who in fact reiterates King Vikram's solution. But if the head controls the body it logically follows that it will transform the body. That is what happens and so far as Padmini is concerned she again remains with Devadatta, her husband. Worse still she is forced to watch the transformation taking place and thus lose Kapila bit by bit. Ultimately she finds herself faced with the same problem which faced her in the first act. She misses Kapila, his impulsiveness and his physicality all the more because she has tested it more intimately through Devadatta's head and Kapila's body in the early days (after the metamorphosis).

In the first act the supernatural element that is the goddess Kali is used to reveal conscious motives behind the actions of the three protagonists. Here he uses the animate dolls as a device to report to us from moment to moment what is going on in Padmini's mind. Her psychological reaction to the transformation in Devadatta is very economically communicated. The sense of time passing is also given by making the dolls report to each other what Padmini dreams, what reveries she indulges in. They also "feel" the change taking place in Devadatta:

Doll I:	His palms! They were so rough, when he first brought us here. Like a labourer's. But now they are soft—sickly soft—like a young girl's . . .
Doll II:	His stomach. It was so tight and muscular. Now . . .

Karnad also uses the dolls as a "device" in the development of the plot. It is because the dolls get old that Padmini can send Devadatta to the Ujjain fair. He could have used the Bhagavata to narrate what is going on in Padmini's mind. But that would have affected his success in making her character individuated and generic (representative) at one and the same time. She, then, would have been more of a representative and less of an individuated character. The Bhagavata has deeper knowledge of Padmini's nature. He knows what kind of person she is, as is clear from his comments when Padmini and Kapila meet in the forest:

> And as I saw him change I could not get rid of you. That's what Padmini must tell Kapila. She should say more without concealing anything: "Kapila, if that Rishi had given me to you, would I have gone back to Devadatta some day exactly like this?" But she doesn't say anything. She remains quiet.

The Bhagavata knows Padmini and therefore he knows what must be going on in her mind. (He is partly like the omniscient narrator.) The dolls on the contrary have only a limited knowledge of Padmini because they are endowed by the dramatist with a special vision (Divyadrishti) which can make them see and only "see" what is going on in the mind of Padmini. It is indeed a very ingenious device.

Padmini tries to act rationally when she first senses the transformation in Devadatta. "I am not going to be stupid again. Kapila has gone out of my life for ever. I won't let him come back again." She, however, is not the one who can act rationally. She yields to the impulse all too soon. Once she knows that her husband can only be Devadatta, he cannot be Kapila, there is an urge in her to accept "Kapila—the—person." So far she knew only "Kapila's body" now she wants to know Kapila the person. When Devadatta goes to the Ujjain fair to buy new dolls for the child, she suddenly, on an impulse, undertakes a strenuous journey carrying the child with her and because he has been taught to accept social norms adds,

"Devadatta and Padmini! Devadatta and Padmini! A pair coupled with the holy fire as witness. I have no place there, no peace, no salvation. Go on, I beg you, Go."

Padmini, however, has realized that she must accept Kapila "totally." Kapila's body which was once Devadatta's body knows Padmini intimately. His head also must know her. That will give "completeness" to Kapila.

When Devadatta appears on the scene with swords and he and Kapila decide to fight he says: "No grounds for friendship now. No question of mercy. We must fight like lions and kill like cobras." He, through his experience of having lived with "Kapila's body," has learnt that the talk about generosity, mercy and friendship with which he hid his subconscious motives earlier is now meaningless. Both Kapila and he accept that both of them living together with Padmini is not possible so long as they live. The only alternative is to kill each other which they do in "resignation."

Padmini prepares to perform "Sati." The very idea of "Sati" is ridiculed here. The song of the female chorus is full of grótesque beauty: "The fortunate lady's procession goes to the street of laburnums, while the makarandas tie the pennants and jacarandas hold lights. Good-bye, dear sister. Go without fear. The Lord of death will be pleased with the offering of three coconuts." It keeps the audience detached from any kind of emotional involvement with the "sad-scene." The audience, as a result, thinks dispassionately about Padmini's death. Padmini's choice of death allows her to assert her will through death. She would have liked to assert it even when she was alive; but she could not, partly because of the social norms and partly due to the realization that her accepting two husbands, namely Kapila and Devadatta, would not solve the problem so long as they themselves could not reconcile themselves to the idea. Padmini solves her problem in an existential fashion. As she dies she says to the Bhagavata:

> My son is sleeping in the hut. Take him under your care. Give him to the hunters who live in this forest and tell them it's Kapila's son. They loved Kapila and will bring the child up. Let the child grow in the forest with rivers and trees. When he's five take him to the Revered Brahmin Vidyasagar of Dharampura. Tell him it's Devadatta's son.

So the fusion of the Dionysian and Apollonian is Padmini's dream which she wants to be fulfilled through her son.

But Padmini and Devadatta's choice of death affects the child's growth adversely. "This child doesn't laugh, doesn't cry, doesn't even smile. There's obviously something wrong with him," as the actor puts it.

The stories of the main plot and the sub-plot lead thus to the same conclusion. Hayavadana's mother, the princess of Karnataka, sought to be a mare and galloped away without thinking in the least of Hayavadana, the product of her marriage with the white stallion. Padmini's act runs parallel to the story of Hayavadana's mother. Hayavadana is thrown into this world neither a beast nor a human being. Padmini's son becomes totally withdrawn from the world, "autistic." The inanimate "dolls" are his only companions—in fact they are the ones he knows intimately in this world. When he meets Hayavadana his innocent smile makes Hayavadana a complete horse and Hayavadana's laughter makes the boy forget his dolls and his regressive tendencies. It makes the child's return to humanity possible. They, thus, cease to suffer from the consequences of the acts of their parents. But this happy ending of a comedy does not prevent the audience from thinking over the other existential problem presented through the story of Kapila, Padmini and Devadatta. Padmini asserts her choice through death, Hayavadana's mother asserts hers through becoming a mare. Both Padmini's son and Hayavadana do not have a choice in the matter. They are brought into this world and they suffer as a result of the parents's act. Is the act of their parents justified?

At this point Karnad makes a very significant change in the story he borrowed from Mann. In Mann's "Transposed Heads" Sita dies thinking that her performing "Sati" will improve the image of her son in society and the son does become a good scholar and a reader to the king of Benares, unlike Padmini's who is autistic and withdrawn.

It now remains to consider a few more formal features of the play. The play borrows heavily from the Yakshagana and many other folk forms. Karnad's contribution is that he introduces (a relatively unknown and partly original) story which a folk form would normally avoid. Karnad had not employed folk theatre devices on such an extensive scale earlier. It is likely that Karnad felt that in the "naturalistic form" the play would never achieve the "universalization" of the theme the way it achieves it in its present form. The "non-naturalistic" form as Karnad employs it is very close to Brecht's Epic theatre. A narrator is used both in Karnad's play as well as in Brecht's Epic theatre. Both make extensive use of songs and music. In both there is linear and loose plot construction avoiding climax and revelation. Actors wear masks in both and in both again the action is presented largely through "miming." This makes the "universal framework" easier. It also succeeds in making the audience think about the problem in a more detached manner. One does not know whether the choice of the form determines the choice of the story or vice versa, but Karnad's choice of a folk tale for his play is very apt because it lifts the play above limitations of time and place.

Karnad has successfully managed to present his characters as "representatives" in spite of having made them highly individuated in some sections of the play and the names given to the characters are generic and suggestive as we have already seen.

The dialogue of the play is at once neutral and contemporary and helps to give contemporaneity to the problem the play discusses. For example:

Devadatta: It's humour for you. It burns my insides.
Padmini: Aw, Shut up. Don't I know how liberal and large hearted you are? You are not the sort to get jealous.

Karnad's use of the character of the Bhagavata contributes a lot to the formal aspect (achievement) of the play. He does not merely borrow the character of the Bhagavata from a typical Yakshagana play. He increases the scope of the role by making the Bhagavata not a mere commentator-narrator but also by making him one of the characters. The scene between the Bhagavata and Kapila before Padmini reaches Kapila's hut and the scene between the Bhagavata and Padmini when she prepares to perform "Sati" are good examples of it. This helps him achieve in a play what Mann achieves in the story through the third person narrator.

The supernatural, i.e. the goddess, is also used as a device. She is "terrible" in appearance but is given all the characteristics of a human being. She is angry at the thought that Devadatta should promise his "head" to Rudra and only his "arms" to her. She is vexed when aroused from her sleep. Through the use of this device

Karnad asserts that there are no ready-made solutions for human problems. The solution offered by the goddess is no solution. She only does what she is asked to do and allows Padmini to carry on her mistake even when she has seen through Padmini's honesty. In short the problem is unresolved and will be solved only through human effort, i.e., by changing the relationships and concepts of relationships which can be done only by the human beings themselves.

One of the striking features of *Hayavadana* is the introduction of the device of making inanimate objects animate. This is a frequent feature in folk literature but not in folk drama. The device, also like the device of the Bhagavata, helps Karnad to prove the psychological reality of the characters in the dramatic form which was achieved through the narrator in Mann's story. He has used the female chorus which is absent in the Yakshagana play. The ludicrous song given to the female chorus when Padmini performs "Sati" has already been discussed. In addition to these masks, the songs, the half curtains and the painted curtains, verbalization of the situation through narration, the continuation of the action without any formal break-up of scenes, the total absence of the front curtain are all devices carefully used to create the effect of alienation.

The most remarkable feature of the play from this point of view is that the entire action of the play is "mimed." This was not done either in *Yayati* or *Tughlaq*. It achieves universalization of the problem to a remarkable degree. Highly individualized subtle emotions cannot be communicated through miming. Fine shades of a particular emotion can be conveyed through soliloquies. In the naturalistic theatre the entire focus is sometimes on a single character and the character is allowed to reveal subtle emotions through the speech given to it and mostly through facial expressions. The speech given to Liubov Andryeevna in *The Cherry Orchard* Act II is a case in point.

> Oh, my sins! Look at the way I've always squandered money, continually. It was sheer madness. And then I got married to a man who only knew how to get into debt. Champagne killed him—he was a terrific drinker—and the worse luck, I fell in love with someone else. We had an affair, and just at that very time it was my first punishment, a blow straight to my heart—my little boy was drowned here, in this river . . . and then I went abroad. I went away for good, and never meant to return.

> I never meant to see the river again, I just shut my eyes and ran away in a frenzied grief, but he, he followed me. It was so cruel and brutal of him! I bought a villa near Mentone because he fell ill there, you see, and for three years I never had any rest, day or night. He was a sick man, he quite wore me out; my soul seemed to dry right up. Then last year when the villa had to be sold up to pay the debts. I went to Paris, and there he robbed me and left me; he went away and lived with another woman. . . . I tried to poison myself. It was all so foolish, so shameful! and then suddenly I felt an urge to come back to Russia, to my own country and my little girl. . . (wipes away her tears). Oh Lord, Lord, be merciful, forgive me my sins, don't punish me anymore! (Takes a telegram out of her pocket) I had this from Paris, today. He's asking my forgiveness, begging me to return. (Tears up the telegram) Sounds like music somewhere. (Listens)

Sometimes the conversation may go on between two characters revealing the interplay of subtle emotions. The dramatist himself suggests through stage directions how the actors should reveal this play of emotions with the help of facial expression. The conversation between Hilde and Solnes in the first act of *The Master Builder* is a good example of this. These function somewhat like the close-up in the film. There is no scope for all this when the entire action is mimed. "Miming," thus is the most important feature of the play so far as the "alienation effect" is concerned.

"This mad dance of incompleteness": Search for Completeness in *Hayavadana*

SUMAN BALA

Girish Karnad is undoubtedly the most important dramatist of the contemporary Kannada stage. In his plays *Yayati, Hittina Hunja, Hayavadana* and *Naga-Mandala*, he makes use of ancient myths and legends to recreate a contemporary consciousness. Karnad delves deep into the traditional myths to spell out modern man's anguish and dilemmas that are created in his mind. In *Hayavadana*, he is seized with the theme of incompleteness and depicts the protagonist Padmini's yearning for completeness, for perfection. K. Narasimha Murthy rightly says, "*Hayavadana* is a Brechtian kind of play employing native folk theatre strategies to present through a folk tale man's tragically futile aspiration for perfection."[1]

The play opens with Ganesh Puja—with the offering of worship accompanied by singing to the God Ganesha. The choice of elephant-headed God is significant because Lord Ganesha with human body and animal head aptly suggests the central theme of incompleteness of being. As the Bhagavata says:

> An elephant's head on a human body, a broken tusk and a cracked belly—whichever way you look at him he seems the embodiment of imperfection, of incompleteness. How indeed can one fathom the mystery that this very Vakratunda-Mahakaya, with his crooked face and distorted body, is the Lord and Master of Success and Perfection? Could it be that his image of Purity and Holiness, this Mangalamoorthy, intends to signify by his very appearance that the completeness of God is something no poor mortal can comprehend?[2]

The perfect combination of the spirit and the flesh in human life is next to impossible. The sub-plot of Hayavadana, the horse-man, is Karnad's own invention. It deepens the significance of the main theme of incompleteness by treating it on a different plane. It provides the framework of the play both as a prologue and as an epilogue. As Krishna Gandhi writes, "The theme of the play is an old one . . . man's yearning for completeness, for perfection. It's this yearning which makes people restless in this ordinary existence, and makes them reach out for extraordinary things. . . . But the ideal of perfection itself is ambiguous. The character of Hayavadana is invented as an example of this ambiguity."[3]

Hayavadana is a man with the head of a horse: "haya" means horse and "vadana" means face. He is the son of the Princess of Karnataka, a very beautiful girl, who fell in love with a white stallion. She was married off to the horse and lived with him for fifteen years. One fine morning, the horse turned into a beautiful celestial being and revealed that he was a *gandhara* cursed by the God Kubera to be born a horse for some act of misbehaviour. After fifteen years of human love, he had become his original self again. Released from his curse, he asked the Princess to accompany him to his Heavenly Abode. But she wanted him to become a horse again. So he cursed her to be a horse herself. She became a mare and galloped away without thinking in the least of Hayavadana, the product of her marriage with the white stallion.

Hayavadana now wants to get rid of his horse's head and become a complete man. Later he goes to the Kali temple and threatens to chop off his head. The goddess grants him his boon "make me complete" but in her hurry to fulfil it, she makes him a complete horse instead of a complete man. However, Hayavadana still retains his human voice. His liberation is complete only when the five-year old son of Padmini asks him to laugh and soon the laughter turns into a neigh. In the "Introduction" to the play, Kirtinath Kurtkoti comments on Hayavadana's transformation into a horse: "The horse-man's search for completeness ends comically, with his becoming a complete horse. The animal body triumphs over what is considered the best in man, the *Uttamanga*, the human head." (vi)

The main plot of the play comes from *Kathasaritasagara*, an ancient collection of Sanskrit stories, and is as simple as that of a folk tale. Devadatta (literally the God-given) is endowed with all the accomplishments expected of a brahmin youth. The only son of a learned brahmin Vidyasagara (ocean of learning), he is comely in appearance, fair in colour and unrivalled in intelligence. Having defeated the mightiest pundits of the kingdom in debates on logic and love and having blinded the greatest poets of the world with his poetry and wit, Devadatta is as it were the apple of every eye in Dharampura. He falls in love with an extremely agile and quick-witted girl, Padmini, the daughter of a rich merchant.

Kapila, the only son of the ironsmith Lohita, with a lithe and handsome body, good in the wrestling pit, and extremely devoted to his friend Devadatta for his poetry and wisdom, mediates and arranges the marriage of Padmini with his friend Devadatta. Devadatta and Kapila are the closest of friends. The Bhagavata describes them as "one mind, one heart." But right at the moment when the match is fixed, Kapila realizes that Padmini is not meant for Devadatta:

> Devadatta, my friend, I confess to you I'm feeling uneasy. You are a gentle soul. But this one is fast as lightning—and as sharp. She is not for the likes of you. What she needs is a man of steel. (19)

And soon enough, Padmini (the lotus plant) who seems to possess something of the Kali, the female deity, in her is attracted to the virility of Kapila. The Female Chorus has already given us an idea of the feeling of Padmini when it sang: "Why should love stick to the sap of a single body? When the stem is drunk with the thick yearning of the many petalled, many-flowered lantana, why should it be tied down to the relation of a single flower?" (11) and "A head for each breast. A pupil for each eye. A side for each arm. I have neither regret nor shame. The blood pours into the earth and a song branches out in the sky." (11) Both Kapila and Padmini start drifting towards each other. He worships her beauty instinctively so much so that she enjoys his company whenever he comes to see her husband. Devadatta becomes jealous of this and shows it in his thoughts:

> Does she really not see? Or is she deliberately playing this game with him? Kapila was never the sort to blush. But now, he only has to see her and he begins to wag his tail. Sits up on his hind legs as though he were afraid to let her words fall to the ground. And that pleading in his eyes—can't she really see that? (22)

He also shows it in his behaviour. He tries to postpone the proposed journey on the cart to Ujjain which disappoints Kapila. In an aside, he tells the audience his thoughts:

> So it's off. What am I to do for the rest of the day? What am I to do for the rest of the week? Why should it feel as though the whole world has been wiped out for a whole week? Why this emptiness. . . . Kapila, Kapila, get a tight hold on yourself. You are slipping, boy, control yourself. Don't lose that hold. Go now—don't come here again for a week.

Seeing Kapila's disappointment, Padmini insists on continuing with the plan of going to Ujjain.

Devadatta is a man of intellect while Kapila is a man of the body. Kapila is more attractive than Devadatta because as representative of the animal energy in the human, he has greater vitality and potential than Devadatta. On way to Ujjain, Padmini describes the charm of Kapila's body when the latter climbs the tree to bring her the fortunate lady's flower:

> How he climbs—like an ape. Before I could even say 'yes,' he had taken off his shirt, pulled his dhoti up and swung up the branch. And what an ethereal shape! Such a broad back—like an ocean with muscles rippling across it—and then that small, feminine waist which looks so helpless. (25)

A little later, she remarks: "He is like a Celestial Being reborn as a hunter. . . . How his body sways, his limbs curve—it's a dance almost." (26) She reaches the conclusion that "No woman could resist him." (26) Ironically, Devadatta also reaches the same conclusion: "No woman could resist him—and what does it matter that she's married." (26)

As Padmini and Kapila go to see the temple of Rudra, Devadatta excuses himself for a moment to go to the temple alone. Then in a sudden outburst of emotion, he decides to sacrifice his head to Kali. That he is doing so because he is unable to bear the pangs of jealousy becomes evident when he says: "Good-bye, Kapila. Good-bye, Padmini. May the Lord Rudra bless you. You are two pieces of my heart—live happily together. I shall find my happiness in that." (28) However, he professes that he is doing so in deference to his earlier vow:

> Bhavani, Bhairavi, Kali, Durga, Mahamaya, Mother of all Nature—I had forgotten my promise to you. Forgive me, mother. You fulfilled the deepest craving of my life—you gave me Padmini—and I forgot my word. Forgive me, for I'm here now to carry out my promise. (28)

His generosity and selflessness are a mere sham because the real reason of the sacrifice is his refusal to share Padmini with Kapila.

The sight of the dead body of his friend shocks Kapila and he follows suit: "No, Devadatta, I can't live without you. I can't breathe without you. Devadatta, my brother, my father, my friend." (30) Kapila says that he is sacrificing himself out of his love for his friend but actually he wants to avert the scandal due to Devadatta's death.

That both Devadatta and Kapila were telling lies is made clear by Kali in the temple. As she points out:

> The rascals! They were lying to their last breaths. That fellow Devadatta—he had once promised his head to Rudra and his arms to me! Think of it—head to him and arms to me! Then because you insisted on going to the Rudra temple, he comes here and offers his head. Nobly too—wants to keep his word, he says—no other reason! Then this Kapila. Died right in front of me—but 'for his friend.' Mind you! Didn't even have the courtesy to refer to me. And what lies! Says he is dying for friendship. He must have known perfectly well he would be accused of killing Devadatta for you. Do you think he wouldn't have grabbed you if it hadn't been for that fear? But till his last breath—"Oh my dear friend! My dear brother!" (33)

Only Padmini is true in what Kali says is her selfishness. She is bold and frank in demanding what will fulfil her. When Kali favours her with the blessing of life of the two friends, Padmini happens to transpose the heads with the result that there are two men now—one with Devadatta's head and Kapila's body and the other with Kapila's head and Devadatta's body.

Padmini stumbles on the opportunity of having the best of the two men—Devadatta's head and Kapila's body. Devadatta scores a point over Kapila because "According to the Shastras, the head is the sign of a man. . . . Of all the limbs the topmost—in position as well as in importance—is the head." (36-37) Kapila is the loser in this ludicrous bargain of mixing up of heads. He has lost not only his body but also his peace on account of the vasanas lodged in Devadatta's body. His mundane logic that body being the real person Padmini should belong to him is rejected by both Padmini and Devadatta.

The extraordinary situation helps Padmini to break out of the moral codes inflicted by society. She wants that her companion in life should be an ideal man—both in brain and brawn. She wants Devadatta's mind and Kapila's body while the society forces her to seek these qualities in one man. But since such a perfect man does not exist, she creates such a man by transposing the heads. Thus for a short while, she succeeds in having both brain and brawn, the spirit and the flesh: "Fabulous body—fabulous brain—fabulous Devadatta." (43)

At the beginning of Act II, the Bhagavata poses the question directly to the audience: "What? What indeed is the solution to this problem, which holds the entire future of these three unfortunate beings in a balance?" (40) He connects the situation to the one way back in the ages, when King Vikrama was ruling the world and was asked the same question by the demon Vetala: "which of the people, thus mixed together, was her rightful husband?" The king had offered a solution to the riddle even without batting an eyelid: "That one of the two, on whom her husband's head was fixed, was her husband, for the head is the chief of limbs and personal identity depends upon it." But the solution King Vikrama gave to the problem is inadequate in the present situation. The Bhagavata raises this question: "Will his rational logical answer backed by the sacred texts appeal to our audience?" (40) It is here that Karnad invests the old legend with a new meaning, making it relevant for the present-day world.

Devadatta, Padmini and Kapila go to a great rishi in search of a solution to their problem who, remembering what King Vikrama had said, gave the solution: "As the heavenly Kalpa Vriksha is supreme among trees, so is the head among human limbs. Therefore, the man with Devadatta's head is indeed Devadatta and he is the rightful husband of Padmini." (40)

Devadatta and Padmini go back to the city where Devadatta enjoys the benefits of Kapila's well-trained body for about a year. He succeeds in exploiting Kapila's body to his and Padmini's satisfaction. But mankind cannot live with perfection for a long time. Padmini's query "Must the head always win" becomes relevant when after about a year Devadatta's head fails to enjoy the liveliness of Kapila's body. Its litheness begins to wear off owing to the lack of physical labour. The mind that controls the body starts transforming the body, making it lose all its virility.

The changes in Devadatta's physical features are conveyed through the dolls. When Devadatta touches Doll I, the latter feels the change and comments: "His palms! They were so rough, when he first brought us here. Like a labourer's. But now they are soft—sickly soft—like a young girl's." (47) The second doll notices the change in stomach: "It was so tight and muscular. Now. . . ." The first doll has noted it too and completes the sentence: "It's loose." Slowly Devadatta's head with Kapila's body regains its former self—a delicate body. Padmini who had felt that she had the best of both the men gets disillusioned. She has known Kapila's body with Devadatta's head. But that physicality in Devadatta is gone. Once again, she starts missing Kapila, his impulsiveness and his physicality. She has enjoyed it for a year but can't do so any more. Consequently, Devadatta loses Padmini to Kapila once again.

Kapila meanwhile has remained in the forest to train the Brahmin's body hanging by his head like a corpse and shape it into form. Kapila cannot live by his head but by labour. He trains the brahmin's body by hard physical labour. Conferring superiority on head entails negation of body and this starts a conflict between the two. Both Devadatta and Kapila realize that sensuous pleasures of the body cannot be escaped. Padmini confirms this when she once again abandons Devadatta to stay with the real Kapila who has trained Devadatta's body.

Practising deceit on her husband, Padmini sends Devadatta to the Ujjain fair to fetch new dolls for the child and herself walks into the embrace of Kapila. She takes the child with her and claims it to be the child of both Devadatta and Kapila. Padmini's visit disturbs Kapila. He had buried all those faceless memories but Padmini has dug them up. He finds himself in a tough situation and asks Padmini: "Why should one tolerate this mad dance of incompleteness?" (57)

The focus of the play however is on Padmini, the woman who is faced with this impossible situation: How would a woman take it if it really happened and would it really solve the problem. Here Karnad takes a leap from the original story and develops it further. Padmini's predicament is the predicament of a modern, emancipated woman in our society who is born between two polarities, a woman who loves her husband as well as someone else for two different aspects of their personalities. Padmini is fascinated by both Devadatta and Kapila and this creates the problem. The two men cannot accept each other when it comes to sharing a woman and all the three destroy themselves in the process. When Devadatta reaches the forest, he asks Kapila:

Devadatta: Tell me one thing. Do you really love Padmini?
Kapila: Yes.
Devadatta: So do I.
Kapila: I know. [*Silence*] Devadatta, couldn't we all three live together—like the Pandavas and Draupadi?
Devadatta: What do you think?
[*Silence. Padmini looks at them but doesn't say anything*]
Kapila [*laughs*]:No, it can't be done.
Devadatta: That's why I brought this. [*Shows the sword.*] What won't end has to be cut.
Kapila: I got your body—but not your wisdom. (60-61)

The two have to die and reduce their beloved Padmini to ashes. Devadatta makes it clear that there are "No grounds for friendship now. No question of mercy. We must fight like lions and kill like cobras." (61)

The play ends with Devadatta and Kapila fighting a duel in which the heads roll again. When both the friends are dead, Padmini decides to perform sati. She asks the Bhagavata to make a large funeral pyre because they are three. Before sacrificing herself, Padmini makes it clear that she cannot hope to get perfection even in her next life. As she prays to "Kali, Mother of all nature," she says: "You must have your joke even now. Other women can die praying that they should get the same husband in all the lives to come. You haven't left me even that little consolation." (63)

It is the child who combines the thematic strands of the main plot and the sub-plot. He grows up as Kapila's child in the forest and at the age of five is given over to a traveller going to the city to be delivered into the hands of his grandparents. This is in accordance with what Padmini had told the Bhagavata:

> My son is sleeping in the hut. Take him under your care. Give him to the hunters who live in the forest and tell them it's Kapila's son. They loved Kapila and will bring the child up. Let the child grow up in the forest with the rivers and the trees. When he's five take him to the Reverend Brahmin Vidyasagara. Tell him it's Devadatta's son. (62)

At the age of five, the child lives in a world of make-believe. He plays with dolls and refuses to talk with any person. What is striking is that the child is found not to be able to laugh like a human child. As Actor I says: "Children of his age should be out-talking a dictionary, but this one doesn't speak a word. Doesn't laugh, doesn't cry, doesn't even smile. The same long face all twenty-four hours. There's obviously something wrong with him." (66) The child is hopelessly incomplete because he has lost the child's natural privilege to laugh and enjoy. The child becomes complete when he laughs in response to Hayavadana's laughter. This abnormal child has never laughed by itself. Hayavadana's laughter restores the boy to normalcy and makes possible his return to humanity. As M.K. Naik suggests, "Modern man must recover his sense of child-like curiosity, wonder and amusement at the sheer incongruity of life in order to achieve integration."[4]

NOTES

1. K. Narasimha Murthy, *Modern Kannada Literature* (Bangalore: Pustakalaya Publications, 1992).
2. Girish Karnad, *Hayavadana* (Calcutta: O.U.P., 1975), p. 1.
3. Krishna Gandhi, "Hayavadana," *Enact*, 68-69 (Aug.-Sept. 1972), n.p.
4. M.K. Naik, "From the Horse's Mouth: A Study of *Hayavadana*," *Dimensions of Indian English Literature* (New Delhi: Sterling, 1984), p. 196.

Hayavadana and the Interminable Quest for Perfection

PRANAV JOSHIPURA

This paper aims at carrying forward the ongoing debate on the quest of perfection evident in Karnad's *Hayavadana*. My attempt is to analyze the thirst for completeness which is lurking in the drama. It is a characteristic of human nature to search for the fulfilment of wants within us, to look for complementation of what looks incomplete. It is also a character of human nature to ignore the importance of what we possess, what we have, what we are. Not contentment but completeness. This is found illustrated in almost all the major characters in this drama. They struggle throughout in the quest successfully or unsuccessfully.

Hayavadana is based on *Kathasaritsagara—Vetal Panchvinshati*, an ancient collection of stories in Sanskrit. Karnad has borrowed the story through Thomas Mann's "The Transposed Heads." The original story poses a moral problem, and Mann treats it to show the mechanical conception of life which differentiates body and soul, while Karnad's play puts forward a different problem, the identification of a human being in this world of strange relationships. For that purpose Karnad deftly uses the conventions and motifs of folk tales and folk theatre—masks, curtains, dolls, the story-within-a story—to create a bizarre world of incomplete individuals, indifferent Gods that speak and children who cannot.

The theme of the play is a complex one. Karnad good-humouredly yet critically manipulates the very concepts of the rational and the physical. The multiplicity of characters and their individual psychic circles playing into each other build up a complex pattern of human relationships. And by projecting these human sympathies against a gradually intensifying clash of personalities, Karnad presents a comprehensive picture of the human beings in search of perfection and completeness.

Karnad in almost all his plays makes use of ancient myths, legends, stories, and traditions to interpret this age-old human situation with reference to contemporary experience. He leads us deep into traditional mythology to reveal the conflict that tears man's mind. Here, in *Hayavadana* he seems to toy with the theme of incompleteness. According to Krishna Gandhi, in *Hayavadana*, "The theme of the play is an old one . . . man's yearning for completeness, for perfection. It is this yearning which makes people restless in their ordinary existence, and makes them reach out for extraordinary things. . . . But the ideal of perfection itself is ambiguous. The character of Hayavadana is invented as an example of this ambiguity."[1]

It is curious to note that the title takes after a minor character of the play. Hayavadana does not play a major role in the weaving of the plot. His is the side story, not directly related to furthering of the principal chain of action. This is because Hayavadana turns himself into a symbol of conscious or unconscious striving after the elusive ideal of perfection illustrated in other characters. He sheds light on the nature of their pursuits. Hence, this seemingly marginal, grotesque, and absurd being becomes the key-figure for the unravelling of the central idea of the play.

The main plot of the play is as simple as that of a folk tale. Devadatta, the only son of the learned Brahmin Vidyasagara, comely in appearance, fair in colour, unrivalled in intelligence, falls in love with Padmini, the daughter of a merchant. With the help of his devoted friend Kapila, the only son of the ironsmith Lohita, he marries Padmini. But unable to seek all the qualities in one man, Padmini drifts towards Kapila. This creates problems. And in the end both of them kill each other, while Padmini performs a Sati.

The play opens with the offering of worship accompanied by singing to the Lord Ganesha. The choice of elephant-headed God is significant because Lord Ganesha with human body and animal head properly suggests the central theme of incompleteness of being. In the words of the Bhagavata: "An elephant's head on a human body, a broken tusk and a cracked belly—whichever way you look at him he seems the embodiment of imperfection, of incompleteness. How indeed can one fathom the mystery that this very Vakratunda Mahakaya, with crooked face and distorted body, is the Lord and Master of Success and Perfection?"[2] Flesh becomes an encumberance in the realization of spiritual pursuits. Karnad himself questions regarding the comprehension of completeness by stating: "Could it be that this Image of Purity and Holiness, this Mangalamoorty, intends to signify by his very appearance that completeness of God is something no poor mortal can comprehend?"(1)

Some critics have accused Karnad of writing with Western audience in mind and of using themes and techniques that might shock or startle the Indian viewers. But this doesn't seem to be true as far as *Hayavadana* is concerned. Karnad wants to illustrate man's universal predicament in a new twentieth century awareness. As banal methods would not do for the purpose, as the established myths were found insufficient, he invented a myth and dramatized it. The play has certainly become provocative. But that is what a good drama should be. Karnad has successfully drawn our attention to what we usually tend to forget in our accustomed pursuits of dangling the carrot before the asses.

In *Hayavadana* there is the question of completion. We, at the moment, are not concerned with the traditional outcome of it. But a couple of questions to a modern man with reference to *Hayavadana* may be asked: What is a complete human being? What constitutes a modern man? What does a man stand for? Is the head more powerful than the body? The answer may be, yes, the head is more powerful than the body. If one has the head of a horse, one will end up as a horse. Instead of a constant tension between a man and a horse, it is better to be just a horse, perhaps. But at the same time it is also true that no one can be a perfect being. For a human being it is better to live with a constant tension rather than try to resolve it through some impossible desire for perfection. Devadatta's head on Kapila's body, therefore, results not in perfection, but in failure in the end. This is perhaps what the text argues.

But suppose one seeks to realize peace through philosophical dismissal of the very desire for perfection or completeness in the Stoical or the Buddhist or the Sthita-Pragna way? Then what would be the implication, the end? Probably Karnad has not taken this matter into consideration. Does he want to argue that man should persist in his folly of trying to realise perfection? Does he really call it a folly? Supposing we look for the Buddhist way. If this is the inevitable destiny of man we cannot call it a folly. This is what we have to live, and this is how people go on living. It has been said that Karnad enlightens us with the age-old situation in new terms. But why enlighten? In order to remedy the situation? Then what are the remedies? One remedy would be that one should reach for the goal of perfection. That is impossible. Another would be to dismiss the desire for perfection. That means one tries to get rid of specific folly. Then what is wrong in this. This is precisely the Stoical way, the Buddhist way, or the Sthita-Pragna way. So, if Devdatta's head on Kapila's body ends up in a failure, it means that man's quest for perfection is futile. That is his folly. However, since it is a part of man's inevitable destiny, there is no way but to accept it.

Karnad depicts the mythological legend in a very interesting and humorous manner. Perhaps the more significant aspect is the description of the Indian belief that one can achieve anything if one visits sacred places like Banaras, Rameshwar, etc. One can achieve even completeness or perfection. In the words of Hayavadana, "Banaras, Rameshwar, Gokaran, Haridwar, Gaya, Kedarnath—not only those but the Dargah of Khwaja Yusuf Baba, the Grotto of Our Virgin Mary—I've tried them all. Magicians, mendicants, maharishis, fakirs, saints, and sadhus—sadhus with short hair, sadhus with beards—sadhus in saffron, sadhus in altogether—hanging, singing, rotating, gyrating—on the skies, in the air, under water, under the ground. . . . I've tried them all." (9) But in spite of this he could not get rid of his horse-head and attain completeness. Towards the end of the play, Karnad describes the horse-man searching for completeness in a very comic vein. Hayavadana becomes a complete horse. The animal body triumphs over what is considered the best in man, the human head. Although the story of completeness has been rendered into lighter tone, its pathos is touching. It implies that the primitive force in a horse is superior to an intellectual.

But if this is the message then it is doubtful whether it is true. What Karnad probably tries to assert is that man ultimately is animal. Then the other way round also may be possible, that is, animal is ultimately man. Man on the one hand looks God-like, and on the other looks animal-like. The riddance of animal from God and God from animal appears impossible in man. If one maintains the tension, it is alright. But if he suggests that man is reducible to animal, I think that will be far from truth. If man were God then there will be harmony. All spirit, no matter. If man were mere animal, there will be all animality. But the tragedy is that man is neither animal nor God. On account of our questioning the Nature, on account of our striving for the spiritual, we are alienated from Nature. If man becomes animal, there will be harmony. Hayavadana becomes a horse and there is harmony. So, Karnad's deliverance is not clear here.

Girish Karnad successfully pictures Padmini's thirst for completeness, for prefection. Probably what Karnad tries to reveal through Padmini is the predicament of a modern, free and bold woman who is torn between polarities, a woman who loves her husband as well as someone else for two different aspects of their personalities. Padmini, after the exchange of heads, had felt that she had the best of both men. But slowly reality surfaces. She has the capacity of complete experience. Karnad has described her situation through the symbols in the Female Chorus. The end of the play is very interesting. The two friends are dead after a duel and Padmini performs a Sati. It is not a tragic end. It applies somewhat absurd meaning to the drama. It is very well to say that one cannot have all these qualities in one man, but does it mean that one should not be satisfied with one man? Should a woman hunt after

> Many for many virtues excellent
> None but for some
> And yet all difference?[3]

Karnad dismsses the quest for perfection on the one hand and on the other pleads for its continuity. What probably Karnad tries to convey is the fact that the world is full of incomplete individuals, indifferent dolls that speak. The world is indifferent to the desires and frustrations, joys and sorrows of human beings. It is conveyed through a superb and ingenious capacity of Karnad who imagines different aspects that transform any situation into an aesthetic experience.

NOTES

1. *Enact*, 68-69.
2. Girish Karnad, *Hayavadana* (Madras: OUP, 1975), p. 1.
3. Shakespeare, *Romeo and Juliet*, ed. Ralph Houghton (OUP, 1974), II. iii. 13-14.

Folk Theatre Strategies in *Hayavadana*

SAVITA GOEL

As part of the great cultural renaissance generated during the post-colonial period, there has occurred a most meaningful encounter with tradition in theatre. The return to and discovery of tradition was inspired by a search for roots and a quest for identity. This was part of the whole process of decolonization of our life-style, values, social institutions, creative forms and cultural modes. During 1960s, dramatists pondered over a significant question, i.e. how to draw upon the various strands in the traditional theatre—some of which had lost contact with urban civilization during the colonial era and many of which seemed deeply rooted in religious sensibility—so as to revitalize and enrich their own work.

Girish Karnad is among those Indian playwrights who have rejected the imitative pursuit of the West and have ventured into indigenous territory for their themes and techniques. Karnad has sought for an appropriate approach, style and form of the theatre which is closer to the consciousness of people, consistent with our cultural traditions, entertaining and yet aesthetically satisfying. He thought over the fact as to how the paraphernalia of folk theatre can become meaningful outside its context and become relevant in the modern context. Karnad points out, "it was when I was focusing on the question of the folk forms and the use of masks and their relationship to theatre music that my play *Hayavadana* suddenly began to take shape in my head."[1]

The present paper explicates how in *Hayavadana*, Karnad draws heavily upon the rich resources of the native folk theatre—Yakshagana and other folk forms with great deftness and how the element of supernatural plays a significant role here. The dramatist employs the conventions of folk tales and motifs of folk theatre i.e. masks, curtains, mime, songs, the commentator-narrator, dolls, horse-man, the story-within-a-story facilitating mixture of the human and the non-human, to create a queer magical world. It is a realm of incomplete individuals, magnanimous gods, of vocal dolls and mute children, a world apathetic to the longings and frustrations, ecstasies and miseries of human beings. In this play Karnad brings back poetry, music, a sense of gaiety and celebration traditionally associated with a theatrical event. The paper proposes to examine how folk theatre strategies are employed as a thematic and technical device by the dramatist and are a means of conveying his ideas and exploring different characters and situations.

The plot of the play is borrowed from Thomas Mann's story, "The Transposed Heads," which in turn, is based on the stories in *Vetal Panchavimshati* and in Somdeva's *Brihatkatha Saritsagara*. Through these folk tales, Karnad deals with the problem of human identity in a world of confused relationships, with the theme of incompleteness and man's desire for perfection. The main plot (in the transposition of heads) and the sub-plot (in the story of Hayavadana) subtly depict that perfection is a humanly unfeasible ideal and the play finally fulfills its aesthetic purpose by portraying the absurdity of the ideal of completeness.

The play initiates with the bringing of the mask of Lord Ganesha, the presiding deity of traditional theatre on the stage and his worship like a typical Yakshagana play. The Bhagavata, accompanied by musicians, sings verses in praise of Ganesha. At the outset, the theme of the play is introduced as Ganesha possessing the head of an elephant and human body symbolizes incompleteness. As the Bhagavata comments, "An elephant's head on a human body, a broken tusk and a cracked belly—whichever way you look at him he seems the embodiment of imperfection, of incompleteness . . . could it be that this image of Purity and Holiness, this Mangalamoorty, intends to signify by his very appearance that the completeness of God is something no poor mortal can comprehend?"[2]

The Bhagavata narrates the story with a formalistic expression in the manner of a folk tale, "this is the city of Dharmapura ruled by King Dharmasheela whose fame and empire" (1) and so on. The protagonists Devadatta and Kapila are intimate friends, "One mind, one heart." (2) Devadatta is an intelligent son of a learned Brahmin Vidyasagara, comely in appearance and fair in colour, has succeeded in defeating the mightiest pundits of the kingdom in debates on logic and love, is an excellent poet and is adored by everyone in Dharmapura. Kapila, the only son of ironsmith Lohita, possesses an agile and handsome body and is adept in activities which require physical strength. Devadatta is deeply in love with a bright, beautiful girl, Padmini, who seems to be "Yakshini, Shakuntala, Urvashi, Inudmati—all rolled into one." (16) He swears that if he does not succeed in getting her as his wife, he will sacrifice his two arms to the goddess Kali and his head to Lord Rudra. Kapila arranges for their marriage and the three seem to be like Rama, Sita and Lakshmana. However, as the play proceeds, their relationships become tangled. Kapila is drawn towards Padmini and admits, "Devadatta, my friend, I confess to you I'm feeling uneasy. You are a gentle soul. But this one is fast as lightning—and as sharp. She is not for the likes of you." (19) He feels that she needs a man of steel like him. Devadatta notices that Kapila was never the sort to blush, but now, "he only has to see her and he begins to wag his tail. Sits up on his hind legs as though he were afraid to let her words fall to the ground. And that pleading in his eyes—can't she really see that." (22) Padmini, too, is fascinated by his physical charm. When she impatiently waits for him, constantly looking out of the window, her husband's jealousy is aroused and he remarks, "you drool over Kapila all day." (20) He tries to postpone the proposed trip to Ujjain and a disappointed Kapila in an aside wonders, "Why this emptiness . . . Kapila, Kapila, get a tight hold on yourself. You are slipping, boy, control yourself. Don't lose that hold." (23)

Their journey to Ujjain is a vital scene in the play. Devadatta perceives the flames of love in his wife's eyes and takes a crucial decision. As Kapila climbs the tree like an ape to procure the fortunate lady's flower for her, she admires his ethereal shape and broad back "like an ocean with muscles ripping across" (25) and in an aside expresses her psychic state, "He is like a Celestial Being reborn as a hunter. . . . How his body sways, his limbs curve. . . . No woman could resist him." (26) Devadatta, too, observes his strong body and manly muscles and realizes that he has been so innocent, so naive all these days. He watched that pleading in Kapila's eyes stretching out its arms, begging for a favour but never looked in his own wife's eyes. He says, "Now! So late! Don't turn away now, Devadatta, look at her. Look at those yellow, purple flames. Look how she's pouring her soul in his mould. Look! Let your guts burn out—let your lungs turn to ash—but don't turn away. Look and don't scream. Strangle your agony. But look deep into these eyes—look until those peacock flames burn out the blindness in you." (26)

Unable to endure this, an envious Devadatta cannot make the agonizing choice of sharing Padmini with Kapila. So he decides to visit the Kali temple and kill himself, while Padmini and Kapila are on their way to Rudra temple. He prostrates himself before the goddess and remarks that as she has fulfilled his deepest desire by giving Padmini to him, so to carry out his promise, he is offering his head. He bids adieu to Padmini and Kapila and says, "May the Lord Rudra bless you. You are the two pieces of my heart—live happily together. I shall find my happiness in that." (28) When Kapila returns, he is stupefied to find that due to intense feeling of abhorrence for him, Devadatta has committed suicide. He, too, picks up his sword, "You spurned me in this world. Accept me as your brother at least in the next. Here friend, here I come." (30) However, Goddess Kali knows the truth and points out, "The rascals! They were lying to their last breaths." (33) Kapila said that he is dying for friendship but deep in his heart he knew perfectly well that he would be accused of killing Devadatta for Padmini.

Unlike the two men, Padmini is intrepid, audacious and candid in pleading for what she desires to attain fulfillment. Unlike an archetypal Indian woman, she does not suppress her desire for Kapila and wants both of them alive, although she is fully aware that her living with two men would be socially unacceptable. She seeks a boon from the Goddess, who admires her for her candidness and says, "Only you spoke the truth because you're selfish." (33) Padmini desires for Devadatta's clever head and Kapila's strong body, i.e. a perfect man, and in her excitement creates such a man by transposing the two heads. The Goddess knows what Padmini has done and remarks that there should be a limit even to honesty and disappears after granting the boon, "Anyway—so be it!" (33) For some time Padmini succeeds in having both the intellect and the flesh, "Fabulous body—fabulous brain—fabulous Devadatta." (43)

Throughout the play Padmini appears as a symbol of emancipated woman. She does not play the part of a demure wife and refuses to accept the passive feminine role. When she is pregnant, both friends express their deep concern for her well-being, but chides them and asserts her will. Karnad depicts her unrepressed nature and her inner feelings through the use of a folk device i.e. the female chorus. The Chorus chants, "Why should love stick to the sap of a single body?" and "A head for each breast. A pupil for each eye. A side for each arm. I have neither regret nor shame."

(11) Kapila epitomizes her character when he says that she is bright like lightning and as sharp.

In *Hayavadana*, as in a folk play, there is no formal division of acts into scenes. Act one concludes on a controversial note as to who is the rightful husband of Padmini and Act two initiates with the Bhagavata posing a question directly to the audience, "What indeed is the solution to the problem, which holds the entire future of these three unfortunate beings in a balance?" (40) Karnad traces the situation back to the story of King Vikrama and demon Vetal. Padmini's resolve to go with Devadatta's head is based on the solution of the Rishi who in fact repeats King Vikram's solution. However, the solution Vikram offered to the problem is not adequate in the present context because if head controls the body it logically follows that it will transform the body. Kirtinath Kurtkoti, in the introduction to the play, asserts, "The original poses a moral problem while Manu uses it to ridicule the mechanical conception of life which differentiates between soul and body. He ridicules the philosophy which holds the head superior to the body. The human body, Manu argues, is a fit instrument for the fulfillment of human destiny. Even the transposition of heads will not liberate the protagonists from the psychological limits imposed by nature." (v)

Padmini is gradually disillusioned and undergoes extreme mental agony as she watches the transformation of her husband's body and loss of Kapila's physicality day by day, inch by inch. Her intense love for her 'perfect' husband diminishes as he goes soft again. Towards the end, their bodies transform again and adjust themselves to the heads so perfectly that the men are physically exactly as they were at the beginning and the problem remains unresolved.

Karnad, through the strategy of the borrowed stories, examines the concept of the rational and the physical and weaves a mazy pattern of relationships. Padmini is quite resolute that she will not let passion overpower her sense of reason. She says, "I'm not going to be stupid again. Kapila's gone out of my life—forever. I won't let him come back." (49) However, she cannot act rationally. Her thoughts constantly drift around Kapila. She wonders, "What could he be doing now? Where could he be? Could his body be still fair and his face dark?" (49) When Devadatta goes to Ujjain to buy new dolls for the child, she undertakes a hazardous journey to meet Kapila, who has been in a state of amnesia. He is distressed as the past is revoked in his mind. He remarks, "why should one tolerate this mad dance of incompleteness?" (57)

Devadatta visits Kapila but they meditate over the possibility whether three of them could live together like the Pandavas and Draupadi and conclude that it is not feasible. "No grounds for friendship now. No question of mercy. We must fight like lions and kill like cobras." (61) The idea of sharing a woman is unendurable to them and results in their annihilation. Padmini's quest for perfection is not satisfied till the end and she decides to perform Sati. She knows that she will not succeed in attaining completeness in the next birth too. She invokes Goddess Kali and says that other women can die praying that they should get the same husband in all the lives to come but she does not have even that little consolation. As Padmini's body's blazes, the female musicians sing a chorus replete with ludicrous beauty, "Our sister is leaving in a palanquin of sandalwood. Her mattress is studded with rubies which burn and glow. She is decked in flowers which blossom on tinder-wood and whose petals are made of molten gold. How the garlands leap and cover her, aflame with love. Good-bye, dear sister. Go you without fear. The Lord of Death will be pleased with the offering of three coconuts." (63) The institution of sati is mocked here and the audience do not get emotionally involved in this tragic scene. Kurtkoti points out, "Neither the death of the lovers nor the subsequent suttee of Padmini is presented as tragic, the deaths serve only to emphasize the logic behind the absurdity of the situation." (vi)

Padmini endeavours to fulfill her dream of perfection through her son. She entreats the Bhagavata to give him to the hunters residing in the forest, tell them it's Kapila's son and they will bring him up. When the child is five years old, he should take him to the Revered Brahmin Vidyasagara of Dharmapura and tell him it's Devadatta's son.

Through the use of stories, Karnad provides a profound insight into the meaning and significance of the play and protrays that the perfect union of the spirit and flesh in human life is not possible. The device of folk tale helps the playwright in transcending the limitations of time and place. The story of the horse-man or 'Hayavadana' in the sub-plot "provides the outer panel—as in a mural—within which the tale of the two friends is framed."[3] At the beginning of the play Hayavadana narrates his tragic story—how his mother, the beautiful Princess of Karnataka, married a white stallion, who is transfigured into a Celestial Being, a gandharva after fifteen years, how her mother is transformed into a horse by the curse of her husband and she runs away abandoning her child. Hayavadana longs to get rid of his horse's head and metamorphose into a complete man.

Towards the end of the play, he tells the Bhagavata that in the temple of Goddess Kali, he prayed, "Mother, make me complete" and even before he could say, "Make me a complete man," (68) the Goddess granted him the boon and he was transmuted into a complete horse, not a complete being as he still possessed the cursed human voice. When Padmini's child asks Hayavadana to laugh, he realizes that his laughter has altered into a neigh and thus he achieves completeness, but not in the shape of a human being. Kurtkoti asserts that Hayavadana's quest for completeness ends comically, with his becoming a complete horse. "The animal body triumphs over what is considered the best in man, the *Uttamanga*, the human head." (vi) Padmini's child links the main and the subplot. It grows up into an abnormal, incomplete child, unable to smile or laugh like human beings, does not cry or speak and constantly plays with dolls. The Bhagavata says, "There is obviously something wrong with him." (66) However, he transforms into a complete child when he starts laughing and clapping his hands in response to Hayavadana's laughter.

The playwright, in an interview, asserts that in the manner of folk theatre, *Hayavadana* depicts "a world of inarticulate and non-human beings who create a typology of functional characters."[4] The dolls speak more fluently than human beings. The character of the Bhagavata is functional in the sense that he simply narrates what he sees. The horseman is not a complete human being and the inarticulate son of Padmini rides him. Goddess Kali mindlessly gives away boons.

Hayavadana is full of mystical wonder and is enshrouded in a realm of magic and supernatural, which is a frequent feature in a folk play. Goddess Kali, a supernatural element in the play, is portrayed as a terrifying figure, her mouth wide open with the tongue lolling out but possesses human attributes, too. She is vexed when she is disturbed in sleep and wakes up yawning and wonders why Devadatta should sacrifice his head to Rudra and his arms to her. The Goddess fully comprehends the motives behind the actions of the characters and is fully aware that the two friends were lying to their last breaths. By employing this strategy, the playwright also stresses the fact that there are no smooth and practical solutions to human problems. She grants boon to human beings when they pray sincerely but ultimately the problem remains unsolved as revealed in the case of Padmini and also Hayavadana.

Karnad, through the use of dolls, who possess a special insight, reveals very effectively to the audience the thought processes and inner psyche of Padmini as she visualizes the gradual metamorphosis of Devadatta's body into its original form and dreams of Kapila's strong body. They report that in her reveries she perceives a man, not her husband, who looks rougher and darker, climbs a tree and dives into a river. Devadatta's transfiguration is also communicated through the dolls. When he touches Doll I, it feels the change and says, "His palms! They were so rough, when he first brought us here. Like a labourer's. But now they are soft—sickly soft—like a young girl's." (47) Doll II notices that his stomach which was so light and muscular has now become so loose. The strategy of dolls helps in developing the plot further. Padmini asks her husband to go to Ujjain and get new dolls, as the old ones have been worn out and Padmini gets an opportunity to meet Kapila.

There is a superb technical achievement in the way in which Karnad uses Brechtian type of narrator figure in the role of the the Bhagavata, who is primarily intended to draw the audience into the play. He is able to step out of the play, talk to the audience, explaining the action with his insightful comments. The playwright widens the scope of his role; he is not only the commentator and omniscient narrator but also one of the characters and this is amply portrayed in act two, when the Bhagavata and Kapila converse before Padmini arrives at Kapila's hut and also when the Bhagavata talks to Padmini before she performs Sati. The dramatist has introduced this device in the play, perhaps, because of his childhood folk theatrical experience in 'Yakshagana.'

Karnad employs the ingenious folk device of masks which is a typical feature of 'Yakshagana,' to project the personalities of different characters. In the beginning of the play, Devadatta appears on the stage wearing a pale-coloured mask and Kapila a dark mask. Later on, to signify the transposed heads, their masks are transposed. Lord Ganesha wears an elephant-headed mask and Kali, a terrible mask. Initially Hayavadana appears wearing the mask of a man and in the end the mask of a horse.

In the play, various conventional elements of stagecraft are used which are integral to the action of the play and the actors' stage business. Half-curtains and painted curtains carried by stage hands are used to convey some facts. For instance, when Padmini performs Sati, the curtain has a blazing fire painted on it and as it is lifted, the flames seem to leap up. The front curtain is totally absent and there is no elaborate stage set up.

The action of the play is mimed, for example, when the three characters proceed to Ujjain, a cart does not appear on the stage, rather, "Kapila followed by Padmini and Devadatta, enter miming a cart ride. Kapila is driving the cart." (25) The play is replete with instances of miming. For all these techniques, Karnad owes a great deal to folk theatre.

In *Hayavadana*, this theatre idiom transcends regional or linguistic barriers without losing its rootedness. It becomes obvious that the main thrust of Karnad's search was not to revive tradition but to understand and assimilate it for creative use, namely, to express the contemporary human situation and its varied manifestations. Thus, through the use of folk theatre strategies, the contours of fresh, innovative and flexible dramatic form have gradually emerged, enabling Karnad and his contemporaries to telescope different points in time and space, to bring in many levels of reality simultaneously, or to negotiate them freely in any order. The new form promises to restore the essential imaginative character of drama suitable for presenting complex human experience.

NOTES

1. Girish Karnad, "Theatre in India," *Daedalus*, Fall 1989, p. 346.
2. Girish Karnad, *Hayavadana* (1975 Delhi: Oxford University Press, 1985), p. 1.
3. "Theatre in India," p. 347.
4. Girish Karnad, "Interview with Kirtinath Kurtkoti," *Contemporary Indian Theatre: Interviews with Playwrights and Directors* (New Delhi: Sangeet Natak Akademi, 1989), p. 82.
5. Girish Karnad, Author's Introduction, *Three Plays* (Delhi: Oxford University Press, 1994), pp. 1-18.

Myth as Fulcrum: Lord Ganesha as Dramatic Presence in *Hayavadana*

JACOB GEORGE C.

Indian English drama upto the 1960s has had an apologetic existence. The rich heritage of Indian classical drama and the vibrant folk tradition seldom attracted the Indian English dramatists of the earlier phase, whose models were Shakespeare, Ibsen and Shaw. When experiments incorporating native traditions were finally conducted, they were often debased to the level of clever and exotic gimmicks flaunted for the sake of gullible Western audience. In addition to an obvious nonchalance in exploiting the potentialities of traditional Indian dramatic modes, the Indian English dramatists also failed miserably in drawing judiciously from the rich reservoir of myth and complex historical heritage. Such a failure became lamentable because their Western models succeeded in bringing new life to their works by going back to ancient Greek myths. In the midst of all these, rays of hope were visible in dramatists like Asif Currimbhoy (*The Dumb Dancer*, 1961), Partap Sharma (*The Professor Has a War Cry*, 1970) and so on, despite the fact that theirs was at best a passive flavouring of Western dramaturgy with Indian ingredients. Winds of change blew in the advanced 1970s with the bolder experiments initiated by the likes of Girish Karnad.

Karnad's trend-setting play *Hayavadana*[1] strikes a significant note by exploring the dramatic potential of the ancient Indian myths, legends and folk traditions. As Tutun Mukherjee points out, in *Hayavadana* Karnad has "made available the rich resources of both the *Great* and the *Little* tradition, the classical and the folk elements of Indian literature."[2]

Of the twin plots which constitute the fabric of *Hayavadana*, the main one comes from Thomas Mann's "The Transposed Heads" which is based on *Katha Saritsagara*, an ancient collection of Sanskrit stories. Devadatta and Kapila are bosom friends, one the rational and scholarly, while the other is the sensual and illiterate. Devadatta falls in love and marries Padmini. Later Kapila too falls in love with the same woman. The two friends, as a way out of this stalemate, kill themselves. Goddess Kali restores them to life, but in her excitement Padmini transposes their heads. The confusion and identity crisis which ensue torment them until they cut the Gordian knot in a duel.

The sub-plot, despite its vague familiarity with several Indian legends, is mostly invented by Karnad himself. A beautiful Karnataka princess falls in love with a white stallion. She marries the horse and lives with him for fifteen years. The horse turns into a *gandharva* (a Celestial Being) and when the princess refuses to accept his new form, curses her to be a horse. She happily gallops away, ignoring her horse-faced (haya-vadana) yet human-bodied child. The two plots come together when Hayavadana, in his quest to become a complete being, meets the five-year old son of Padmini who is also in search of completeness.

Karnad begins his play with the *nāndi* (singing of benedictory verse) and concludes it with the *Bharatavakya* (valedictory prayer), recalling the tradition of ancient Sanskrit drama. But the ritualistic invocation of Lord Ganesha, the elephant-headed God, in the *nāndi* and the *Bharatavakya* goes beyond the fulfillment of a traditional prescription and assumes symbolic significance. In the play, the image of Lord Ganesha "suggests a major development in the action as well as the central theme of completeness of being."[3] The play revolves around the myth of Ganesha which operates at several levels.

One of the major issues in the play is the conflict between two polarities which could be categorized as the *Satwa-guna* and the *Rajo-guna.*[4] Devadatta, "comely in appearance, fair in colour, unrivalled in intelligence . . . logic and love . . . poetry and wit," (3) is portrayed as *Satwic* in nature. Kapila, the only son of an ironsmith "is dark and plain to look at, yet in deeds which require drive and daring in dancing, in strength and in physical skills, he has no equal." (3) *Rajo-guna* obviously dominates in Kapila. The play firmly establishes the opposition between reason and instinct; culture and primitive nature; brains and loins; mind and body; and spirit and flesh; through Devadatta and Kapila. The ritualistic invocation to Lord Ganesha does release certain resonances on such a polarization, which contribute to the thematic and structural unity of the play.

While elucidating the complex symbolic connotation of the elephant-headed Lord, whose divine form appears to be so ridiculous and absurd, Swami Chinmayananda comments on the issue of being *dwandwaatita.*[5] The trunk of an elephant is a unique organ which symbolises great adaptability, sensitiveness, strength and discriminative power. The discriminative power functions only where there are two factors or opposites to discriminate between. The tusks and the trunk of an elephant signify this. The image of Lord Ganesha with one broken tusk suggests the relevance of going beyond the pairs-of-opposites or in other words, of becoming *dwandwaatita*, the only condition which can make one complete.

In *Hayavadana*, both Devadatta and Kapila are deluded by *Prakriti* or *Maya* (illusion) and are trapped in their own respective *gunas* which in the context of the play act as the opposites. The *Satwic* Devadatta does not seek higher knowledge which gives true happiness or bliss. Under the intoxication of *Maya* he aspires only for the knowledge of this world. He dreams of possessing Padmini so that he "could outshine Kalidasa." (14) Though it is underplayed, thirst for possession and ropes of hope also tie down Kapila. Paradoxically, Devadatta and Kapila who occupy extreme poles at the socio-cultural as well as metaphysical levels are also "one mind, one heart." (2) The complementary nature of their relationship gets evoked when they are placed alongside "Lava and Kusha, Rama and Lakshmana, Krishna and Balarama," (2) the classical, quasi-divine pairs. The much yearned for and near impossible achievement of fusion between the polarities, materializes in the play after the transposition. It is such a fusion between intellect and flesh which is also sought by *Prakriti*, seen manifested in the woman (Padmini), in order to further the creative purpose. But the golden solution which involves the reconciliation of the irreconcilable, instead of bringing integration and completeness, only intensifies the feeling of incompleteness. Though such a feeling of incompleteness arouses existential angst, in *Hayavadana* it does not move towards existential despair. Instead, the play goes towards the achievement of an integration which becomes graspable only in relation to the Ganesha myth.

In *Ganapathi Atharva Seersha* which is an *Upanishad* of the *Atharva Veda*, Mantra no. 6 invokes Lord Ganapathi as one "beyond the three *gunas*."[6] The three *gunas* (*Satwa, Rajas* and *Tamas*), which literally mean "ropes," shackle a *jeeva* (soul) to *Maya*; and therefore quest for completion involves the attainment of release from the fetters of *gunas*. Lord Ganesha, being "Gunapathy" (the master of all the three *gunas*), represents the ultimate desired by all aspirants for completeness. Hence his intercession which is sought and gained in the context of the play by the Bhagavata, the typical Sanskrit narrator figure, on behalf of all those who suffer from fractured personality, becomes meaningful and makes the attainment of 'totality of being' through the integration of the self, convincing.

The figure of Lord Ganesha which represents a perfect blend of three different worlds of experience—the divine, the human and the animal—becomes central within the frame of the sub-plot too, since it foreshadows the character of Hayavadana.

Hayavadana's problem is one of alienation as well as incompleteness. The incompatibility of his head and body and his inability to find his society, haunt him. He cannot join the world of Divine since he is rejected by his father; the animal world is denied to him because he has not his mother's advantage of having a complete animal body; and the equine face makes him a stranger among men.

If the attainment of integration in the main plot is linked to the Ganesha virtue of being *dwandwaatita* and *gunateeta*; the achievement of completeness in the sub-plot touches the issue of yet another Ganesha virtue, namely that of being *dehateeta* (reaching beyond the three bodies). It is the attainment of the distinction of being *dehateeta* which connects Hayavadana's predicament to the Ganesha myth. Hayavadana from this standpoint represents a deluded *jeeva* who due to ignorance forgets its true nature which is full and complete. With the desire to make up for his imaginary incompleteness, he tries to acquire things and beings of the world. Such desires in their subtle form are called *vasanas*. A *jeeva* is trapped in the wheel of birth and death till all the *vasanas* are exhausted; and therefore only the dawn of knowledge or attainment of the ability to go beyond the three bodies, can bring Salvation. The *jeeva* then becomes *dehateeta* and achieves the goal of desirelessness. It is this unfathomed mystery of Lord Ganesha, looked upon as Brahman who is always full and complete and devoid of any trace of *vasana* which makes Him *dehateeta*. Hayavadana's attainment of completeness comes from such an awareness of the mystery and hence the prayer of gratitude voiced by the Bhagavata at the end of the play, "Unfathomable indeed is the mercy of the Elephant-headed Ganesha. He fulfils the desires of all—a grandson to a grandfather, a smile to a child, a neigh to a horse. How indeed can one describe his glory in our poor, disabled world?" (71) perfectly rounds off the play and elevates the *Bharatavakya* into something much more than a conventional stipulation.

Through the attribution of a pivotal role to the Ganesha myth in *Hayavadana*, Karnad achieves an admirable equation which accommodates classical and folk conventions within the frame of contemporary theatre strategies. A play of such a unique nature remains opaque to an application of conceptual tools transplanted from the western dramaturgy. The lukewarm response towards *Hayavadana* from the Western critical world often stems from this. Indian socio-cultural ethos and tradition sustain Karnad's play which remains mostly open to an essentially native explication based on indigenous critical apparatus.

NOTES

1. Girish Karnad, *Hayavadana* (Madras: Oxford UP, 1975).
2. Tutun Mukherjee, "Persistence of Classical Categories in Modern Indian Drama: Girish Karnad's *Hayavadana*," *Literature and Popular Culture: A Festschrift to Isaac Sequeira*, ed. R.S. Sharma et al (Hyderabad: Cauvery, 1990), p. 134.
3. M.K. Naik, "From the Horse's Mouth: A Study of *Hayavadana*," *Dimensions of Indian English Literature* (New Delhi: Sterling, 1984), pp. 197-98.
4. *Maya* (illusion) has *Satwa*, *Rajas* and *Tamas* as its three ingredients called *gunas*. Different proportions of three *gunas* in any individual determine his nature. A person dominated by *Satwa-guna* will be a gentle, contemplative seeker of knowledge. A *Rajaswic* will be an active and dynamic person who thirsts for possession. Being deluded by *Maya*, we see only the predominantly manifested demerits in these *gunas*. But *gunas* can themselves help Man to reach his goal, namely *moksha* or salvation.
5. Swami Chinmayananda, "Shri Ganapati-Vinayaka," *Glory of Ganesha* (Bombay: Central Chinmaya Mission Trust, 1987), p. 3.
6. S.G. Savarkar, "Two Mantras from *Ganapati Atharva Sheersha*," *Glory of Ganesha* (Bombay: Central Chinmaya Mission Trust, 1987), pp. 132-38.

Drama as Criticism of Life: *Hayavadana*

V.B. VINOD

There is a continuing text in Girish Karnad: the search for a moral order.[1] His plays locate this problem in different contexts to generate discourse about Man as both subject and object. The engagement with this theme which began with *Yayati* (1961) continues into *Tughlaq* (1964), *Hayavadana* (1971), *Naga-Mandala* (1988) and *Talé-Danda* (1989). Karnad meets the spectator as a romantic who is game for serious philosophical reflections. And the idea of morality outlined by a similar philosopher-romantic, D.H. Lawrence, may be remembered as the delicate equilibrium "between man and his circumambient universe."[2] (127) The Karnad character seeks to achieve such a moral order. The drama explores the possibilities before the seeker using a very refreshing and inventive dramatic idiom. It invariably ends in "knowledge" and self-illumination. It is the point at which the seeker realizes the price exacted by life. Bruised and brutalized he learns the essential nature of "truth"—as being elusive though it appears to be within one's reach.

Karnad's source for *Yayāti* is the *Mahabhārata*. Yayati who borrows Puru's youth is initiated into the morality of 'give' and 'take.' Confronted by Chitralekha (Karnad's innovation to give the play its polemical twist), Yayati is forced to choose between Chitralekha as daughter-in-law and Chitralekha as wife. Mughal history is where Karnad goes to for the political allegory in *Tughlaq*. The emperor, Muhammad-bin-Tughlaq, is checkmated every time he makes a move. The visionary King-emperor is upstaged by the pawn—Aziz. Magnificent schemes for the welfare of the subjects end up in a shambles and the whole court resembles, at the end of the play, the chess-board, in the words of one of its characters, a veritable, "market of corpses."[3] (55) Kannada folk tales supply *Naga-Mandala* its story line. As a folk tale, it combines realistic elements with mythical or surreal elements to present the domestic drama featuring Appanna, Rani and the Naga. The roots given by Kurudavva are consumed by the snake who satisfies Rani's desires. What was expected of the husband is realized through a proxy. The snake, with all his mythical and surreal dimensions is instrumental in the deification of Rani who turns the wife-beating husband into the deity-serving devotee overnight. Karnad turns to the history of Karnataka, the twelfth century AD, for *Talé-Danda*. The idealistic aspirations of Basavanna, of assembling in the city of Kalyan a gallery of notables in the land: poets, philosophers, sages and social engineers, with a view to rooting out the ossified social evils, has an ironic conclusion in bloodshed and pandemonium, reminiscent of the way the French Revolution culminated in the Reign of Terror of Robbespierre. Hence the title *Talé-Danda* meaning "Death by Beheading."

Hayavadana is a link in this continuing thesis of Karnad—that life is a conundrum. The man who sets out to crack the puzzle is a seeker, with the attributes of the romantic and the adventurer. The tendency to ask questions does not yield answers (as is the grand illusion created by the positivists and rationalists who assume that answers are possible) instead, it leads on to more questions. There is a continuity from one kind of problems to another. The seeker who expects certitude is rudely shaken to accept the fundamental indeterminacy at the core of human existence.

Hayavadana is a 'play' in more than one sense of that word. It communicates both as 'theatre' and as 'theme.' The play as theatre chooses for its narrative the ambience of folk drama. As folk drama which incorporates the elements of *Yakshagāna* it makes a few large statements. These statements become clear when set against the backdrop of classical Sanskrit drama which has a longer tradition in India.[4] Karnad's choice of the 'folk' form instead of the 'Classical' speaks about the deliberate choice with regard to the 'mindset' that dominates the play. Classical Sanskrit drama has an inflexibility about it: be it the script, or the enactment, or the communication of the message and maybe, even about the expected spectator response. One gets the standard idea of being inside a 'concrete' playhouse with 'fixed' seats from which to watch a drama whose thesis is pre-determined with a providential finality about Cause and Effect. One is tempted to look at the classical dramatist as better described in Lucien Goldmann's phrase, *Diem Caché* , a kind of "hidden god," who remote-controls the action on the stage.[5]

The choice of the Bhagavata to speak to the spectator on the one hand and, to act with the actors on the other lends to the narrative of *Hayavadana* an aspect of 'folk' drama that opens it up for a 'free' play of responses.[6] It must, however, not be read as a free-for-all of responses. For the Bhagavata only allows a long leash on the narrative while he never lets go off the leash completely. As very articulate theatre, it must be said about the play that it does not insist on any 'given' idea but multiplies them. After all, real life is not a series of well-calculated and laid out moves but a series of stumblings upon one choice after another and the consequences set off by each one. As theatre then, the play is an invitation to look at the various options open before the individual before he can speak or think coherently. This is the 'mindset' of the play.

Hayavadana as theme is a 'play' of ideas: it is 'absurd in a Beckettian sense and 'fractured' in a Freudian sense. It is laced with Cartesian elements, the conventional hierarchical idea of society, the mythical idea about gods and goddesses, besides, the folk legends. Just as the characters on the Beckett stage are maimed, the characters in *Hayavadana* appear as 'complete' halves seeking their 'others.' Devadatta as 'mind' and Kapila as 'body' must realize their completeness. But every effort in this direction only takes them away from this end.

What is common to all these ideas is the theme of incompleteness. Some of the instances in the play are as follows: the stage props, the *Rangadaivata* , the spoken word, the vows made, the desire of Padmini and so on. One of the most important stage props is the "half-curtain." It is effective in the presentation of Hayavadana. By gradually bringing down the curtain the horse is exposed and concealed a few times. In the meanwhile, "the all-knowing" spectator has moved in and out of illusion and reality by virtue of the half-curtain. The fact that it can reveal and conceal even as the spectator is all eyes, makes the half-curtain the most visible symbol of the play's theme. It effectively demonstrates the *maya* which teases him who thinks he sees the most.

The next instance of incompleteness is a meta-theatrical exploitation of the image of the *Rangadaivata* or the presiding deity. Here, *Ganapati*, who also has epithets like *ādivinayakā, siddhivinayaka, vigneshwara* , which mean, respectively, the ruler of the divine aspects of Shiva, the first God to be worshipped, the god who can assure achievement, the remover of obstacles. The Bhagavata uses the ritual of *nandi* or invocation to underscore the problem of the play by asking the spectator to look at the God of "the goal" (*ga*) and the God of "the source" (*ja*)—hence the Alpha and the Omega—as himself an embodiment of incompleteness.[7] Hence the irony in the name *Gajānanan.* The ritual opening is thus turned into a real opening.

The elusiveness of meaning and the menace of language is explored. The child Hayavadana who wants to be made complete (implying a complete human being) is made a complete horse. The inexactitude of language is further evidenced in the reaction of an indignant Kali. Devadatta who promises Rudra his head and right hand to Kali, ends up offering the latter his head. The incompleteness in the language of the body (action) to reflect the language of the mind (thought) exposes the profanity of vows and promises and even prayers.

The incompleteness of human desire is symbolized by Padmini. As the ideal of all womanly attributes she is the lotus (*padmam)* itself. Rooted to the earth and with the flower turned skyward, she symbolizes the fundamental nature (*prakriti*) of the human body: it is torn between the downward (*tāmasic*) earth and the upward (*sāttvic*) heavens, itself being impressionable (*rājasic*). Thanks to the incompleteness in nature, even when the eyes see, a lot of things cannot but be taken on trust:

Padmini:	How about your eyes? Do they work properly?
Kapila:	Yes.
Padmini:	So there is nothing wrong with your eyes. As for the other thing, I'll have to take you on trust. (17)[8]

The feminine principle, Padmini, "born of Kalidasa's magic description—as Vatsyayana had dreamt her," (13) takes the "other thing" of Kapila on "trust." Kapila who is acting as Devadatta's messenger of love is himself in love with her. Padmini who answers Kapila's call (knock on the door) humming the tune, "Here comes the rider—from which land does he come?" (16) suggests the unconscious craving of the female for completeness. Her desire for the body of Kapila and the mind of Devadatta comes to a head:

Padmini:	(back at the window) where is Kapila?
Devadatta:	. . . and drool over Kapila all day. (20)

The tension mounts in the dialogue between husband and wife.

Devadatta is against Padmini undertaking the journey to the Ujjain Fair. Kapila who is expected to bring the cart is the cause of Devadatta's sexual jealousy and anger. Padmini is unrelenting.

Devadatta (mind) finally surrenders to the pulls of Kapila (body). The journey to Ujjain which is a journey to a sacred place, a heavenly abode in traditional thinking, becomes an allegory of the sexual act. The cart (symbolic of the phallus) driven by the oxen makes Padmini comment on the performances of Kapila and Devadatta:

> How beautifully you drive the cart, Kapila. Your hands don't even move, but the oxen seem to know exactly where to go. . . . What a terrible road. Nothing but stones and rocks—but one didn't feel a thing in the cart! You drove it so gently—almost made it float. I remember when Devadatta took me in a cart—that was soon after our marriage— . . . The oxen took everything except the road. He only had to pull to the right, and off they would rush to the left! I've never laughed so much in my life. But of course he got very angry, so we had to go home straight! (25)

On way to Ujjain, passing through the forest, the two friends behead themselves before Kali. Padmini who moves the goddess to grant her wish, commits, what appears like a Freudian slip,[9] the transposition of heads. For when Kapila insists on being accepted, Padmini asks Devadatta to "Let him [Kapila] scream away. Don't pay him any attention." (38) There is only a brief period of this wish-fulfilment for Padmini as Devadatta soon wastes Kapila's body. She soliloquizes wistfully, "Kapila? What could he be doing now? Where could he be? Could his body be fair still." (49)

The dolls brought from Ujjain are brilliant expressionistic devices which convey the mental processes of Padmini. The rider who comes in her lullaby for the child and who keeps returning in her thoughts is identified by the dolls. So when Devadatta prepares to visit Ujjain a second time for new dolls, Doll II makes a comment exposing the disturbance in Padmini. In an aside it says, "Cover your wife." (52) This marks the second wave of seeking in Padmini. She addresses the child: "How can I describe it to you? There's so much. Long before the sun rises, the shadows of twigs draw *alpanas* on the floor. . . . Then the day dawns and the fun begins." (52) On her second journey into the woods, Padmini takes on the guise of the archetypal seeker. "I asked the villagers. . . . And the pilgrims. And the hunters. And the tribesmen. When there wasn't anyone anymore, I asked myself. Everyone saw to it that I didn't lose the wrong road." (54) The words reinforce the idea of the search for completeness as a series of stumblings. The individual is educated everytime but is disillusioned the more for that reason. The answers to the "Why"-questions do not fetch answers:

Kapila:	(suddenly) Why have you come away from him?
Padmini:	What do you want me to say? (They freeze)
Kapila:	(to Padmini) Why have you come here?
Padmini:	I had to see you.
Kapila:	Why? (No reply) (56)

The "why"questions culminate in a crescendo of more questions than answers:

Padmini:	Why should one buy anything?
Kapila:	Why shouldn't one? Why should one tolerate this mad dance of incompleteness?
Padmini:	Whose incompleteness? Yours? (57)

The questions fade into and lose themselves into the choric song of the Bhagavata:

> You cannot engrave on water
> nor wound it with a knife,
> which is why
> the river
> has no fear
> of memories. (58)

There is a pattern of thinking which is exercised in the play. Generally the adult is expected to know the 'answers' while it is the lot of the child to be curious about the phenomena of the world. The child's curiosity is expressed, generally, as questions to the adult. By that score, Hayavadana amplifies the perplexities of the 'child' who, startled by reality, relates with the world with an almost endless series of questions. The adults in the play, Kapila, Devadatta, and Padmini, at some point of time identify each other as 'children'—suggestive of a lack of knowledge or the characteristic incomprehension of the child:

Devadatta:	(to Padmini) You've no sense of what not to say. So long as you can chatter and run around like a child . . . (20)
Padmini:	(to Devadatta) But you are so fragile! I don't know how you're going to go through life wrapped in silk like this! You are still a baby . . . (21)
Padmini:	(to Devadatta about Kapila) Please don't get angry. Poor boy, he looked so lost and disappointed, I couldn't bear to see it. (24)

The significant unit of the play, in terms of which all the characters are delineated, is the 'child.' Hence, Kapila, Devadatta, Padmini, 'their' son, Hayavadana, the Dolls from Ujjain, are alike, proper children.

The Bhagavata is the only prominent presence on the stage. He initiates the discussion of the *drishya* (the spectacle). He invites responses to the actions of the characters. He empathizes with Kapila when he is forsaken by Devadatta and Padmini after the transposition. It is to the Bhagavata's charge that Padmini entrusts her baby before she performs sati. Besides, the Bhagavata takes charge of the play's opening when the Nata, frightened by a 'speaking' Hayavadana creates a commotion on the stage. He also decides the time when the half-curtain must be brought in or withdrawn, symbolic of a God who decides the amount of illusion to be purveyed. The Bhagavata, who is a God-like omnipresence in the "theatre" of the play, is involved intimately with every character. He is the Tiresian-witness presiding over the everyday reality that keeps turning into the "problem" of the play.

In the main plot, Devadatta, Kapila, and Padmini, seeking completeness come to the temple of Kali. Devadatta's vow to offer his right hand in the event of his marriage to Padmini is yet unrealized. The goddess appears bored and aloof as the language of human promises and prayers has become too mechanical and ritualistic to be exact. She plays a practical joke on Hayavadana by granting his wish. His wish to be made complete is realized when he becomes a complete horse. Kali, who is a Goddess, and omnipotent in the "theme" of the play handles the destinies of the characters (everyone is her "child" as they address her as "Mother") to serve as 'eye-opening' problems for the spectator. The Bhāgāvata-Kāli complex is the factor that weaves together the main plot of the play—Padmini's search for completeness—and its sub-plot—Hayavadana's search for completeness into one seamless whole.

NOTES

1. In this paper the search for a moral order is meant to be synonymous with the search for completeness. The plays of Karnad locate the idea of the search for a moral order in different spheres: it is a philosophical problem in *Yayati*; political in *Tughlaq; Naga-Mandala* is located in the social sphere; in *Hayavadana* it is a mental puzzle and in *Talé-Danda* it is a socio-political problem.
2. D.H. Lawrence, "Morality and the Novel," *20th Century Literary Criticism: A Reader*, ed. David Lodge (London: Longman, 1989), pp. 127-31.
3. Girish Karnad, *Tughlaq* (Delhi: OUP, 1972)
4. For a separation between Classical Sanskrit Drama and Folk drama I consulted *The Tradition of Kannada Theatre,* ed. K.D. Kurtkoti (Bangalore: IBH, 1986).
5. Goldmann's phrase is taken from the second chapter of *Structuralism or Criticism? Thoughts on How We Read*, Geoffrey Strickland (London: Cambridge Univ. Press, 1981).
6. There is a distinction between the *sūtradhara* in Classical Sanskrit drama and the Bhagavata in the folk drama. "The *Sūtradhārā* in Sanskrit drama does not enjoy a high status. Apart from his appearance at the beginning of the play to invoke the blessing of Gods and to conduct formalities with the audience, he is seldom seen on the stage again. But in the Bhagavata or Yakshagana . . . the Bhagavata even today justifies the Sutradhara, as he is seen on the stage from the beginning of the performance to the end of it. . . . He is responsible for the movement of the play and its climax." H.K. Ranganath, *The Karnatak Theatre* (Dharwad: Karnatak University, 1982), p. 29.
7. A useful discussion on the symbolism of Ganesha is the article by Nancy Patchen, "Rationale Behind Ganesha," *Tattvāloka*, Vol. XII, No. 6. Feb./Mar. 1990, pp. 9-12.
8. Girish Karnad, *Hayavadana* (Madras: OUP, 1991).
9. *Dictionary of Eponyms* by Mansel Martin H. Wordsworth (Hertfordshire, 1996), p. 73.

Dionysian Ego in *Hayavadana*

M. SARAT BABU

Norman O. Brown, a psychoanalyst, uses the Greek myths of Apollo and Dionysus in interpreting the alienation of mind and body and their unification.[1] According to psychoanalysis, human mind is divided into three organs; the id, the ego and the superego. The id consists of instinctual drives and always seeks gratification irrespective of external reality and cultural values (Pleasure principle). The ego perceives and responds to external reality (Reality principle). It, being the leader, tries to satisfy the id and the superego within the limits of external reality. The superego irrespective of external reality and biological impulses (the id) contains ideals, values and morals and urges the ego to lead an ideal life. When the ego wants to be ideal under the pressure of the superego, the mind starts functioning independent of the body. This naturally leads to a split between the mind and the body. Consequently they become strangers to each other. That is, the experiences of the body do not reach the mind, and the feelings of the mind do not spread through the body. The ego which causes this self-alienation is called Apollonian ego in which the soul leaves the body as Brown puts it. On the other hand when the ego wants to be natural or really human and when the superego accepts the biological reality (the id), the mind and the body work together. There is no split between them. There is perfect harmony between them. The mind feels the bodily experiences and the body rocks with the feelings of the mind. This is what Blake describes as 'the undivided body-soul.' Such an ego as allows the undifferentiated, unified body-mind is called Dionysian ego in which the soul returns to, and resides in, the body as Brown explains.

According to psychoanalytical interpretation of history as expounded by Brown, human history is divided into three phases: primal unity, differentiation and final unity. The primitive man enjoyed the primal unity of the body and the mind. As man civilizes himself through ages, the body and the mind are differentiated, divided and finally alienated. All human suffering is only due to this culture of self-alienation (Apollonian Culture). When the intense suffering brings about awareness, man stops feeling ashamed of being human. As human knowledge reaches its zenith, he evolves Dionysian culture through which he retains the undifferentiated unified mind-body. This final unity is the salvation that the future human society attains according to the optimistic prediction of psychoanalysis. This concept helps us solve such riddles in *Hayavadana* as why Hayavadana's mother chooses for her husband a stallion rather than a man and why Goddess Kali makes Hayavadana a complete horse instead of a complete man.

The theme of *Hayavadana*[2] is the problem of alienation. The play starts with the worship and then the description of Lord Ganesha, the elephant-headed god, who symbolizes alienation since his head and his body are incompatible. A little later Hayavadana, the eponymous character, comes and like Ganesha he too is a symbol of alienation since he is a horse-headed man. Karnad makes use of these mythical figures to throw light on the alienation of man and its consequences in human society. He tries to show suggestively the hegemony of Apollonian culture that has captured the racial unconscious of mankind. The modern man represented by Devadatta-Kapila suffers from self-alienation. Goddess Kali's power proves to be very weak since the transposition of their heads fails to liberate Devadatta and Kapila from alienation.

Padmini: Must the head always win?
Kapila: That's why I am Kapila now. (56)

It is the hegemonistic culture which wins through the head. Devadatta discontinues physical exercise and gradually loses his physical vigour while Kapila regains his physical vigour by taking rigorous physical exercise. This is because the cultural roles of Devadatta, a brahmin and Kapila, a blacksmith, carried in their heads respectively, successfully undo what is granted by Goddess Kali. As Devadatta says, "All the muscle and strength. But how long can one go on like that? I have the family tradition to maintain—the daily reading, writing and studies." (46)

Devadatta is a brahmin. He reads and writes. He develops his mind and ignores his body. Kapila is a blacksmith. He is adept in making and repairing carts and other things. He plays games and participates in sports. He develops his body and neglects his mind. While describing their friendship, the Bhagavata says "one mind, one heart." Devadatta is "the mind" and Kapila is "the heart." Actually their friendship is based on the fact that they depend on each other for what each lacks. That is why Raykar says, "They are thus complementary to each other."[3] Since the mind is considered superior to the body in human society, the caste of Brahmins occupies a higher rung than all other castes in our hierarchical society. That is why Devadatta sits on a chair while Kapila squats on the floor. Since real love is not possible between two unequal persons, their friendship is not real. The dishonesty of their friendship is well exposed by Goddess Kali. "Kali . . . says he is dying for friendship. He must have known perfectly well he would be accused of killing Devadatta for you." (33) The covert conflict between Devadatta and Kapila which comes out after the transposition of their heads stands for the antagonism of human mind and body. It culminates in the duel that kills them both. This shows that alienation is lethal to both the mind and the body.

Devadatta is 'the mind' and Kapila 'the body.' Devadatta falls in love fifteen times in a period of two years. (12) Yet he fails to get married to any one of the girls. Even his sixteenth love seems to be a fiasco. He feels utterly hopeless and helpless: "I swear, Kapila, with you as my witness I swear, if I ever get her as my wife, I'll sacrifice my two arms to the goddess Kali, I'll sacrifice my head to Lord Rudra." (14) Unlike Devadatta, Kapila does not fall in love. He does not feel it difficult to arrange the marriage of Devadatta and Padmini. Devadatta's body does not respond as adequately as his mind readily loves and Kapila's mind is not nimble enough to feel the sensations of his body. Thus both suffer from self-alienation. Therefore the problem is more than the passiveness of Devadatta's body and Kapila's mind. There is little or no communication between their body and mind. Padmini, not realizing the real problem, juxtaposes the active mind (head) of Devadatta and the active body of Kapila. So, even after the transposition of their heads, their self-alienation continues since each head carries deep in itself the Apollonian ego.

The alienation of the mind and the body is unnatural and artificial while their unification is natural. Apollonian culture strives for alienation while nature seeks unification. Libido (life impulses) of

Freud or the Life Force of Bernard Shaw tirelessly try to bring about unification. It can be seen functioning through Hayavadana's mother (the princess of Karnataka) and Padmini. The Princess therefore prefers a stallion to a human prince because animals are free from alienation. When the stallion becomes a gandharva after fifteen years, she requests him to remain a horse. She does not regret her becoming a mare when the enraged gandharva curses her. As Hayavadana says: "He cursed her to become a horse herself. So my mother became a horse and ran away happily." (9) The stallion's becoming the gandharva symbolizes the primitive man's becoming the civilized man. Mother Kali also favours nature. She therefore grants Hayavadana's wish to become complete. He becomes a complete horse instead of a complete man. By doing so, the Goddess liberates Hayavadana from self-alienation. Thus Hayavadana as also his mother attain Dionysian ego.

Padmini fails to achieve the reunification of the mind and the body in Devadatta-Kapila. She realizes her mistake and perceives the real problem. She explains the problem to Kapila whose mind is frigid to the sensations of his body on account of self-alienation: "Be quiet, stupid. Your body bathed in a river, swam and danced in it. Shouldn't your head know what river it was, what swim? Your head too must submerge in that river—the flow must rumple your hair, run its tongue in your ears and press your head to its bosom! Until that's done, you'll continue to be incomplete." (58) She wants to achieve her aim through her son. So she requests the Bhagavata to let her son be brought up as the son of Kapila by the hunters in the forest for five years and then as the son of Devadatta by Vidyasagara, her father-in-law and learned brahmin. Thus she wants to provide both physical and mental training for her son so that he may attain unification. After passing her oral will to the Bhagavata, she commits sati on the pyre of Devadatta and Kapila who have died in a duel. Thus she ends her life of alienation and averts the possible dilution of her will.

Padmini's son is brought to the Bhagavata again after five years. He is as morose as Kapila after his transposition. Hayavadana who becomes a complete horse comes and expresses his grief over his human voice. When he laughs with human voice, Padmini's son throws away his dolls and starts laughing and clapping as if he were freed from a spell. Similarly Hayavadana loses human voice when Padmini's son rides him and sings a nursery rhyme. Thus

Hayavadana and Padmini's son symbolizing the primal unity and the final unity respectively attain Dionysian ego. Padmini succeeds in achieving her aim posthumously. As the Bhagavata says: "So at last Hayavadana has become complete. (To the Actors) You two go and tell the Revered Brahmin Vidyasagar that his grandson is returning home in triumph, riding a big, white charger." (71) Padmini's son representing the future man achieves harmony not only between the mind and the body but also between himself and nature represented by Hayavadana.

Most of the critics including M.K. Naik[4] and Shubhangi S. Raykar think that it is humanly impossible to achieve perfection. Raykar in her brilliant paper on *Hayavadana* argues that the unification of Apollo and Dionysus symbolized by Devadatta and Kapila is not possible. This present study being based on psychoanalysis is entirely different from the earlier ones of *Hayavadana*. In the primitive man, the body and the mind are in perfect harmony which Brown calls Dionysian ego. As man has been vainly striving to be above biological principles for ages, he has evolved Apollonian culture which causes alienation. Devadatta and Kapila, like the people of modern society, are victims of self-alienation while Hayavadana, his mother and Padmini's son attain Dionysian ego (the undifferentiated body-mind).

NOTES

1. Norman O. Brown, "Apollo and Dionysus," *Life against Death* (London: Routledge and Kegan Paul, 1959), pp. 155-76.
2. Girish Karnad, *Hayavadana* (New Delhi: Oxford University Press, 1988).
3. Shubhangi S. Raykar, "The Development of Girish Karnad as a Dramatist: *Hayavadana*," p. 177 of this book.
4. M.K. Naik, "From the Horse Mouth: A Study of *Hayavadana*," *Dimensions of Indian English Literature* (New Delhi: Sterling, 1984), pp. 191-201.

Hayavadana and *Nagamandala*: A Study in Postcolonial Dialectics

A. JAGANMOHANA CHARI

There is no gainsaying the fact that the Indian psyche has been reeling under the colonial burden of the past. It is compounded of the effects of the alien rule and the oppressive ethos left over from the *varnashrama dharma*. What appears to be at work in consequence in the present day Indian culture and literatures weaving the webs of hegemonistic structures is an imperialism of the ruling class ideas both of the west and ancient India.

The Indian bourgeoisie-comprador and brahminical in character and interests—became a willing prey or an easy collaborator with the British design to perpetuate their economic hold over the people of India since the middle of the nineteenth century. As a result the new entrepreneurial middle-class which emerged in India, taking its succour from the traditional mores while absorbing the contemporary post-Enlightenment Western ethic, found itself in a division. Girish Karnad explains this division thus: "whereas in public it [the new entrepreneurial class] accepted the Western bourgeois notions of secularism, egalitarianism, and individual merit at home it remained committed to the traditional loyalties of caste, family, and religion." He further says: "Only a society which is honest enough to face the implications of this division squarely could produce meaningful drama out of it."

It looks as though Girish Karnad is talking of his own predicament as an Indian English playwright. A close look at two of his plays—*Hayavadana* and *Nagamandala*—will also tell us the same. It also presses upon the mind of the reader that he has written the plays not as a matter of self-clarification alone, but as therapeutic device also. In the plays he is seized with the theme of incompleteness as he makes it explicit. He seeks to exorcize himself of this demon of incompleteness by dramatizing the predicament; which is also the predicament of the class to which he belongs.

Let us now have a brief look at *Hayavadana* from this viewpoint. The plot of the play, as everyone knows, is as simple as that of a folk-tale although the playwright crams it with everything in the world. Devadatta endowed with all the accomplishments expected of a brahmin youth falls in love, for the seventeenth time, with an extremely agile and quick-witted girl, Padmini, the daughter of a rich *shresti*. Kapila, the son of an ironsmith with a lithe and handsome body, good in the wrestling pit and extremely devoted to his friend Devadatta for his poetry and wisdom, mediates and arranges the marriage of the girl with his friend. Padmini who seems to possess something of the Kali, the female deity, in her is attracted to the virility of Kapila who also worships her beauty instinctively so much so that she would enjoy his company whenever he came to see her husband. Devadatta becomes jealous and tries to postpone the proposed journey on the cart at Ujjain but with no success on account of Padmini's insistence. On the way, Devadatta decides to sacrifice his head to Kali ostensibly in deference to his earlier vow but in fact, unable to bear the pangs of jealousy. On finding the dead body of his friend, Kapila sacrifices his head too, out of his love for his friend as he likes to tell himself but only to avert the possible ignominy. Padmini who goes in search of the friends stumbled on an opportunity of having the best of the two—Davadatta's head and Kapila's body. Kali the primordial deity favours her with the blessings of life of the two friends. Padmini happens to succeed in transposing the heads with the result that there are two men now, one with Devadatta's head and Kapila's body and the other with Kapila's head and Devadatta's body. Since head is superior according to *Shastras* Devadatta scores a point over Kapila. Kapila is the loser in this ludicrous bargain of mixing up of heads. He has lost not only his body to Devadatta but also his peace on account of the *vasanas* lodged in Devadatta's body. His mundane logic that body being the real person Padmini should belong to him is spurned by both Devadatta and Padmini. Finally Devadatta and Padmini go back to the city where Devadatta enjoys the benefits of Kapila's well-trained body for about a year before it loses its verve. Kapila who feels hurt and cheated remains in the forest to train the brahmin's body dancing by his head like a corpse and shape it into form.

Padmini, in the end, cheats on her husband and walks with her child in her arms into the embrace of Kapila who once again succeeds in his effort to "live" in the forest. She claims that child to be the child of both Devadatta and Kapila. The play ends with Devadatta coming in on Padmini and Kapila and fighting a duel with the latter in which the heads roll again.

The child who grows as Kapila's child in the forest to be delivered as Devadatta's at the age of five into the city combines in him the thematic strands of the main plot and the sub-plot. When he is given over to a traveller going to the city to be delivered into the hands "of his grandparents, he is found not to be able to laugh like a human child. He laughs only when the horse born of a princess and *gandharva* cursed to live like a horse until he loved a human, laughs a real laughter in his attempt to make the child laugh.

This story in which folk conventions and motifs are used in plenty holds out the possibility of several layers of meaning such as: (1) man's quest for his origins, (2) status of friendship and love, (3) city versus forest, (4) innocence versus guilt, (5) the primordial relation between man and woman, (6) life versus death, (7) man's struggle for completeness, and so on. Nevertheless, what Girish Karnad has consciously tried to create, it appears, is the last of the above-mentioned themes. But if one deconstructs all these, one could arrive at a space which throbs with a neo-colonial dialectic which is brought into being by the absorption of metaphysical traditions of both the West and ancient India. What is common for these traditions is the world view which splits everything into the real and the ideal and looks upon the latter as more valid. It also views things or phenomena as given and disconnected. It has come to be called metaphysical dualism which justifies the existence of classes or castes. In its discourse, it is status-quo-ist. But when confronted squarely it also gives the lie to itself.

In Karnad's *Hayavadana*, the metaphysical dialectic or discourse we come across consists in its essence in the statement made by Devadatta: "According to the *Shastras*, the head is the sign of a man" and also in the text uttered by Padmini: "Must the head always win." If we examine the logic which is pre-given, Devadatta's head should succeed in explicating Kapila's body to his and Padmini's satisfaction, after it is hooked on to Devadatta's head. But after about a year his head fails to enjoy the liveliness of the body. Its litheness begins to wear off owing to the lack of physical labour.

Consequently, Devadatta loses Padmini to Kapila once again. And Kapila who finds the brahmin's body a drag and a torture trains it by hard physical labour in the forest. And he "lives" unlike his friend. The subversionist folk element in the play also plays on this text "live" into a disruptionist comment on the quality of life of the city, the knowledge of *Shastras* and *Varnashrama dharma* as dead and oppressive. The question is: how has he come to live? Not by head as Padmini seems to think but by labour. The idea of metaphysical dualism of body and head corresponding to that of real and ideal is not merely unscientific. Conferring superiority on head entails negation of body which starts off a self-negating conflict between the two. The relation becomes one of opposition and oppression instead of dialectical unity. If we translate it into social terms, a brahmin head is the repository of abstract ideas divested of all sensuousness. Abstract ideas of ritualistic nature which tradition has sanctified are useful for a brahmin like Devadatta in exercizing authority or dominance over a non-brahmin like Kapila and also a woman like Padmini. But he finds in reality or in his experience sensuous pleasures of the body inescapable. So he discovers the lie inherent in his own being. He refuses to come out of it because it represents the mystique on which his class/caste thrives. Kapila too, who has bowed to the hegemonistic mystique yields to the lie and sacrifices his own passion for Padmini, when he cuts off his head in Kali temple.

That both of them—Devadatta and Kapila—are victims of the metaphysical mystique which is at the base of *varnasharma dharma* is aptly conveyed by Kali to Padmini in the dilapidated temple. Kali does not hide her disgust in saying that both Devadatta and Kapila "were lying to their last breaths." Only Padmini is found to be sincere in her selfishness and she speaks the truth when she mixes up the heads.

Woman, like Padmini, is yet another victim of postcolonial dialectic. If Kapila the ironsmith is oppressed by the hegemonistic violence of the ruling class ideology, Padmini, the woman is also repressed by the power of patriarchal values of the ruling class ideology. But she appears to be relatively more free and more capable of distancing herself from the hegemonistic contexts. She may rest content in her consent to the hegemonic structures; yet she adopts the more indirect mode of facing up to reality. Owing to her naturalness and to the degree in which she is away from the matrix of power, only she can be sincere to herself.

Similarly, Padmini in *Hayavadana* acts within the space the post-colonial dialectic allows her. Originally she tries to save the situation for herself by mixing up heads. But as she herself subscribes to the ideology of head, not physical labour, which is against nature, she becómes a victim of the lie herself. When she realizes her mistake, she practises deceit on her husband whom she sends to fetch dolls for her child from Ujjain and she herself makes yet another symbolic journey to Ujjain, i.e. to Kapila and his abode in the forest.

This in the language of dialectics of nature also amounts to the rejection of the metaphysical dialectic or the brahminical ideology. That being determines consciousness, not the other way round is vindicated. But the author Girish Karnad does not rest the problematic in the play at that. He stretches it on account of his collaborationist hegemonistic psychology beyond the natural bounds of the story and sacrifices the men at the altar of status-quo-ist values and drives the woman to *suttee*. But the subversionist folk-tale nature of the story gives the lie to the author's ideology, all the same.

Same thing happens in *Nagamandala* too. The postcolonial matrix embedded in the play opens up yet another space for the working out of the theme of patriarchal oppression.

The concept of ritualistic purity of the metaphysical tradition has structured the hierarchical vertical line-up of gods at the top, men below and women still underneath. So with the classes and castes. The plot of *Nagamandala* unfolds thus: Appanna marries and fetches home Rani to keep her locked inside the house. She is allowed only to cook his lunch. He exercises absolute supremacy over her while he arrogates to himself the power of spending the night with another woman. This vulgar display of power instead of love and treating woman as a disposable object accrues to him owing to the postcolonialist ethos and the mystique of tradition.

Kurudavva who plays the Kali in this play provides Rani with some roots with pseudo-magical powers to make her husband come round to her. But in her fear of, as well as for, her husband, for the magical potion she has prepared out of the roots is poisonous red, Rani pours it into the anthill in which lives a king-cobra. The aphrodisiac works on the Naga and he tuns into her lover. Naga begins to call on Rani in the shape of her husband in the nights and makes love to her. Appanna who notices Kurudavva and her son near the house keeps a watch dog. Later he keeps a mongoose to keep off the snake. Naga destroys both the watchposts by killing them.

Rani becomes pregnant and she thinks she has conceived for her husband, Appanna. The husband comes in on her secret eventually and accuses her of infidelity. She is put to test in the presence of the village elders. Naga comes to her in the shape of her husband once again to tell her that she should opt for the snake ordeal to escape punishment. That is, she should put her hand into the ant-hill, pull the cobra out, take her oath by the Cobra and "speak the truth." The cobra will not bite her if she speaks the truth, he tells her. Truth is what she believes the fact to be, in her innocence.

When exactly Rani perceives that the man who comes to her in the nights is not her husband Appanna but the cobra in his shape is never the moot point here. The woman in her might have experienced it through and through—as the difference between love and authority of one and the same person, her husband. The dichotomy of lover and husband is in the tradition she has inherited. When she discovers in her experience in the end the difference between Naga's love and that of her husband the feeling of experience hardly crosses the threshold of her consciousness because her experience or her head or her consciousness hardly matters in the world of patriarchal hegemony. In fact, it had already been decreed as a taboo by the dominant set up.

The test of her fidelity, after which her husband, a victim of metaphysical mystique himself will become her slave for good—is a lie which gives the lie to the lie or mystique itself. Thus, the negation is negated for a moment. And the woman takes it out on the husband by making him agree that their son should perform the rituals for the snake that dies like a real lover in the coils of her hair.

As it occurs in one of the folk-tales blended into the play, "'The Story' in the form of a woman dressed in a new colorful sari, 'the song'" tells the story of Rani, Appanna, and Naga to the playwright. He snatches the opportunity of listening to it in a bid to escape the curse of death for the sin of boring his audiences, by keeping himself awake for at least one night as is enjoined on him. Thus the story of *Nagamandala* is the story told by "The Story" of the folk tradition which opens up enough space for the writer's predicament, both as man and playwright to place in the context of postcolonial dialectics.

The Concept of Chastity and *Naga-Mandala*

M. SARAT BABU

Srilatha Batliwala says in her article "Why do women oppress women?": "Since the beginning of civilization, every society has lived by certain values and beliefs which are cleverly transformed into immutable truths. In reality, these ideologies are specifically created and disseminated to justify the inequalities and injustices of prevailing social structure, and thus protect the rights and privileges of the powerful."[1]

Chastity is such a value invented by patriarchal culture and accepted by women. It is one of the most powerful yet invisible cultural fetters that have enslaved women for ages since the dawn of patriarchy. There has been enough literature, both oral and written, glorifying this enslaving value and deifying the women characters who observed it faithfully. The *Ramayana* in which Sita undergoes the fire ordeal to prove her chastity to Rama has been a cultural guide to Indians for more than two thousand years. The concept of chastity goes with, and gets its indispensable support from, another morbid concept that sex is mean and sinful. Prostitution and erotic literature, the morbid inventions of patriarchy, have been a safety valve protecting the unnatural ideal of chastity from the excess pressure of libido. Every mother along with father and other elders enslaves her daughters to patriarchy by teaching them verbally and non-verbally that chastity is more important than life and that its loss which brings an unbearable social stigma is worse than death. Many women lose their lives to protect their chastity and many other women bear in silence all the oppression and violence of their sadistic husbands. If any brave woman violates these values, she is not only looked down upon but also culturally excommunicated. Another major harm of these values is that they have weakened natural spontaneous love among human beings which is feared to lead to 'immoral' sex. In spite of pernicious nature of these values, neither men nor women can tolerate attack on these values. Therefore, any sensible intuitive writer has to use a kind anaesthesia while operating on culture to remove the morbid tissue.

Myths, legends and folk forms function as a kind of cultural anaesthesia and they have been used for introducing and eliminating, in our racial unconscious, cultural pathogens such as caste and gender distinctions and religious fanaticism. Like Jean Anouilh, Girish Karnad makes use of myths and folk forms in his plays to exorcise socio-cultural evils. He says, "The energy of folk theatre comes from the fact that although it seems to uphold traditional values, it also has the means of questioning these values, of making them literally stand on their head." In his recent English play, *Naga-Mandala*,[2] he not only exposes male chauvinism, the oppression of women, the great injustice done to them by men and patriarchal culture but also stealthily deflates the concept of chastity. He seems to suggest that matriarchy which according to Bachofen's theory of Mother Right is the lost paradise of mankind will come again.

Naga-Mandala is the story of Rani, narrated to a playwright by Story. Story is a woman character in the play. She narrates certain incidents and conducts the play. She is the Bhagavata of *Naga-Mandala*, a modified version of Yakshagana (folk theatre of Karnataka). Appanna marries Rani and brings her to his house when she reaches womanhood. She arranges for his bath and serves him lunch. After lunch, he locks her in and goes to his concubine. Rani feels lonely and miserable. She is mentally a child craving for parental affection. So she moons 'Oh mother, Father!' in her sleep. The next day before Appanna leaves, she expresses her plight.

Rani:	Listen—(Fumbling for words) Listen—I feel-frightened—alone at night—
Appanna:	What is there to be scared of? Just keep to yourself. No one will bother you. Rice!
Rani:	Please, you could—
Appanna:	Look, I don't like idle chatter. Don't question me. Do as you are told and you won't be punished. (Finishes his meal, gets up) I'll be back tomorrow for lunch. (7)

Rani remembers her favourite nursery tale and day-dreams that an eagle takes her to her parents who caress her affectionately. When she comes into the real world she sobs. Her miserable days roll by in this manner. Appanna treats her as if she were a non-human thing, without any feeling and a robot-cook following his oral instructions. As a male chauvinist, he has utter contempt for his wife. This mental torture forces her to fly mentally into the lap of her parents.

One day Kurudavva, an intimate friend of Appanna's mother, comes to Rani. Since she is blind and old, she is brought by Kappanna, her son. She talks to Rani and feels her through the window. She learns that Appanna still visits his concubine though he has a beautiful wife. So she gives Rani a piece of aphrodisiac root and instructs her to grind the root and mix it in Appanna's food. Rani for the first time has someone to speak to her sympathetically and moreover she is granted a miraculous thing to solve her problem. So she feels very happy. When Appanna comes, Kurudavva expresses her wish to talk to Rani. He says: "She won't talk to anyone. And no one need talk to her." (14) Later he brings a watch-dog to prevent people from talking to his wife. It is clear that Appanna does not want Rani to come into contact with other people and to know more. While he enjoys extra-marital sex, he does not allow her to enjoy even the affection of others. He mercilessly keeps her starved of affection and love which are indispensable for the growth and sustenance of human mind. This solitary confinement of Rani by Appanna in the house symbolizes the chastity belt of the Middle Ages, the reduction of women's talents to house work and the exclusion of women from enlightenment and enjoyment.

Rani mixes the paste of the aphrodisiac root in the curry. As the curry turns red and looks sinister, she throws it on the anthill in front of the house. Then Appanna slaps her so hard that she collapses onto the floor. "There is not a trace of anger in anything he does. Just cold contempt." (17) Rani as a typical wife does not want to cause her husband any harm which she fears will be caused by the root though her husband has been treating her badly since she came. Appanna as a typical husband punishes her severely even for a small thing like her going out though she has been serving him without any grudge since he brought her. He as a male chauvinist thinks he has a right to do whatever he likes and whatever he does is always right. He is insensitive to the feelings of others. Of course he, like many men who are slaves of patriarchal culture, is only playing the role expected of him. He will be so until somebody or something opens his eyes to the reality.

A King Cobra, called Naga, consumes the aphrodisiac paste and falls in love with Rani. He assumes the form of Appanna and visits Rani at night. He takes pity on Rani for her pathetic condition and showers parental affection on her. All her pent-up sorrow bursts out.

Naga:	Did it hurt . . . the beating this morning?
Rani:	No.
Naga:	Locked up in the house all day . . . you must be missing your parents.
Rani:	(Struggles to hold back a sob) No.
Naga:	They doted on you, didn't they? (She suddenly bursts out into a fit of weeping) . . . (Startled) What is it? (Rani continues to howl.) I know, you want to see your parents, don't you? All right. I'll arrange that. (She looks at him dumbfounded) Truly. Now, smile. Just a bit. Look. I'll send now to them only if you smile now. (Rani tries to smile. A new outburst of barking from the dog) (19-20)

Rani cannot comprehend the situation since Appanna cannot be so affectionate and compassionate. Yet she willingly suspends her disbelief and enjoys the concern and affection of Naga who is in the guise of Appanna. She feels happy and secure in his company. She becomes bold enough to talk to him and falls asleep in his embrace. Naga is happy about his success. He lays her gently down on the bed. He becomes a cobra and leaves.

Appanna comes in the morning next day. He unlocks the door and steps in. Rani comes out running and laughing, obviously thinking that her hardships have ended as Appanna has changed for better. She learns that she is wrong.

Rani:	But when did you go away? I'm . . . (Freezes when she sees the expression of distaste on his face)
Appanna:	Yes?
Rani:	Oh! Nothing. (21)

She thus becomes frigid again. As usual, after lunch, Appanna leaves. It gets dark. Naga comes out of the anthill and fights with the dog. He kills the dog to stop the disturbance to Rani's sleep but gets injured in the fight. Then he enters the house through the drain and assumes the form of Appanna. He washes his blood in the bath-room and comes in. He sees Rani, smiles and sits on her bed. She closes her eyes and opens them. Then she bites her finger and gives a cry of pain. She is not sure whether she is dreaming. The gentleness and warmth of Naga (Appanna to her) is incomprehensible to her.

> (To herself.) His visit last night—I assumed, I must have dreamt that. I am certainly not dreaming now. Which means I am going mad. Spending the whole day by myself is rotting my brain. (22)

Then Naga assures her that what she sees is real, not a figment of her imagination. He asks her to tell about herself and her parents. She expresses her doubt about him.

Rani: You talk so nicely at night. But during the day I only have to open my mouth and you hiss like a . . . stupid snake. (Naga laughs) It's all very well for you to laugh. I feel like crying.

Naga: What should I do then . . . stop coming at night? or during the day.

Rani: Who am I to tell you that? It's your house. Your pleasure.

Naga: No, let's say, the husband decides on the day visits. And the wife decides on the night visits. So I won't come at night if you don't want me to.

She feels sorrowful and says that she can say nothing if he spins riddles like this. Naga knows that his identity will be revealed unless he suppresses her reason and intuition by using patriarchal authority.

Naga: (Seriously) I am afraid *that* is how it is going to be. Like *that* during the day. Like *this* at night. Don't ask me why?

Rani: I won't.

This shows how the men of patriarchal culture suppress the intellect of women and how their ignorance gives men the freedom of doing whatever they like. Thus male chauvinists are able to prove that women are foolish and ignorant. This injunction of Naga proves to be so powerful that Rani does not know the real identity of Naga until Appanna sleeps with her.

Rani moves into Naga's arms as a child when he invites her to sleep in his lap. She sees wounds on his cheeks and so brings the mirror box for ointment. She sees an image of a cobra instead of Naga in the mirror and screams with fright. He at once shuts the box and pushes it away. She says, by miming, that she has seen a cobra in the mirror.

Naga: Why shouldn't it come with love?
Rani: May God bless our house and spare us that calamity. The very thought makes me shudder.
Naga: I am here now. Nothing more to fear. (24)

Then she gently touches his wounds and finds his blood peculiarly cold. The mother in her advises him not to wander in cold weather and spoil his health. In spite of the hints, she fails to suspect the identity of Naga.

Rani in her happiness forgets everything. She does not realize what Naga is doing to her until he completes love-making. At once she goes to a corner away from him and starts weeping. She feels that sex is mean and sinful. Naga is astonished at her erotic ignorance. He does not know why she is crying.

Naga: What is it now?
Rani: Go away! Don't talk to me.
Naga: But why are you crying?
Rani: I said be quiet. (Pause) I didn't know you were such a bad man. I should have known the moment you started using honeyed words. Had I known, I would never have agreed to marry you. What will Father and Mother say if they come to know?

Naga takes the trouble of explaining to her that sex is natural and enjoyable but not sinful. He makes a long speech, giving examples to justify love-making. Yet she is not convinced and says that human beings should have some sense of shame unlike animals. Then it is almost dawn and he is about to go. She expresses her unhappiness over his going out. Before leaving, he repeats his injunction that she should not ask why his behaviour at night is different from that during the day. She accepts it like a dumb animal: "No, I won't. The pig, the whale, the eagle—none of them ask why. So I won't either." She cannot suspect Naga's identity in the bed because Appanna has never made love to her.

Kurudavva comes in the morning. Kappanna, her son, sees Naga and mistakes him for Appanna. They find the front door locked. She thinks that Appanna is doing like this (locking the door outside and making love to Rani inside the house) for fun. She is happy that her root has worked the wonder. She speaks to Rani. They do not understand how Appanna has gone out while the lock is still there. Kappanna sees a cobra coming out of the house. Kurudavva advises Rani to burn incense and block the drain to prevent the entry of reptiles. After they leave, Appanna comes and finds the dog dead. He discovers that a cobra has bitten it to death. Rani does not find any wound on his cheeks. As she goes about her usual house work, her doubts sink into her unconscious. After lunch Appanna goes out, locking her in as usual. He brings a mongoose. The mongoose gives a tough fight to the Cobra before it dies. Naga thus receives severe injuries and does not visit Rani for fifteen days. She spends her nights crying and pining for him. When he comes after fifteen days, his body is covered with wounds. She applies ointment to his wounds. During the day Appanna has no scars on him. But she does not question her husband (Naga/Appanna) since questioning her husband is made a taboo.

Naga visits Rani every night. He cures her of frigidity with affection, patience and tact. Naga here functions as a male sex surrogate in curing Rani of frigidity. Thus he and she bring to our mind Paul Brandon and Nan Whitecomb in *The Celestial Bed*, a novel on sex education, by Irving Wallace. Rani starts enjoying erotic pleasures. The days roll by. After five months one day she says she is happy because she has a concrete evidence that her happiness is not a fantasy.

Rani: All these days I was never sure I didn't just dream up these nightly visits of yours. You don't know how I have suffered. When I saw your scowling face in the morning, I would be certain everything was a fantasy and almost want to cry. But my real anxiety began as the evening approached. I would merely lie here, my eyes shut tight. . . . Every night the same anxiety. The same cold feeling deep within me! Thank God. That's all past now.

Naga: Why?

Rani: I have definite evidence to prove I was not fantasizing.

Naga: What evidence?

Rani: I am pregnant. (He stares at her, dumbfounded)

Naga is not happy because her pregnancy can reveal his identity; he does not know what to do. He just asks her to keep it secret from him as long as possible. She feels utterly confused and helpless because she can neither hide the pregnancy of five months nor have it aborted. She must have thought that the man is a mystery.

The next day, Appanna discovers that Rani is pregnant. Since he has never slept with her, he knows that she has committed adultery. This infuriates him and he pushes, kicks and curses her.

Appanna: Aren't you ashamed to admit it, you harlot? I locked you in, and yet you managed to find a lover! Tell me who it is. Who did you go to with your sari off?

Rani: I swear to you I haven't done anything wrong!

(33)

He does not accept her innocence. He cannot stand the shame that she has caused him. He drags her out and tries to throw a huge stone at her to smash her illegitimate child to be born. At the moment, the Cobra (Naga) comes out and hisses loudly. Appanna throws the stone at the snake which escapes into the anthill. Rani at once gets in and bolts the door behind her. He demands her to open the door and she does not obey her husband in order to escape his wrath. He goes out to request the Village Elders to sit in judgement and punish her severely. That night Naga comes and finds her crying. He sits glumly nearby and Rani asks: "Why are you humiliating me like this? Why are you stripping me naked in front of the whole village? Why don't you kill me instead? I would have killed myself. But there's not even a rope in this house for me to use." He says that the trial by the Elders cannot be avoided and he advises her to take the snake ordeal. He assures her that everything will be all right: "All will be well. Don't worry. Your husband will become your slave tomorrow. You will get all you have ever wanted." (35) She suddenly runs to him and embraces him. She says "please hold me tight. I am afraid." (35)

She notices his heart-beat which betrays his great anxiety. The mother in her tries to console him, "I mustn't let you go. I must listen to my head and hold you back. Take you like a baby in my arms and keep you safe." (35) When she turns to him, he is gone.

The Village Elders sit in judgement the next day. They listen to Appanna and Rani. They ask Rani to prove her chastity by taking the oath while holding a red-hot iron rod. But she requests them to permit her to take the snake ordeal. They concede to her request. She puts her hand in the anthill and takes the Cobra out. While holding it, she says that she has never touched anybody other than her husband and the Cobra. The Cobra slides up her shoulders and spreads its hood like an umbrella over her head. It sways its hood gently for a while, moves over her shoulder like a garland, slides down and goes into the anthill. Rani stares with confusion while people prostrate before her and praise her.

Elder-I: A miracle! A miracle!
Elder-II: She is not a woman. She is a Divine Being!
Elder-III: Indeed, a Goddess—! (39)

While Appanna stands uncomprehending, the people take Rani and Appanna in a palanquin to their house. The couple is taken in procession to their house.

Elder-I: Appana, your wife is not an ordinary woman. Don't grieve that you judged her wrongly and treated her badly. That is how goddesses reveal themselves to the world. You were the chosen instrument for revealing her divinity.
Elder-II: Spend the rest of your life in her service. You need merit in ten past lives to be chosen for such holy duty.
Elder-III: Bless us, Mother. Bless our children. (40)

When all the people are gone, Appanna also falls at her feet and says, "Forgive me. I am a sinner. I was blind." (40) She gently takes him in her arms. Thus as promised by Naga, she gets everything. Appanna becomes a devoted husband. Appanna's concubine becomes her servant-maid. In due course, Rani gives birth to a beautiful child.

In spite of all this, Appanna is not convinced of Rani's chastity. He says, "Have I sinned so much that even Nature should laugh at me?" (41) When Rani sleeps with her husband on the day of judgement, she comes to know that Naga in the guise of Appanna has been with her all these nights. She expresses her gratitude to Naga for all the help by making her son cremate the dead Cobra who commits suicide. Appanna also concedes to her request that their son should not only light the funeral pyre of Naga but also perform the annual rituals every year to commemorate his death. Appanna has never bothered about the purity of his wife and he and Rani have enjoyed happy marital life. They must have considered the problem of chastity a mere inconvenience as Story says: "When one says, 'And they lived happily ever after,' all that is taken for granted. You sweep such headaches under the pillow and then press your head firmly down on them. It is something one has to live with, like a husband who snores, or a wife who is going bald." (41)

Naga-Mandala is a feminist play. It questions the patriarchal moral code which demands the faithfulness of a woman to her husband but not the faithfulness of a man to his wife. This is accepted not only by men but also by women. Appanna openly and unashamedly commits adultery but nobody objects to it; the Village Elders who sit in judgement do not find fault with him. Nobody believes the innocence of Rani. She sleeps with Naga without knowing it. She does not discover the identity of Naga who assumes Appanna's form by using his magical power. Her failure to discover the truth is the suppression of her reason and intuition by the injunction of Appanna and Naga not to ask any questions (to remain ignorant). If she had discovered the real identity of Naga, she would not have allowed him to enter her bedroom. As a typical woman, she is frigid and despises sex. What she craves for is affection which Naga gives her in plenty by functioning as a surrogate parent for a while. By using his erotic art, Naga cures her of frigidity. Because of this later Appanna and Rani are able to enjoy marital life.

Rani is a simple, innocent and ignorant girl. She has grown

physically but not matured mentally. She behaves as a frightened child in the presence of Appanna. She grows as she receives the affection of Naga. She, a little helpless diffident girl, gradually becomes a confident and courageous lady. This can be seen when she speaks to Naga: "I was a stupid, ignorant girl when you brought me here. But now I am a woman, a wife, and I am going to be a mother. I am not a parrot." (32) She later shows the same courage which shocks Appanna: "(Snarling at Appanna) If you don't let go, I'll—(Taken aback by her fury, Appanna lets her go)." (38) After judgement, Rani becomes the head of the family. Appanna accepts her superiority and says to her, "You are no common person. You are a goddess." However the matriarchal Rani, unlike the past patriarchal Appanna, never orders him; she requests him if she needs a favour from him.

Rani:	(Almost to herself) A Cobra. It has to be ritually cremated. Can you grant me a favour?
Appanna:	As you say. (44)

Thus by showing a trace of matriarchy at the end, the play anticipates that matriarchy is to follow patriarchy if our society is to change for better.

The Dough Cock, *Hayavadana* and *Naga-Mandala* prove that chastity is a myth. If chastity is spiritual or psychological, Rani has not lost it though she sleeps with Naga before the judgement. The Queen in *The Dough Cock* loves a singer for his melodious voice without seeing him. He turns out to be ugly when she sees him; yet she sleeps with him since she has already committed adultery mentally. Padmini in *Hayavadana* enjoys marital life with Devadatta who gets Kapila's body after the transposition of heads. In addition, chastity is a patriarchal concept that has been used to oppress and weaken women for ages. The raped women and the women deceived by their lovers commit suicide while the men culprits go unpunished. It is clear that the concept of chastity is gender biased and that women care more for chastity than men. In Ben Jonson's *Volpone,* there is an incident similar to that in *Naga-Mandala*. Carvino has a very beautiful wife called Celia. He locks her in when he goes out. When he sends her to sleep with Volpone in order to inherit his property, Celia refuses to do so. This shows that the concept of chastity proves to be more powerful than the strongest lock.

Mandala is a tantric concept indicating inner concentration, a source of energy. Naga-Mandala is a magico-religious ritual involing Naga, the snake-god of Hindus who grants the wishes of his devotees, especially the wish for fertility. In the play, Naga grants Rani all her wishes which she does not express openly. She grows mentally and becomes a confident lady. She is cured of her frigidity. She gets a devoted husband. Her husband's concubine becomes a life-long servant-maid for her. And she begets a good son. Naga, in addition, makes Appanna's heart fertile with love and affection for his wife. At a higher level of symbolism, Naga represents a cultural leader who is instrumental in bringing about a socio-cultural reform.

NOTES

1. Srilatha Batliwala, "Why Do Women Oppress Women?" *The Hindu*, Sunday Magazine, May 2, 1993, p. iii.
2. Girish Karnad, *Naga-Mandala* (Delhi: Oxford University Press, 1990).
3. V. Rangan compares this with the episode of Ahalya in the *Ramayana* where Indra in the guise of Gautama visits Ahalya at midnight when Gautama goes out for meditation.

Naga-Mandala: A Story of Marriage and Love

SANTOSH GUPTA

Girish Karnad's plays reflect upon contemporary Indian cultural and social life through the use of folk tales, myths and historical legends. He weaves together timeless truths about human life and emotions contained in ancient Indian stories with the changing social mores and morals of modern life. His plays are particularly concerned with the psychological problems, dilemmas and conflicts experienced by the modern Indian men and women in their different social situations. His play *Naga-Mandala* (1988) is a powerful portrait of the agony and anguish faced by both men and women in their development into adult roles and social adjustment in a society where the individual is given little space for self-development, awareness and independence as a being.

The source-material of the *Naga-Mandala* comes, as Karnad informs the reader in his Introduction to the *Three Plays*, from a folk tale that he had heard from A.K. Ramanujan, who had collected many folk tales and their variants as they existed in different parts of India. The folk tale of a Prince whose extreme mistrust of women prevented him from loving any woman, and whose encounter with a woman's desire for love, has, as Ramanujan writes about this tale, as many as forty variants.[1]

The central theme of all these tales is, as Ramanujan remarks, "the narcissism" of the "self-involved hero," who undergoes a test put to him by the wife, in order to survive. The psychological inadequacy that the young man is caught in prevents his self transcendence, causing acute lack of understanding and communication between him and a woman. It is a threat to family and society, standing in the way of continuity of the race, and the story, and most of its variants have tragic ending.

This existential problem that perhaps every young man faces as he passes through adolescence, and must learn to overcome, becomes in Girish Karnad's play more comprehensive. For the *Naga-Mandala* is not only about the male difficulty to trust and love women, and transcend his narcissism. It seems to be about the socialization process of both men and women, particularly in the Indian society where marriage is, more often than not, the first experience of sex and love for most people. The transition from childhood into adolescence, and then into adult roles has, in India, very different stages and psychological and cultural relationships than in other less tradition-bound societies. The *Naga-Mandala*[2] probes into the female and the male growth into selfhood, and their mature adjustment with the social roles appointed for them by the traditional society.

Myths and folk tales in a patriarchal society represents primarily the male unconscious fears and wishes (Ramanujan, 12), and are patriarchal constructs and "man-oriented."[3] In these stories the woman's experiences and inner feelings often do not find adequate expression. They do not give much information about the women's fears, anxieties and psychological problems. Sudhir Kakar finds that these factors make it difficult for social scientists to gain insight into women's psychological inner being. It is a remarkable achievement of Karnad's play that he adapts this 'man-oriented' folk tale in such a manner that it becomes a representation of the experience of man and woman in the psychologically transitionary phase.

Naga-Mandala is the story of a young girl, Rani, newly married to Appanna, and their gradual understanding of the role, function and responsibilities of the institution of marriage. This story is presented in the play by a woman-narrator, a "flame" which has come to tell a story. The play begins in a temple on the outskirts of a village, where a passer-by stops at night for shelter. He then finds many tiny 'flames' entering the premises, who then start talking to each other. All the 'flames' have come from different households in the village, who, after the lights have been put out for the night, escape their houses, to collect, gossip and have some entertainment. Each flame is a female, a story-teller, sharing with the others her observations and new experiences. The stranger, a writer himself, enters into their conversation, and listens to a 'new' tale that has just escaped from an old woman's head.

The identification of the flames with young, sprightly and 'vocal' women, and stories that they tell each other is a brilliant device used by Karnad for creating a particularly female context and content in the 'man-oriented' folk tale. He brings within the play the strong association between oral narrative tradition and women's sub-culture, existing within the patriarchal societies. Women tell many of these folk tales, myths and legends, and in their telling, often reinvent and transform them. In the Introduction, Karnad says that women tell stories when putting children to bed or while doing their household chores. In the presence of other women and children, women give expression to their own point of view and experiences which are not perhaps permitted or recognised by patriarchal, classical stories. Their stories represent, Karnad says, a "distinctly woman's understanding of the reality around her, a lived counterpoint to the patriarchal structures of classical texts and institutions." (17) The female experience expressed in female narratives is woven within the folk tale as the "flame" tells her story to the professional, male playwright.

The flame begins her story of Rani and Appanna. The dramatization of the tale now begins. Both Rani and Appanna do not know how they can relate to each other. The young girl misses her parents, feels home-sick and lonely, while Appanna comes home only in the day, asks for food, stays for some time and then goes away. Every night he visits the concubine, which reflects his awareness of the biological aspect of sex.

This initial stage is painful for Rani, who is still very attached to her parents. The absence of any new attachment makes it difficult for her to mould herself in her new role of the wife, although she takes over the charge of the household. The pain and loneliness of Rani are emphasized by the narrator, drawing attention to her emotional state.

Appanna's behaviour reflects his divided emotional and physical selves. In fact the emotional aspect of his personality seems to be underdeveloped, as he treats both Rani and the prostitute in an unfair manner. Neither of the relationships is complete and satisfactory. Rani and Appanna are strangers to each other, as Appanna treats her with contempt, aggression and mistrust. He locks her in the room, and scolds the old lady Kurudavva and her son Kappana when they attempt to become friendly with Rani.

In her isolation Rani begins to build a world of stories around herself. She imagines herself to be a princess locked up by a demon, "So the demon locks her up in the castle. Then it rains for seven days. Then a big whale comes to Rani and says, 'Come, Rani, let us go.'" (35) Her story grows and perhaps it is in her fantasy that she takes a lover. Her story expresses her psychoerotic needs which she does not fully understand. But she needs to relate to someone, for it is through her relation with some other that she, as a woman is likely to realize herself.

Women's close-knit relationships with the other members of family and their lack of freedom to explore the world on their own is one of the reasons why identity for them is usually a matter of relationships. Sudhir Kakar points out that the "dominant psycho-social realities of a woman's life can be condensed into three stages. First, she is a daughter to her parents; second, she is a wife to her husband (and daughter-in-law to his parents); and third, she is a mother to her sons (and daughters)." It is through these three important relationships that a woman realizes her self and social significance. Rani's developmental struggle meets the first obstacle, as she lives with a man who does not give her the full physical and emotional relationship that should exist between a husband and wife. Rani's confusion is increased at the schizophrenic behaviour of the man who behaves so differently in the day and at night. The gap between the private and public selves is so great that it seems almost irreconcilable.[4]

The folk tale gets over this psychological self-division through the device of the snake-lover. In the folk tale there is a magician/snake who assumes the form of the Prince, enters the palace and woos the beautiful princess, locked in the palace. When the prince gets to know about it, he gets the snake/magician killed and the wife then sets him a riddle. If he fails to answer the riddle, he was to die. This existential crisis in the folk tale is treated in different ways in the different variants of the tale. In Karnad's play, the story takes a happy turn, both Rani and Appanna adjusting to the family and community in a socially useful manner. But this is achieved after upsetting the male egoism and exaggerated sense of power over women. The male assumption of keeping full control over the body, sexuality and virtue of women through the institutions of family and values like chastity, are mocked in the story, in the play, where the absent husband finds his substitute wooing his wife and taking his place. The woman's experience of her desires, dreams and ability to find means of satisfying them is expressed in the story, creating laughter.

The next important stage for facing the situation and their roles in it comes as Rani becomes pregnant. It is a moment of public acknowledgement of the private desire and act. Appanna is aghast at this development and takes his wife to a public trial. Rani finds herself alone in this crisis, for the lover as well as the husband fail to provide moral or emotional support. Rani is asked by the man at night, whom she takes to be her husband, to "speak the truth . . . what you think is not of any consequence. It must be the truth." (54) The truth for Rani is that she has been faithful to her husband. This conviction comes into the public. The nervous, frightened young girl finds within herself a new courage and confidence and gains social respectability. She emerges triumphant from the public trial, as the snake does not bite her. The cold, aggressive and indifferent husband is subdued, mildly tamed and accepts the judgement even if he is not fully convinced.

Appanna's violent reaction to his wife's 'infidelity' does not make him consider for a moment his own infidelity towards her. The other villagers also ignore this lapse on his part but they emphasize the institution of marriage and the procreative function of the couple. The importance of the family and progeny are established over and above personal self-seeking. The husband and wife turn towards each other, with a greater sense of relationship. The girl-bride now becomes the "mother-to be" and as such receives a new social recognition.

This stage of Rani's social integration brings her a new sense of respect and her own worth. This is another significant aspect of the Indian social and cultural life in its treatment of women. In Sudhir Kakar's words, "an Indian woman knows that motherhood confers upon her a purpose and identity that nothing else in her culture can." (56) As a mother, Rani is seen, in the last part of the story, to be in command of the household, with some authority and decision making power. Appanna even agrees to her rather strange demand that their son should perform an annual "pinda-daan" in the memory of the dead snake.

Naga-Mandala depicts the man and woman pass through several stages of doubt, uncertainty and even failures before they become mature and learn to live harmoniously as husband and wife, within the family-fold. Appanna becomes a caring and subdued husband, accepting Rani's decisions which may at times baffle him. This change in Rani's status comes through her motherhood, and the public trial, where her bold acceptance of the 'truth' gains her public respectability. This transformation of both Appanna and Rani presents the significance of the institution of marriage. It is through their adjustment that they gain a status within the life of the community. As individuals, they gain full selfhood only after going through these roles. Both man and woman accept the social pressure in putting aside personal feelings about selfhood, fantasies and dreams about love and freedom, and learns to surrender to the other, for the sake of family and community. Rani's dreams of a lover who had awakened her and loved her as a woman, and Appanna's self-centred and physical relationship with the prostitute, are given up, and they work together in the interest of the family and the community.

The public and private selves become connected through the acceptance of socially responsible roles. But does that completely dry up the hidden, suppressed desire for greater love and personal fulfilment? The double ending of the play *Naga-Mandala* presents this duality through the structural device. In End One of the story about Rani and Appanna, the Naga enters Rani's bedroom again and dies for the sake of Rani and her family. Though Rani grieves for her lover, the naga's sacrifice paves the way for Rani's happy married life.

In End Two of the play, the snake does not die. He is allowed by Rani to live in her tresses, her "dark, long and cool tresses, like snake-princess." (57) The lover is always present, he lives with her, within the family. The danger to male authority as a husband and patriarch lives on constantly, at close quarters, but mostly within the woman's imagination. The dutiful and loyal wife may observe the social, moral code entirely, yet within her live the memories of the perfect lover who had given her her first emotional and erotic experience. These desires may haunt her or lie dormant within. What matters most to Rani during the period of her relationship with the snake-lover is the awakening of desire and introducing her to love rather than to sex. Rani can understand sympathetically why Kapanna the young man who was bound by filial duty to his old and blind mother, runs away one night. He was pursuing his dream of a beautiful woman. Though he resisted the alluring voice and presence of the dream girl, trying to be a dutiful son and carried his old mother on his back, finally he is pulled away when the dreams become too powerful. Rani has gone through these new desires, the day-dreaming and fantasizing about love and she understands their power over other social and moral duties. She questions her 'story':

"Do desires really reach out from some other world beyond right into our bed?" (54)

The tremendous power of Eros in human life brings turmoil within the person and upsets the social life if it is denied proper recognition and expression. Publicly approved expression may not be possible due to oppressive norms and values of the society. The story of Rani as told by the woman narrator transforms the tale of the Prince which is tragic in its endings, to a mockery of the misogyny and self-centredness of the male world. The men who seek sexual satisfaction only and deny the importance of love and trust of woman in family and personal relationship are mocked in the exposure of the fragile hold they have over woman's mind, heart and even body. The need to provide great space to the woman is accepted by the village elders, who respect the procreative role of woman, compel the man to accept and respect his wife and change his egoistic and violent behaviour. It is an extremely ironic moment in the play when Appanna is left holding in public another man's child and asked to respect his wife as a "goddess."

Though the woman's tale mocks exaggerated male claims and ambitions to control female sexuality and virtue, the tale is not in the end disruptive. All the persons in the story surrender their self-centred seeking to the larger claims of the family, and community. The family structure is honoured and harmony prevails within the family. It paves the way for the happy ending, "and they lived happily ever after." (58)

The woman's story expresses the female point of view about her needs, problems and experiences within the patriarchal institutions. It provides an understanding into the complex nature of human relations while also showing women's ways of adjusting into their difficult social roles. The snake-lover's story has become a "vrat-katha," a story told as a festival of cobra worship, where women pray to the cobra for granting safety, and progeny to their family. A.K. Ramanujan writes that the "ritual tale itself is a public event told during the cobra festival to propitiate snake, to ensure safety and fertility within marriage." (12) This tale he feels socializes the "self-involved hero." More than that, it seems to be a public acknowledgement of the dangers to which marriage is always open, and a recognition of the blessing and goodwill of the outsider for bringing together the husband and the wife. Karnad uses the folk tale in its feminized form to present the problems faced by both man and woman in marriage and the process of transformation of the immature and emotionally under-developed person into a mature and fully grown adult.

At the end of the play, the male, professional playwright takes the responsibility of taking the "story" to a larger audience. This is another instance of the female narrative being assimilated into the 'patriarchal, classical' texts. But the structure of this play retains the individuality of the female narrative, centrestaging the women's experiences within marriage.

NOTES

1. A.K. Ramanujan, "The Prince Who Married His Own Left Half," *Aspects of India*, ed. Margaret Case and N. Gerald Barrier (New Delhi: Manohar, 1986), pp. 1-15.
2. Girish Karnad, *Three Plays* (New Delhi: Oxford Univ. Press, 1994).
3. Sudhir Kakar, *The Inner World*, rpt. *The Indian Psyche* (Oxford Univ. Press, 1996), p. 57.
4. Appanna's division into the Snake-Lover, the youthful Kappanna reflects the extreme division of the male persona, unable to come together in an integrated whole.

Naga-Mandala Reconsidered

PRANAV JOSHIPURA

This paper aims at studying some of the important aspects of *Naga-Mandala*. Girish Karnad, while using mythology, has put forward a question mark to some of the values of today. While we are busy satisfying ourselves, our desires, thirsts, we forget or overlook certain values which may lead us towards a stage from where we feel satisfied with ourselves, with what we have, what we possess. Although we live in this so-called 'society' where we are closely "related" to one another, we are totally 'alien' to each other. Our *Brihadaranyaka Upanishad* describes the formation of a human being as following: "In the beginning, this universe was nothing but the self in the form of a man. . . . He was as large as a man and woman embracing. This Self then divided itself into parts; and with that, there were a master and a mistress." This symbolizes the split of a whole human being into a man and a woman. The same symbolism can be found in the creation of Adam and Eve by God, as described in the *Bible*.

We are born whole human beings, but gender-based division of labour breaks us into male and female fragments. Each fragment retains only half of the human potential. The retained part overgrows to compensate for the other part which remains underdeveloped. These two polarized, deformed fragments are called men and women. Gender deformities are thus caused and gradually 'canonized' by socio-cultural programming of sex roles.

It is significant to note that the title of the play comes not from any human character, but from a snake—Naga. The story of the Cobra suggests that the play not merely dramatizes the folk tales in modern interpretation, it also implies a deeper meaning at various levels. In our Hindu mythology, the Naga represents several images. In South India, many houses have their own shrine which is often a grove reserved for snakes, consisting of trees, festooned with creepers, situated in a corner of the garden. Snakes are also the symbols of human maleness and strength. Nagas are sometimes portrayed as handsome men, or as half-man and half-snake, the top half using the torso of a man, the lower half a coiled snake. Karnad in *Naga-Mandala* has made use of the folk tales and the "mixing of human and non-human worlds" as a distancing device which brings in the element of alienation in the play. The folk tale element of *Naga-Mandala* and the magical power which the Cobra possesses remind us that we are watching a play. Moreover, the role of the Man and the Story is as the narrator-character. So, the play is interspersed with their analyses, observations and narrations which continually remind the spectator that he is only 'watching' a play.

In *Naga-Mandala*, Karnad has rejected the value of emotional identification. According to Girish Karnad: "The energy of folk theatre comes from the fact that although it seems to uphold traditional values, it also has the means of questioning these values, of making them literally stand on their head. The various conventions—the chorus, the mask, the seemingly unrelated comic episodes, the mixing of human and non-human worlds—permit the simultaneous presentation of alternative points of view, of alternative attitudes to the central problem. To use a phrase from Bertolt Brecht, these conventions then allow for 'complex seeing.'"

Rani, in *Naga-Mandala*, can be seen as a metaphor for the situation of a young girl in the bosom of a joint family where she sees her husband in two unconnected roles—as a stranger during the day and as a lover at night. The empty house Rani is locked in could be the family she is married into.

Kurudavva, the blind woman, plays a significant part in *Naga-Mandala*, though the only way she is connected with the plot of the play is that the Cobra falls in love with Rani because of the magical influence of the root given by Kurudavva to Rani. We can easily identify similarities between Goddess Kali of *Hayavadana* and Kurudavva in the sense that as Goddess Kali helps Padmini in relivening Devadatta and Kapila, in the same way, Kurudavva gives 'solution' to Rani's problem. But an error of destiny leads both of them, and, subsequently, the entire story towards a literal disaster. Can we call this disaster a part of human destiny, or a result of human error, or owing to a thirst, is a matter of debate.

Rani, too, resembles Padmini in many ways. Like Padmini at the Kali temple, she hurriedly, without thinking of the possible outcome, pours that magic 'blood like,' 'poisonous' paste in the ant-hill. It is from here that the entire story takes a turn. But the events which take place in Act Two raise many questions. Rani is sleeping in her bedroom. Naga moves near her and caresses her. Rani, not recognizing Naga disguised as Appanna, submits to Naga's advances. Rani's gesture is questionable because there are sufficient reasons to believe that Naga is not Appanna. On the night when the Cobra enters the darkened frontyard of Rani's house, she hears the sounds of the dog's growling and fighting, mixed with the hiss of the snake, whlch ends shortly after the dog gives a long painful howl. On the night when she moves into his arms, she notices blood on the Naga's cheeks and shoulders. She opens her mirror-box for the healing ointment. She screams in fright as she sees in the mirror a cobra in the place where the Naga was sitting. The next morning when Appanna comes, Rani's confusion is worst confounded. She says: "But last night . . . he had blood on his cheeks and shoulders. Now . . . " (29)

Another episode is that of the Cobra and the mongoose in which the Cobra is badly bitten by the mongoose. Therefore, he could not visit Rani for fifteen days. In the words of the story: "Rani spent her nights crying, wailing, pining for him. When he started coming again, his body was covered with wounds which had only partly healed. She applied her ointment to the wounds, tended him. But she never questioned him about them. It was enough that he had returned. Needless to say, when her husband came during day, there were no scars on him." (29)

Aren't these enough reasons to believe that the person who comes at night and the person who comes at day are different? If she takes it as an illusion, or a dream, then there are enough instances in the drama to come to reality. Moreover, the outcome of this situation applies to the fact that in this modern world the physical satisfaction is to be given high priority. This is clearly evident in Rani's words: "The smell of the blossoming nightqueen! How it fills the house before he comes! How it welcomes him! God, how it takes me, sets each fibre in me on fire!" (30)

If it is so, then what about the spiritual or moral situation of a person? Will one's soul accept it? What does Karnad have to say about it? In spite of the tangible proofs that the Naga is not Appanna, it is not clear whether Rani at all discovers the reality. The argument is very well supported by the Story when she expresses her doubts as to whether Rani could have lived happily even after. She reveals Rani's anguish in her narrative speech: "No two men make love alike. And that night of the Village Court, when her true husband climbed into bed with her, how could she fail to realise it was someone new? Even if she hadn't known earlier? When did the split take place? Every night this conundrum must have spread its hood at her. Don't you think she must have cried out in anguish to know the answer?" (41)

Thus both Rani and Appanna know that she has lost her chastity. But they do not bother about it. The story aptly comments: "It is something one has to live with, like a husband who snores or a wife who is going bald." (41)

In *Naga-Mandala*, if the Cobra is regarded as a totem possessing magical powers, the play is a folk drama. But if the Naga alludes to Rani's paramour, the play arouses our critical faculties, sets our mind to thought, and poses many problems. It leaves the audience to reflect on the efficacy of the social law which discriminates a woman from a man and which demands a wife's faithfulness even to her callous husband. Rani is required to undergo the trial by ordeal to prove her innocence. But Appanna can afford to indulge in adultery with impunity. Since neither Rani, nor Appanna, nor the Cobra is chaste, we may ponder over the idea that this world which is dominated by 'compromise' happiness, is incompatible with purity. It uncovers the injustice of the patriarchal moral code which demands the faithfulness of a woman to her husband but not the faithfulness of a man to his wife. The name Appanna means 'any man' and it is a wry comment on any man who tries to enforce chastity on his wife, while he himself indulges in extra-marital relationships. Marulasiddappa expresses an opinion similar to what the play argues: "The irony of the term 'fidelity' comes through in this sequence of events. Appanna and Naga—the two faces of one man, one seen at day, the other at night—symbolize the exploitation and double standards of man, while Rani is the symbol of a woman's eternal endurance of this oppression."

The notable features of this drama are the use of a chorus and music. In *Naga-Mandala* all the songs are sung by the Flames. At night the Man hears female voices outside the temple. He hides himself behind a pillar. Several flames enter the temple, giggling, talking to each other in female voices. The Man, addressing the audience, says: "I had heard that when lamps are put out in the village, the females gather in some remote place and spend the night together, gossipping. So this is where they gather!" (24) Here, the flames are the metaphors of the women of the village who have gathered at this time of night to tell tales and sing songs. The story of the flames comments on the paradoxical nature of oral tales in general: they have an existence of their own, they are independent of the teller and yet live only when they are passed on from the possessor of the tale to the listener. Similarly the status of a tale becomes akin to that of a daughter, for traditionally a daughter too is not meant to be kept at home too long but has to be passed on.

Shape shifting is another device very cleverly and effectively used by Karnad. Shape shifting in Karnad is not merely a central structural strategy but a means of reviving the ancient and sacred function of drama as ritual. *Naga-Mandala* has several examples of shape shifting. The main one is the Cobra assuming the form of Appanna to make love to Rani. Earlier, the flames take on human shapes to gossip at the temple after they have been 'put out' in the houses. In the New Flame's story of the old woman, who knew a story and a song, the story becomes a young woman and the song a sari. Wearing a sari, the story walks out of the old woman's house. The point is that stories mustn't be stingily confined to oneself as the old woman did, but shared. As Flame I puts it, "So if you try to gag one story, another happens." And later, the woman Rani, after her Cobra Ordeal, is apotheosized into a living goddess, an extraordinary woman.

The alternate dramatic criticism offered by the Man and the story and the enchantment of the action is in the nature of a workshop, of drama which appeals to the spectator's reason, contributes to the effect of the alienation, and suggests that the play mustn't be seen only as a folk drama. The Man argues that the "present ending just doesn't work," and that Appanna "will spend the rest of his days in misery." (41) At this Appanna suddenly moves out of Rani's embrace and makes a long aside which unravels his dilemma: "What am I to do? Is the whole world against me? Have I sinned so much that even Nature should laugh at me? I know I haven't slept with my wife. Let the world say what it likes. Let any miracle declare her a goddess. But I know! What sense am I to make of my life if it's worth nothing?" (41)

Naga-Mandala is a play about narrativity or the truth of fiction. The union of Rani and Naga is fruitful though the latter is not a man. This is simply because reality—Appanna—is harsh, unkind, and cruel, but fantasy, art, love—Naga—is more fulfilling, satisfying, and energizing. So, here recreation is literal—Rani and Naga have a child but not Rani and Appanna.

Girish Karnad explains the reason behind the 'nature' of the drama: "Whereas in public our middle-class has accepted the Western bourgeois notions of secularism, egalitarianism, and individual merit, while at home it remained committed to the traditional loyalties of caste, family, and religion." He further says: "Only a society which is honest enough to face the implications of this division squarely could produce meaningful drama of it."

Even Karnad seems to be torn between his Western mind and his affinity towards his religion, his mythology, which is very well reflected in *Naga-Mandala*, as well as in *Hayavadana*. It presses upon the mind of the reader that he has written the plays not as a matter of self-clarification alone, but as therapeutic device also. In the plays he is seized with the theme of incompleteness, as he makes it explicit. He seeks to exorcize himself of this demon of incompleteness by dramatizing the predicament, which is also the predicament of the class to which he belongs.

It is obvious that in *Naga-Mandala* Karnad has cut below the surface to reveal the burning core of mental or spiritual reality. The main concern of the playwright here becomes centred on human being in combination, interacting, entering into one another's lives, becoming part of one another. What Karnad seems to be primarily interested in is a real contact, a real meaning of the selves, depending on mutual knowledge. The abandonment of realism in this play takes us to a world that appears to be weird and even metaphysical. The primarily psychological treatment of character seems to embody a philosophy of life which emphasizes that events have meaning only in relation to the characters. And yet there is a patterning of human affairs by an agency which remains inscrutable. Karnad here presents a world where things happen inexplicably, and the schemes and intentions of people do not seem to control the action. Indeed Karnad's art can be described as a vision of reality.

Epic Theatre Revisited: A Study of *Naga-Mandala*

S.R. JALOTE

Girish Karnad (b. 1938) wrote his play *Naga-Mandala* originally in Kannada. In his note to the play, Karnad writes that his English translation of the play must be "seen only as an approximation to the original."[1] He observes, '*Naga-Mandala* is based on two oral tales from Karnataka which I first heard several years ago from Professor A.K. Ramanujan." (20) In his "Introduction" to *Three Plays* Karnad says: "These tales are narrated by women—normally the older women in the family—while children are being fed in the evenings in the kitchen or being put to bed. The other adults present on these occasions are also women. Therefore these tales, though directed at children, often serve as a parallel system of communication among the women in the family." (16-17)

Karnad admits Brecht's influence on his play. He observes: "And it must be admitted that Brecht's influence, received mainly through his writings and without the benefit of his theatrical productions, went some way in making us realize what could be done with the design of traditional theatre." (14)

Bertolt Brecht (1898-1956), the German poet and playwright, is the codifier of Epic Theatre. From the late 1920s dates his formulation of Epic Theatre which is a reaction against the traditional "Aristotelian" theatre of illusion. The essential point of Epic Theatre is that it appeals less to the spectator's feelings than to his reason. Brecht discusses the concept in his various works, but his main theoretical work on the topic is *Little Treatise on the Theatre* (1949). After emigration from Nazi Germany, he returned and settled in 1949 in East Berlin, where he founded and directed the Berliner Ensemble, his own company. The ensemble under Brecht exercised a profound influence in England, France, Italy, and the United States. Brecht used the platform as an arena unmasked the full stage, and exposed the lighting equipment that negated all Romantic-Symbolic-Illusionist-Idealistic theatre. Epic Theatre demonstrates the principles of multiplicity and simultaneity.

In a traditional theatre though the audience knows that it is watching an illusion of reality, it accepts it engaging in what S.T. Coleridge calls "that willing suspension of disbelief for the moment, which constitutes poetic faith."[2] In challenging the traditional principles of drama, Brecht questions the value of identification or empathy (*Enfuhlang*—translated as "to feel oneself into"). The theatrical alternative to empathy according to Brecht is Alienation or Estrangement (*Verfremdung*). According to Brecht we should not identify ourselves with the characters, but we should stand back from them. Brecht assumes that when we abandon empathy we can see the object in itself as it really is. He observes: "If the intercourse between stage and public were to occur on the basis of sympathetic understanding, then at any given moment the spectator could have seen only as much as the hero saw with whom he was joined in sympathetic understanding. . . . The stage could scarcely generate emotions, permit observations and facilitate understanding which are not suggestively represented on it."[3]

Brecht renounces the classical principle of pity and terror, "the twin-yoked classical cause of Aristotle's Catharsis,"[4] in favour of the process of alienation or estrangement. Instead of becoming emotionally involved in the stage action, the spectator should remain a dispassionate observer and judge. Brecht's aim was to teach men to think, to shake or enrage them into revolutionary action against social injustice. Brecht's theory of Epic Theatre is illustrated in its most significant form in *The Life of Galileo* (1937-9), *The Good Woman of Setzuan* (1938-41), *Mother Courage* (1941), *Puntilia and His Servants* (1948), and *The Caucasian Chalk Circle* (1948).

Though Karnad doesn't fully exploit the Brechtian artifice of Epic Theatre in *Naga-Mandala*, he claims that the play strikes a departure from the emotion-based world of traditional values. He observes: "The theatrical conventions Brecht was reacting against—character as a psychological construct providing a focus for emotional identification, the willing-suspension-of-disbelief syndrome, the notion of a unified spectacle—were never a part of the traditional Indian theatre. There was therefore no question of arriving at an 'alienation' effect by using Brechtian artifice. What he did was to sensitize us to the potentialities of non-naturalistic techniques available in our own theatre." (14-15)

In *Naga-Mandala* Karnad attempts at instilling an "alienation" effect by deriving the material of the play from the folk tales, and also by using the "non-naturalistic techniques" of the traditional Indian theatre. The title of the play is not the name of a human character, but it is that of a snake. The story of the cobra suggests that the play is intended to dramatize not merely the folk tales, but to imply a deeper meaning at various levels. In South India, many houses have their own shrine which is often a grove reserved for snakes, consisting of trees, festooned with creepers, situated in a corner of the garden. Often a stone with a snake depicted on it is set up, and women desiring children visit it. The Shaiva Lingayats worship snakes, which are often depicted with Shiva. Snakes are also the symbols of human maleness and strength. On the Naga-Panchami, the festival held in Sravana on the fifth day of the first half of the lunar moon, wrestling matches are organized, and women pour offerings of milk and cereals into the snakes' holes. Nagas are sometimes portrayed as handsome men, or as half-man and half-snake, the top half being the torso of a man, the lower half a coiled snake. Karnad has made use of the folk tales and the "mixing of human and non-human worlds" as a distancing device which brings in the element of alienation (*Verfremdung*) in the play. The folk-tale element of *Naga-Mandala* and the magical power which the cobra possesses continually remind the spectator that he is only watching a play. In *Naga-Mandala* Karnad has rejected the value of emotional identification and catharsis. The play leaves the audience in possession of their critical faculties, so that they may learn something conducive to social realism. Karnad observes:

> The energy of folk theatre comes from the fact that although it seems to uphold traditional values, it also has the means of questioning these values, of making them literally stand on their head. The various conventions—the chorus, the masks, the seemingly unrelated comic episodes, the mixing of human and non-human worlds—permit the simultaneous presentation of alternative points of view, of alternative attitudes to the central problem. To use a phrase from Bertolt Brecht, these conventions then allow for 'complex seeing.' (14)

In an Epic Theatre there are scenes of narration and commentary. In it a neutral area near the wings is occupied by the narrator—

character, who analyses the action or comments on it. Epic Theatre presents a series of loosely connected episodes in a simple way and in a kind of linear narration. It dispenses with the tradition of "dramatic" excitement and uses songs as an integral element. Neither the play nor the stage production maintain any consistent illusion to actuality. On the contrary such illusion is to be destroyed by fragmentation of scenes and settings and by the interruption of action. In a Brechtian theatre:

> The playwright was able to propose his play to the actors and the scenic designer in uninterrupted collaboration, to influence as well as be influenced. Painters and musicians at once regained their independence and were able through their own artificial means to make their presence felt on the subject matter: the collective art project appeared before the spectator as a series of dissociated elements.[4]

According to Brecht this new technique and style of production may not be complete and that experiments must continue.

Naga-Mandala, a play within the play, begins with the "Prologue." The characters of the "Prologue" are the narrator-characters of the play proper, and their story constitutes the sub-plot of the play. The setting of the "Prologue" is the inner sanctum of a ruined temple. A man, in a "morose stance," is sitting in the temple. He is sad because a mendicant has told him, "You must keep awake at least one whole night this month. If you can do that, you'll live. If not, you will die on the last night of the month." (22) The man has been dozing off every night, and tonight is the last night of the month. His guilt is that he has "written plays," says the mendicant, and thereby caused so many good people "to fall asleep twisted in miserable chairs." Hence there is "the Curse of Death" on him. (22-23) He swears that if he survives this night, he will "abjure all story-telling, all play-acting." (23)

The notable features of epic drama are the use of a chorus and music. In *Naga-Mandala* all the songs are sung by the Flames. At this time of night the Man hears female voices outside the temple. He hides himself behind a pillar. Several Flames enter the temple, giggling, talking to each other in female voices. The Man, addressing the audience says: "I had heard that when lamps are put out in the village, the flames gather in some remote place and spend the night together, gossipping. So this is where they gather!" (24) Here the Flames are metaphors of the women of the village who have gathered at this time of night to tell tales and sing songs. According to Karnad:

> The story of the flame comments on the paradoxical nature of oral tales in general: they have an existence of their own, independent of the teller and yet live only when they are passed on from the possessor of the tale to the listener. Seen thus, the status of a tale becomes akin to that of a daughter, for traditionally a daughter too is not meant to be kept at home too long but has to be passed on. This identity adds poignant and ironic undertones to the relationship of the teller to the tales. (17)

There also enters the Story, in the form of a woman dressed in a new, colourful sari. She goes and sits in a corner, and the Flames gather around her to listen to her. The Man is also keen to listen to her, because he doesn't want to doze off this night in order to remain alive. "Throughout the rest of the play, the Man and the Story remain on the stage. The Flames too listen attentively though from a distance." (26) In the rest of the play the Man and the Story play the part of the narrator-characters. The play is interspersed with their analyses, observations and narrations which continually remind the spectator that he is only watching a play.

When the curtain rises, there is seen on the stage the locked house with its front door and the interior. The opening speech of Act I is the long narrative speech delivered by the Story, the narrator-character:

> Story: A young girl it doesn't matter. But she was an only daughter, so her parents called her Rani. Queen. Queen of the whole wide world. . . . Her fond father found her a suitable husband. The young man was rich and his parents were both dead. Rani continued to live with her parents until she reached womanhood. Soon, her husband came and took her with him to his village. His name was—well, any common name will do . . .
>
> Man: Appanna?
>
> Story: Appanna.

Rani's problem in Appanna's house could be the problem of any bride in a Hindu family. Appanna treats Rani very rudely. He comes home only for his lunch, locks the house from outside and goes away. Rani tells Appanna that she feels frightened alone at night, but he pays no attention to her. The story, in her brief speech, narrates, "And so the days rolled by." (28) Thus the play *Naga-Mandala* offers a study in the patriarchal structures of the traditional families. Karnad says: "The position of Rani in the story of *Naga-Mandala*, for instance, can be seen as a metaphor for the situation of a young girl in the bosom of a joint family where she sees her husband in two unconnected roles—as a stranger during the day and as lover at night. . . . The empty house Rani is locked in could be the family she is married into." (17)

As in an Epic Theatre, so in *Naga-Mandala* there are loosely connected episodes in a kind of linear narration. Though Kurudavva, the blind woman, plays a significant part in *Naga-Mandala*, her marriage to a boy distantly related to her, her intense love for her son, Kappanna, and her subsequent insanity form the subplot of the play. The only way in which Kurudavva is connected with the plot of the play is that the Cobra falls in love with Rani because of the magical influence of the root given by Kurudavva to Rani. Kurudavva has been the best friend of Appanna's mother. Kurudavva feels very much concerned for Rani's miserable plight that Appanna has "got himself a bride—and he still goes after that harlot?" (29) She gives Rani the piece of a root, which was given to her by a mendicant, saying, "Take it! Grind it into a nice paste and feed it to your husband. And watch the results. Once he smells you he won't go sniffing after that witch." (34) When Appanna comes as usual for his lunch, Rani takes out the paste of the root, but she dares not pour it into the curry. She exclaims: "On my god! What horrible mess is this? Blood. Perhaps poison. Shall I serve him this? That woman is blind, but he isn't. How could he possibly not see this boiling blood, this poisonous red? And then—even if he doesn't see it—how do I know it is not dangerous? Suppose something happens to my husband? What will my fate be? That little piece made him ill. Who knows. . . ?" (37) Rani resolves that she must get rid of the paste before Appanna notices anything. She runs to the tall ant-hill and pours the liquid into it. A King Cobra lifts its hood out of the ant-hill. The paste of the root tasted by the Cobra has its effect on him and he at once falls in love with Rani.

Act One ends with a brief narrative speech of the Story. She says that as a cobra can assume any form it likes, that night it enters into the house through the bathroom drain and takes the shape of Appanna. In the rest of the play the Cobra in the disguise of Appanna is called Naga.

The events which take place in Act Two may be seen both from the temporal as well as the spiritual points of view. Rani is sleeping in her bedroom. Naga moves nearer her and caresses her. Rani, not recognizing Naga disguised as Appanna, submits to Naga's advances. Naga tells Rani that he wants her to be fresh and bright when he comes home every night from now on. He spends the night with her in her bed, and as it dawns he goes to the bathroom, turns into his original self and slithers away. In the morning Appanna comes, unlocks the door, steps in, has his lunch and goes away. It goes on like this for many days.

Thus it may be seen that there is a dichotomy in the Naga's relationship with Rani. On the supernatural level the Cobra is a totem for the Hindus. It falls in love with Rani, and it takes the human shape and form in order to extend happiness to her. But on the temporal level the Cobra alludes to a lover who is enthralled by Rani's beauty and visits her in the night. Rani is puzzled to think as to whether she has been dreaming or she has gone mad. The diametrically opposed behaviour of the Naga and Appanna confound her. She says to Naga: "Goodness! Goats have to be sacrificed and buffaloes slaughtered to get a word out of you in the morning. But at night—how you talk! Snakes and lizards may do what they like, but human beings should have some sense of shame." (45)

Moreover Rani has sufficient reasons to believe that the Naga is not Appanna. On the night when the Cobra enters the darkened front yard of Rani's house, she hears the sounds of the dog's growling and fighting, mixed with the hiss of the snake, which ends shortly after the dog gives a long painful howl. On that night when she moves into his arms, she notices blood on the Naga's cheeks and shoulders. She opens her mirror-box in which she has kept the healing ointment. She screams in fright as she looks at the Naga in the mirror. At the place where the Naga is sitting, she sees a Cobra. The next morning when Appanna comes, Rani's confusion is worst confounded. She says: "But last night . . . he had blood on his cheeks . . . and shoulders. Now . . ." (48)

The next episode relating to the Cobra and the mongoose, and

Rani's increasing suspicion about the Naga's identity is narrated by the Story. The mongoose dies in its fight with the Cobra. But the mongoose gives a tough fight, and the Cobra is badly bitten by the mongoose. The Naga, therefore, could not visit Rani for the next fifteen days. The Story continues: "Rani spent her nights crying, wailing, pining for him. When he started coming again, his body was covered with wounds which had only partly healed. She applied her ointment to the wounds, tended him. But she never questioned him about them. It was enough that he had returned. Needless to say, when her husband came during the day, there were no scars on him." Rani is so much enamoured of the Naga's love that in spite of the tangible proofs relating to the striking differences between the Naga and Appanna, she never cares to resolve the riddle. She says: "The smell of the blossoming nightqueen! How it fills the house before he comes! How it welcomes him! God, how it takes me, sets each fibre in me on fire! (49)

In spite of the tangible proofs that the Naga is not Appanna, it is not clear in the play whether Rani at all discovers the reality. In Act II the love of the Naga and Apanna is presented in an exotic manner when they embrace and dance as the Flames surround them and sing. One day as the Naga and Rani are lying together on the bed, Rani tells the Naga that she is pregnant. She is very happy because she feels that all her anxieties are over. Now she has the definite evidence to prove that she has not been fantasizing. But the news doesn't make the Naga happy and he asks her to keep it a secret as long as possible. The audience is aware of the dramatic irony in the play, when Rani says to the Naga in an agony: "Why don't you take it on trust that I have a mind and explain this charade to me? Why do you play these games? Why do you change like a chameleon from day to night? Even if I understood a little, a tiny bit—I could bear it. But now—sometimes I feel my head is going to burst!" (51)

In the Epic Theatre by means of numerous "distancing" devices the spectator is continually reminded that he is only watching a play. Epic stage directors press into service moving or revolving platforms, treadmills carrying pieces of scenery, charts, cartoons, and projected films. In *Naga-Mandala* the setting changes abruptly as in a cinematograph. As soon as it dawns and the Naga takes a step to go, the lights change sharply from night to mid-day. "In a flash, Naga becomes Appanna: pushes her to the floor and kicks her." He charges Rani: "Aren't you ashamed to admit it, you harlot? I locked you in, and yet you managed to find a lover! Tell me who it is. Who did you go to with your sari off?" (52)

Appanna exits and the lights change to night. Rani is crying on the floor, Naga comes and sits glumly nearby. He says that her being summoned by the Village Elders cannot be avoided, and that she should take the snake ordeal to prove her innocence. A King Cobra lives in the enormous ant-hill under the banyan tree. She should put her hand into the ant-hill, pull out the King Cobra and take her oath by the Cobra. If she tells the truth by holding the Cobra, it won't bite her. He says, "Your husband will become your slave tomorrow. You will get all you have ever wanted." (54) As he turns to go, she runs to him and embraces him. He slowly moves her away, moves down the steps, turns into a snake and goes away. There is a sudden commotion on the stage. Crowds of villagers fill the stage from all sides, and the stage becomes the village square. The three Elders come and take their positions near the ant-hill.

The scene of Rani's trial reminds us of Sita's trial in the *Ramayana,* and it shows its affinities with the traditional Indian values. The traditional test in the Village Court has been to take the oath while holding a red-hot iron in the hand. But Rani insists, "I must swear by the King Cobra." (55) She steps up to the ant-hill, plunges her hand into it, pulls the Cobra out and says: "Since coming to this village, I have held by this hand, only two. . . . My husband and . . . And this Cobra. . . . Yes, my husband and this King Cobra. Except for these two, I have not touched any of the male sex. Nor have I allowed any other male to touch me. If I lie, let the Cobra bite me." (58) The Cobra doesn't bite Rani. Instead it slides up her shoulders, spreads its hood like an umbrella over her head, moves over her shoulder like a garland, and then slips back into the ant-hill. There are hosannas and cheers from the crowd. The Elders fall at her feet and the crowd surges forward to prostrate itself before her. The couple, being seated in a palanquin, is taken in a procession to their house. The Elders tell Appanna that his wife is a goddess incarnate, and that he should spend the rest of his life in her service. All disperse, except Rani and Appanna. Appanna falls at her feet and begs her forgiveness. Rani gently takes him in her arms. The story narrates the following subsequent events which are not presented on the stage: "So Rani got everything she wished for, a devoted husband, a happy life. She even got a life-long servant to draw water for her house. For Appanna's concubine was present at the trial. When she saw Rani's glory, she felt ashamed of her sinful life and volunteered to do menial work in Rani's house. In due course, Rani gave birth to a beautiful child. A son. Rani lived happily ever after with her husband, child and servant. (59)

There is a hubbub created by the Flames as they prepare to leave. The conversation which follows is in the nature of a panel discussion between the Man and the Story about the popular tastes and concerns regarding the appropriate ending of the play. The discussion brings home to us that in this play the Man is the metaphor of the playwright and his critical faculty, the Story is that of his poetic imagination, and the Flames may stand for both the village women and the audience:

Man: (Exasperated) These Flames are worse than my audience. Can't they wait till the story is over?
Flame 1: But isn't it?
Man: It can't be. No one will accept this ending.
Story: But why not?
Man: Too many loose ends. Take Kappanna's disappearance, for instance . . .
Story: Oh, that is Kurudavva's story. . . . I am only Rani's story. (59-60)

The alternate dramatic criticism offered by the Man and the Story and the enactment of the action is in the nature of a workshop, of drama which appeals to the spectators' reason, contributes to the effect of alienation (*Verfremdung*), and suggests that the play may not be seen only as a folk drama. The Man argues that the "present ending just doesn't work," and that Appanna "will spend the rest of his days in misery." (60) At this Appanna suddenly moves out of Rani's embrace and makes a long aside which unravels his dilemma: "What am I to do? Is the whole world against me? Have I sinned so much that even Nature should laugh at me? I know I haven't slept with my wife. Let the world say what it likes. Let any miracle declare her a goddess. But I know! What sense am I to make of my life if that's worth nothing?" (60)

The Story, in modification of her earlier statement, expresses her doubts as to whether Rani could have lived happily ever after. She reveals Rani's anguish in her narrative speech: "No two men make love alike. And that night of the Village Court, when her true husband climbed into bed with her, how could she fail to realize it was someone new? Even if she hadn't known earlier? When did the split take place? Every night this conundrum must have spread its hood out at her. Don't you think she must have cried out in anguish to know the answer?" (60) The Man suggests that the ending of the play at this point is unsatisfactory in the sense that the Cobra's story is yet incomplete. The Story, therefore, continues: "Yes, the Cobra. One day the Cobra was sitting in its ant-hill and it thought of Rani and said: 'Why should I not go and take a look?'" (61) During the above dialogue, the Cobra enters the house and becomes the Naga. It is night and the Naga is besotted with Rani. Rani is sleeping next to her husband and her child is by her side. The Naga cannot bear to see this scene and decides that someone must die. He cannot kill Rani, because of his passionate love for her. Moreover he thinks that Rani belongs to one "who is forever a man." (61) The Naga summons his magical powers and becomes as thin and small as the size of Rani's tresses. He ties a tress into a noose and places it around his neck. In the morning Rani feels as if her head "weighs a ton." (62) Something has caught up in her tresses. Appanna, therefore, combs her hair and a dead cobra falls to the ground. Appanna, overwhelmed with awe, says: "Your long hair saved us, Rani. The Elders were right. You are no common person. You are a goddess." (63)

It is not explicit in the play as to whether Rani regards the Cobra merely as a totem. She says that the Cobra has given the gift of life to her son, as by a father. Therefore, the Cobra has to be ritually cremated and that "the fire should be lit by our son." (63) She adds, "And every year on this day, our son should perform the rituals to commemorate its death." (63) Appanna thinks that Rani is going too far, because these rituals are performed by the son for his deceased father. But he has come to believe that Rani is "the goddess herself incarnate." (63) He, therefore, accedes that every wish of Rani will be carried out Rani's eyes are filled with tears. She picks up the dead snake and presses it to her cheeks.

The Story exits and the subject of the brief discussion which ensues is the ending of the play as tragedy. The Flames prefer happy endings, but the Man holds the view that death is the inescapable truth. However, for the gratification of others, the Man gives the alternative ending in which the play ends happily. Rani and Appanna are sleeping with the child next to them. Rani suddenly moans and sits up. Holding her hair she says that something hurts her. She tries to comb her hair, but cannot. She gives the comb to Appanna. As he combs her hair, a live snake falls out of her hair and lies writhing on the floor. Appanna runs out to search for a stick in order to kill the snake. Rani lets her hair down to the floor and hides the snake in her tresses. Patting her hair she addresses the snake, "This hair is the symbol of my wedded bliss. Live in there happily, for ever." (64) The Flames disappear one by one. It is morning and the Man is sitting alone in the inner sanctum of the temple. He bows to the audience and goes out.

In many ways epic drama has much in common with documentary theatre. Though not overtly a propagandist drama, much of epic drama is devoted to the expression of social and political ideas and the ideals. In *Naga-Mandala* if the Cobra is regarded as a totem possessing magical powers, the play is a folk drama. But if the Naga alludes to Rani's paramour, the play arouses our critical faculties, sets our minds to thought, and poses many problems. It leaves the audience to reflect on the efficacy of the social laws which discriminate a woman from a man and which demand a wife's faithfulness even to her callous husband. Rani is required to undergo the trial by ordeal to prove her innocence. But Appanna can afford to indulge in adultery with impunity. Since neither Rani nor Appanna nor the Cobra is chaste, the spectator may ponder over the idea that in this world dominated by compromise happiness is incompatible with purity. Though in the heart of their hearts both Appanna and Rani know that their child is born out of wedlock, they accept the child as their own. They do not share the secret even with each other. They probably think it better to let the secret remain buried in their hearts, and keep the family together.

NOTES

1. Girish Karnad, *Three Plays: Naga-Mandala, Hayavadana, Tughlaq* (Delhi: Oxford University Press, 1994) 20.
2. Coleridge, *Biographia Literaria* (1817) Chapter XIV.
3. Bertolt Brecht, "On Experimental Theatre," in *Perspectives on Drama*, ed. James L. Calderwood and Harold E. Toliver (New York: Oxford University Press, 1968) 271.
4. *Ibid.*
5. *Ibid.* 274.

Psychology of Social Development: A Study of *Naga-Mandala* and *Tale-Danda*

VEENA NOBLE DASS

In its original version, a series of essays, Sri Aurobindo's *The Human Cycle* was called *The Psychology of Social Development.* The work is too little known for its importance. Its major importance lies in the fact that we have in him an eastern visionary as aware of western thought and history as of the perennial insights, models that are not fools of time. Secondly, the insights are more forward-looking rather than backward. Thirdly, he gives to the idea of evolution a prophetic perfectionist dimension, assimilates it to mankind's oldest yearnings for a holistic and higher harmony, the plentitudes of deeper harmony.

The essays offer not only a creative critique of contemporary theory and practice but also the rationale of man's need of integrality and his impulse of self exceeding if we would fix rightly the meaning of his individual existence and the perfect aim and norm of his society.[1] Here is not only the crisis but its psychological cure, one that can counter, in a richer synthesis the dialectics of other-worldly and this-worldly bias.

But why psychology? Sri Aurobindo puts the explanation or hypothesis thus: there are necessarily three stages of the social evolution. It starts with the infra-rational stages, proceeds towards a rational age, finally must move through a subjective towards a spiritual age. These stages, or periods need not be naturally exclusive and absolute but are much inevitable in the psychological evolution of mankind than the stone or other ages for they depend on the very nature of his being.[2] The Aurobindean view presents a dynamic ontology according to which we say that self-realization is the sense, secret or overt of individual and social development.

The paper aims at projecting a psycho-analytical interpretation of Karnad's plays which in turn reflect the Indian social milieu and the role the individual character or group of characters play for individual or social development.

The play *Naga-Mandala* as the name suggests revolves around a woman and a serpent. This play is based on a folk tale and it is interesting to observe that the serpent forms an important ingredient in most narratives all over the world. Martin S. Day (1984) states that there exists a theory that the mothers of great men in history such as Scipio Africans, Alexander the Great and Augustus Caesar were all impregnated by serpents. He also says that snake myths are found extensively in Brahamanism, Buddhist, Lamaistic and Javanese writings.

Snake worship is still practised in the southern states in India such as Kerala, Karnataka and Madras. The play *Naga-Mandala* presents a fantasy world. It has the ingredients present in dreams of every individual. The action begins in an abandoned temple. The fantasy is enhanced by the arrival of the flames who talk. Their talk brings out intimate details of the households they inhabit. Their talk is tinged with eroticism and this again serves as a precusor to the events that follow. Finally the story and the song disguised as a young woman and her sari make their appearance and contribute to the finishing touches of the fantasy world.

It is interesting to note how the story is born. One of the flames recounts the details. The flame was from a house in which an old man and an old woman lived. This old woman knew a story and a song which she had always kept to herself. That afternoon while she was sleeping the story and the song emerged out of her and hid in the attic. At night the story took the form of a young woman and the song became her sari.

This event needs to be looked into in detail. Freud's main contribution is the division of the mind into the conscious and unconscious. He felt that the individual puts away unwanted or asocial elements into the unconscious. But depending on the experiences they can only do so through dreams from where they can come back once again. Freud divided the conscious mind into the Id, Ego and super ego. This play is narrated by the story woman and this is a clever device to allow for further displacement and disguise. The play thus can be interpreted in Freudian terms by applying his views on dreams. In dreams the individual does not matter, for sometimes one or many individuals can constitute one form. (This is called condensation.) What matters is the ideas they represent. Hence the story states that the main characters' names are not important. It gives the names Rani and Appanna and adds, "any common name would do."[3] We can even go to the extent of calling them every man and woman because the experience that they undergo is typically the experience of many young men and women.

Rani enters her wedded life like most girls with a lot of expectation but is shocked by Appanna's neglect. Marriage is a milestone in a person's life and since it presents a hostile environment her mind indulges in dreams in order to calm her troubled self. She, like a hurt child, dreams of a fairyland which can be reached only after crossing seven seas and seven isles. And in a magic garden her parents wait for her and receive her with love. This act of combating the present circumstance by withdrawing into an earlier pleasant state is known in psychology as Regression.

Rani's further encounters with her husband leave her disappointed and her dreams about her parents recur more frequently. They comfort her and now a new dimension enters her dream content. She dreams of a male deer which asks her to come away with her. But she is afraid to accept her invitation and he replies: "I am not a stag, I am a prince." (28) According to Karnad, "The position of Rani in the story of *Naga-Mandala* can be seen as a metaphor for the situation of a young girl in the bosom of a joint family where she sees her husband only in two unconnected roles—as a stranger during the day and as lover at night. Inevitably, the pattern of relationships she is forced to weave from these disjointed encounters must be something of a fiction. The empty house Rani is locked in could be the family she is married into."[4]

Many of these narrated tales here talk about the nature of tales. The story of the flames comments on the paradoxical nature of oral tales in general: they have an existence of their own, independent of the teller and yet live only when they are passed on from the possessor of the tale to the listener. Seen thus, the status of a tale becomes akin to that of a daughter, for traditionally a daughter too is not meant to be kept at home too long, but has to be passed on. This identity adds poignant and ironic undertones to the relationship of the teller to the tales.

The story for his other play *Tale-Danda* which literally means beheading is borrowed by Karnad from an important historical movement that took place in the city of Kalyan in 1168 A.D. The movement was started by a group of poets, philosophers, mystics and social revolutionaries which wanted to revolutionise the society as well as change the age old practices of the evils of caste system. It resulted in an age of creativity, courageous questioning and social commitment which was unmatched in the hisotry of Kannada. They used the language of common man, instead of Sanskrit and talked to people about god in the language which they could understand. They even went to the extent of condemning idolatry and temple worship. They wantned to bring about a complete change and believed in the principle of movement and progress in human enterprise and opposed any kind of static situation. Even in that age they believed in the equality of sexes as well as committed hard work. Because of their commitment to oppose caste system they were humiliated and the anger and displeasure of the orthodox community came down heavily on them. Finally the movement ended in terror and bloodshed.

In the words of Karnad, "I wrote *Tale-Danda* in 1989 when the Mandir and the Mandal movements were beginning to show again how relevant the questions posed by these thinkers were for our age. The horror of subsequent events and the religious fanatics that has gripped our national life today have only proved how dangerous it is to ignore the solutions they offered."[5]

The language of the play is also quite relevant to the situation. According to Karnad, "In Karnataka as elsewhere in India, a man has only to open his mouth and his speech will give away his caste, his geographical origins, even his economic status. In the original Kannada version of *Tale-Danda* the language of the play engages with the implications of this fact for a situation in which a group of people are trying to fight caste and social inequality."[6] This view can be justified by taking few lines from the text:

> Mallibomma: Don't be silly. I shouldn't have even stepped into this brahmin street. And you want me to come into your house? No. Thank you. (2)
>
> Damodara: Indrani, the Rig Veda tells us that the four varnas flowed out of the primordial Man: the brahmin from the head, the shudra from the feet.

These two quotations show us clearly the deep-rooted feelings of caste that were imbedded in the psyche of the people which affected the society at large.

NOTES

1. Sri Aurobindo, *The Human Cycle* (MacMillan India, rpt. 1987), p. 89.
2. *Ibid.*, p. 6.
3. Girish Karnad, *Three Plays* (OUP, 1995), Act I, p. 27.
4. "Introduction," *Ibid.*, p. 17.
5. Girish Karnad. "Introduction," *Tale-Danda* (New Delhi: Ravi Dayal, 1993).
6. Note to the text. *Ibid.*

Social Deformity in *Tale-Danda*

M. SARAT BABU

> From this moment all *sharanas*, foreigners, and free thinkers are expelled from this land on pain of death. Women and the lower orders shall live within the norms prescribed by our ancient tradition, or else they'll suffer like dogs.
>
> *Tale-Danda*

> Disregarding for the moment the ideological distinctions among various Vedic cosmogonies, they all seem to be in agreement concerning one matter: the world we live in and know it emerged from a powerfully disruptive partition of a precosmogonic unity in accordance with the dictates of the law of necessity (Rta).[1]

The Vedic cosmogonies symbolically reveal that the division of labour is an indispensable evil of civilization. These divisions did not remain horizontal for long but were hierarchized by the human urge to overcome the feelings of inferiority caused by the alienation of human beings from Nature and to prove their power and superiority. The hierarchization, a major process of civilization, gave rise to competition which replaced cooperation. And the urge for superiority, as Adler would have argued, effected privatization, another major process of civilization. This process caused private family and private property. Even human love underwent privatization and so individualism emerged and replaced collectivism. Hierarchization and privatization have supported and sustained each other. All this has caused and consolidated social deformity and inequality.

Exploitation and oppression have become a 'natural' norm in our society as it has absorbed and observed individualism and competition. Consequently everybody takes inequality for granted. Steiner aptly points out, "The difficulty which we have in feeling equality with all other human beings is the result in part of our banal training in competitiveness and individualism."[2] He later talks about the dehumanizing effect of competition: "In our mad scramble to the top we forget how to love, how to think, and we lose track of who we are and what we really want." (187) Marx also comments on the evil effects of the division of labour and social deformity: "It proved, incontrovertibly, the disastrous effects of machinery and division of labour; the concentration of capital and land in a few hands; over-production and crises."[3]

The social deformity in the Hindu society took the form of 'caste system.' The Hindu society consists of four recognized classes called *Varnas* and one unrecognized class called *avarnas*. They are Brahmins (priests, poets, teachers and ministers), Kshatriyas (Kings and Warriors), Vaishyas (tradesmen), Shudras (craftsmen) and Panchamas (menial workers). Shudras and Panchamas toil and produce wealth which the people of higher classes enjoy. According to a Hindu myth, the four recognized classes emanated from the mouth, the arms, the thighs and the feet of Brahma, the God of Creation, respectively. Such myths and literature, created and perpetuated by Brahmins, seek to justify the social hierarchy and sanction their superiority. Stanley Rice rightly observes:

> If, then, it be admitted that Brahmans, at least in the earlier stages, became the superior caste by reason of their priestly office and all that is thereby implied, it is not unnatural that they should have made use of their position to glorify themselves, as the priesthood has shown itself apt to do in other countries. That they did this in extravagant fashion, claiming privileges unheard elsewhere and even arrogating to themselves the position divinities[4] may be admitted.[5]

Shudras and Panchamas are subdivided into various castes. Ambedkar elaborates on this: "Caste system is not merely a division of labourers—which is quite different from division of labour—it is an hierarchy in which the divisions of labourers are graded one about the other."[6] The gradation of the various castes of labourers prevents them from being united and makes them easily exploitable. Moreover Manu says: "A Brahmana may compel a Shudra, whether bought or unbought, to do servile work; for he is created by the

Creator to be the slave of a Brahmana."[7] He prescribes severe punishment to Shudras for reading Vedas[8] and for insulting higher caste people. Panchamas are humiliated, oppressed and exploited more than Shudras for they are considered untouchable. This is the most inhuman part of Hindu culture and so Gandhiji considers it a great stigma on Hinduism. Since caste system gives Brahmins and other higher castes a privileged position, they have never tolerated any violation, including an inter-caste marriage and have punished the people most cruelly for violating the conventions of the caste system.

The social deformity of the Hindu society has not changed much for ages. Gross atrocities are committed on Shudras and Panchamas by high caste Hindus at one place or another, even now in the modern age of democracy.[9] Like Mulk Raj Anand and Bhabani Bhattacharya in Indian English fiction, Badal Sircar and Mohan Rakesh in Indian English drama, Girish Karnad is concerned with social deformity and exposes the evil effects of caste and class in his play *Tale-Danda*.

Karnad's *Tale-Danda* exposes the ugly deformity of the Hindu society by depicting the twelfth century communal struggle in the city of Kalyan in North Kanara when Bijjala was the king. In his court, there were great scholars and poets. Basavanna, the king's officer and the great poet-philosopher, united those brilliant people and fought for equality. They shed their castes and became *sharanas* or devotees of Lord Shiva. They talked about God in the language of common people. They considered their body the very abode of God and denounced idolatry. They condemned all the inhuman traditions and believed in social and gender equality. Finally their noble movement ended in a disaster when the marriage of a Brahmin girl to a Panchama boy led to the fateful war between *sharanas* and orthodox people.

Bijjala, a Shudra, a barber by caste, becomes the king of Kalyan. He himself says how he has become a Kshatriya: "For ten generations my forefathers ravaged the land as robber barons. For another five they ruled as the trusted feudatories of the Emperor himself. They married into every royal family in sight. Bribed generations of Brahmins with millions of cows. All this so they could have the caste of Kshatriya branded on their foreheads."[10] Bijjala also marries a royal princess, Rambhavati and has a son, Sovideva. He loves Sovideva but detests his unprincely behaviour. So he does not favour him while he makes the sons of his other wives local lords. Sovideva resents this greatly.

Bijjala knows that the people of higher castes do not respect him properly. He admits: "In all my sixty two years, the only people who have looked me in the eye without a reference to my lowly birth lurking deep in their eyes are the *sharanas*: Basavanna and his men." (15) Moreover his city flourishes because of their hard work and devotion. While accounting for his love of *sharanas*, the king himself says:

> Every *sharana* seeks only to earn the day's keep, makes no extra demands, treats profits with contempt. So who profits? From every corner of the country, trade and commerce have come pouring into Kalyan, and now the city is bursting at its seams with money and activity. Even those who despise the *sharanas* for their beliefs need them for their economic enterprise—as indeed I do— and they pour money into the *sharana* coffers. (24)

Thus Bijjala feels grateful to Basavanna and his men. But his son, Sovideva is not happy about it. He dislikes Basavanna and his philosophy. He knows that Basavanna spends large amounts of money on his hospitality to his guests. So he suspects that Basavanna has stolen money from the royal treasury. He therefore decides to prove this by opening the treasury. Thus, he wants to win his father's favour by making Basavanna unpopular.

Jagadeva, a *sharana*, comes to know Sovideva's plan to open the royal treasury. At once, he gathers thousands of *sharanas* and encircles it. Thus, he prevents Sovideva from tampering with it. Meanwhile Basavanna comes and immediately sends Jagadeva to attend to his ailing father. He takes Sovideva into custody, finds the treasury intact after verification and then releases him. People consider it miraculous that the treasury is intact. Bijjala scolds Sovideva severely for his misdeed. So, Sovideva feels deeply frustrated, humiliated and hurt. He, therefore, decides to avenge this on his father and Basavanna. Damodara Bhatta, Queen's priest and Manchanna Kramita, the Brahmin adviser to the king, are very unhappy about Basavanna's mission and Bijjala's support to it. So, they join hands with Sovideva in the plot against Bijjala and Basavanna.

Jagadeva goes home and finds his father on death bed. His father's death makes him remorseful of neglecting home and so performs all the funeral rites for his father though it is contrary to his new faith. His emotion gets reversed as Basavanna visits him to express his condolences. Disturbed by the feelings of guilt for betraying the *sharana*-faith, Jagadeva blames Basavanna for his bereavement. He complains that Basavanna gets the credit though he prevented Sovideva from tampering with the treasury. Basavanna repudiates the miracle attributed to him and criticizes miracle-mongers for this. He is on his way to Maddur to stop the violence of *sharanas* against Jains which Jagadeva approves. He, then, condemns all violence whatever may be its cause. He understands the agitated soul of Jagadeva and pacifies it through prayer. Then he goes out to see the people who are clamorous for his *darshan*.

Sharanas assemble at Basavanna's house. They propose the marriage between Kalavati, a Brahmin girl and Sheelavanta, a *dalit* boy. Their parents invite Basavanna to the betrothal. Basavanna is shocked so much that he cannot say anything. *Sharanas* are unhappy about his hesitation. So Basavanna explains his apprehension: "It's a question of life and death for these children. From tomorrow the wrath of the bigoted will pursue them like a swarm of snakes, to strike as they pause to put up a roof or light an oven. Who will protect them then?" (38) Overwhelmed by the fervour of performing an inter-caste marriage, *sharanas* misunderstand Basavanna.

Basavanna, then, asks Sheelavanta for his opinion about the marriage. Sheelavanta likes Kalavati but does not want to marry her because she cannot stand even the smell of leather. Then, Lalita, the bride's mother, confirms his statement. Haralayya, the bridegroom's father, regrets that his son will not be allowed to change his vocation by other castes on account of the rigidity of the caste system. Lalita aptly quotes the intuitive prediction of Haralayya's mother: "Rivers of blood will flow if the marriage takes place." (41) Madhuvarasa, Lalita's husband, feels angry with her and orders her to keep quiet. Immediately, Gangambika, Basavanna's wife strongly objects to his male chauvinism: "Women and cattle, they are all the same to you, aren't they?" (42) In spite of all the discussion, *sharanas* stubbornly stick to their stand and one of them questions Basavanna: "So how many more generations have to roll by before a cobbler marries a Brahmin?" (44) At last Basavanna gives blessings and *sharanas* leave.

Bijjala requests Basavanna to stop the inter-caste marriage as it leads to communal violence. Basavanna replies that he cannot make decisions for *sharanas*. He will sit with his *sharanas* in front of his palace if Bijjala bans the marriage. Bijjala knows that the act of Basavanna will paralyse the life of Kalyan. So, he uses his army to avert the blood-bath during the marriage. Thus, the marriage takes place peacefully. While *sharanas* feel jubilant about their great achievement, the marriage infuriates orthodox Hindus.

Damodara Bhatta rushes to Indrani's house in the Courtesan's Quarter to talk to Sovideva about the marriage. Indrani, the courtesan, sees no reason in their going hysterical about it. So, Damodara explains her how the inter-caste marriage is a great sacrilege: "Indrani, the Rig Veda tells us that the four Varnas flowed out of the Primordial Man: the Brahmin from the head, the Shudra from the feet. So what we have here in this wedding is desecration of the body of the Purusha. How horrifying!" (55) Indrani is not convinced and praises Basavanna and his followers: "But the *sharanas* have done so much for the downtrodden and the destitute." (56) Damodara criticises Bijjala for protecting the *sharanas*. As Manchanna arrives with some courtiers, tradesmen, soldiers and citizens, he starts proclaiming the titles of Sovideva as if he had become the king of Kalyan.

Sovideva, Damodara and Manchanna hatch a plot against the king. They first get the loyal servants of Bijjala killed and then imprison him in his own palace. Basavanna knows this and requests *sharanas* to stand by the king. But most of them refuse to save him from Sovideva. So he himself, followed by a few *sharanas*, visits Bijjala who is greatly perturbed. He advises him to cling to Lord Shiva who alone can save him from any danger. As he leaves for Kappadi, Bijjala frenzily sobs and laughs.

Sovideva follows the advice of Damodara and Manchanna and persecutes the *sharanas* violently and mercilessly. As Basavanna is away, the *sharanas* lose heart and go helter-skelter. Damodara and Manchanna feel satisfied with it. But Manchanna is afraid of Basavanna: "The *sharanas* have lost their drive and in course of time are bound to revert to caste for sheer survival. Unfortunately Basavanna is alive and we can take nothing for granted." (79) Damodara pleads with Sovideva for forgiveness and generosity. But Manchanna advises him to get all the *sharanas* decimated without any discrimination and pay a brief visit to his father-in-law for his safety. Sovideva therefore leaves with Damodara, keeping Manchanna in charge of the kingdom.

Jagadeva and other *sharanas* are enraged about the persecution of their fellow-*sharanas* by Sovideva. So, they decide to avenge this on Sovideva. For this, they enter the palace through a secret passage. But, they do not find the Prince and feel greatly frustrated. Jagadeva leads them to the inner shrine of Shiva where the old king hides. Bijjala firmly embraces the *Linga*[11] to protect himself. Then, Jagadeva lies that Basavanna has sent them to him. Believing this, Bijjala comes out of the shrine. In spite of the request of the other *sharanas* not to kill him, Jagadeva stabs him to death. When they all leave on his request, he commits suicide. Basavanna returns from Kappadi and learns all this. He is greatly agitated and talks to himself philosophically.

Sovideva learns from messengers that 'the city reels under gruesome tales of rape, murder, looting and rioting.' (89) He blames Damodara for this. He orders the guard to shut him up when Damodara tries to reply. The guard kills him at once. Another messenger says, "The *sharanas* flee Kalyan." Sovideva then instructs:

> Pursue them. Don't let them escape. Men, women, children—cut them all down. . . . From this moment all *sharanas*, foreigners, and free thinkers are expelled from this land on pain of death. Women and the lower orders shall live within the norms prescribed by our ancient tradition, or else they'll suffer like dogs. Each citizen shall consider himself a soldier ready to lay down his life for the King. For the King is God incarnate! (90)

The crowning ceremony of Sovideva goes on as the city of Kalyan is ablaze. The screams of the victims and the eulogies of Sovideva by Brahmins are heard simultaneously.

Karnad says: "you can perceive deep irony, because, after all the martyrdom of the *sharanas*, when they re-emerged after three centuries of underground survival as lingayats, they were totally caste-ridden."[12] It happened as Manchanna had predicted, "The *sharanas* have lost their drive and in course of time are bound to revert to caste for sheer survival." (79) Karnad tries to trace the cause behind the failure of Basavanna's movement, "Ultimately the final betrayal was not by the enemies, but by the followers." He feels that *Tale-Danda* is relevant even today as religious fundamentalism is strong enough to destroy the Babri masjid and claim the lives of thousands of people. He adds: "When people all around us are slaughtered in the name of a temple, I hear echoes from those times long past."[13] That is why the words of Basavanna point to mandir-masjid violence: "Violence is wrong, whatever the provocation. To resort to it because someone else started it first is even worse. And to do so in the name of a structure of brick and mortar is a monument to stupidity." (29) Therefore what happened in the twelfth century is still happening now. So Karnad rightly remarks: "It seems 800 years have solved no problems. We are back exactly where we started."[14]

Social deformity is thus illustrated in its various aspects in Karnad's *Tale-Danda.* The ugly face of the caste system in India is exposed in *Tale-Danda.* Most of the people accept it and observe the customs that sustain it. Moreover state protects it with military force. Basavanna is betrayed by his own followers in his ideal struggle to eradicate the caste system gradually. Consequently, not only does Basavanna's movement fail but also his followers emerge as a new caste after a few hundred years. Thus Karnad exposes the evil effects of social deformity at cultural, social and psychological levels.

NOTES

1. J. Bruce Long, 'Life out of Death,' *Hinduism*, ed. Bardwell L. Smith (Leiden: E.J. Brill, 1982), p. 172.
2. Cluade M. Steiner, *Scripts People Live* (New York: Bantam, 1980), p. 186.
3. Marx and Engels, *Manifesto of the Communist Party* (Moscow: Progress Publishers, 1977), p. 64.
4. Brahmins are called *Bhusuras* (Gods on earth) in Sanskrit.
5. *Hindu Customs and their Origins* (Delhi: Low Price Publications, 1993), p. 122.
6. *Dr. Babasaheb Ambedkar: Writings and Speeches* (Bombay: Government of Maharashtra, 1987), p. 67.
7. Qtd. Ambedkar, p. 418.
8. Lord Rama beheaded Shambuka, a shudra, for reading Vedas.

9. Venkatesan, "Caste Crimes," *Frontline*, July 29, 1994, p. 104. (This can be illustrated by the incident reported by Venkatesan in *Frontline*. Subhash, a shudra boy of twelve years, allegedly broke the glass shell of 'akhand jyoti' on 28 May 1994 in Jaitsar, a village of Rajasthan. For not allowing him to be caught, Prakash Kaur, his mother, was most inhumanly punished. She was stripped naked, dragged with her legs tied around the Durga Temple and beaten with sticks all the time by upper caste men and one of them allegedly pushed hard a stick into her genitals. Then her head was tonsured, her face was blackened and she was paraded on a donkey in the market. Hot water and then kerosene were poured down into her mouth. She could not survive the heinous torture and died. This is only one of the incidents that often happen throughout India).
10. Girish Karnad, *Tale-Danda* (Delhi: Ravi Dayal Publisher, 1993), p. 14.
11. Linga is the holy phallic symbol of Lord Shiva.
12. "Where is the tradition?" (Interview), *Frontline*, September 25, 1992, p. 76.
13. *Loc. cit.*
14. *Loc. cit.*

Caste and Religion in *Tale-Danda*

A.R. SHUKLA

Girish Karnad has attempted various themes concerning past history, past and present values, and religious beliefs and myths of India. In that way he is deeply concerned with India and the Indianness. Karnad, it seems, has taken up a job to re-interpret and, if necessary and if possible, to re-structure the traditional values of social and political systems concerning caste. He is also concerned with the subtle meaning of Religion. In "his first play *Yayati* (1991) he re-interprets an ancient Hindu myth on the theme of responsibility."[1] But in *Tughlaq* (1972), a historical play on the life of Sultan Muhammad-bin-Tughlaq of the fourteenth century India, he shows Tughlaq as a complex personality who is "at once a dreamer and a man of action, benevolent and cruel, devout and godless."[2] M.K. Naik notes that "Karnad himself has suggested that he found 'Tughlaq's history contemporary' in that the souring of his idealism had a close parallel in the mood of disenchantment of the sixties after the passing away of Nehru; and this is another reason why the play was a success on the Kannada stage." (262) Here Karnad draws correspondences from the past to the present, from history to the real life to meet his thematic needs. In *Tale-Danda* (1993) he re-examines the need and structure of the caste system of India that was once, in the past, hailed as an ideal one. Picking up historical-cum-political background for his plot, he moulds his theme of Tale-Danda to serve his present needs. He writes, "I wrote *Tale-Danda* (1993) in 1989 when the 'Mandir' and the 'Mandal' movements were beginning to show again how relevant the questions posed by these thinkers were for our age."[3] These thinkers are those who condemned idolatry and temple worship. Indeed, they reflected anything 'static' in favour of the principle of movement and progress in human enterprise. They believed in the equality of sexes and celebrated hard, dedicated work. They opposed the caste system, not just in theory but in practice. This last act brought down upon them the wrath of the orthodox. The movement ended in terror and bloodshed." It is through the *sharanas* that the author advocates his philosophy. Basavanna, the great *sharana* saint poet is the mouthpiece to announce the author's views. However, the author's views are expressed also through the King Bijjala who is very close, in thinking and nobility, to the dukes in Shakespeare's plays. He also shares his views with Kakkayya, a *sharana* and an untouchable saint aged about seventy.

Ancient saying in the form of commandments, shariyats or Vedic mantras need to be reassessed and reviewed with the change of time and growth in understanding. A fresh outlook is inevitable to analyse the literary and the cultural stores which the past masters have left for us. Prakriti, a Chandal girl in Tagore's *Chandalika* (1933), says, "A religion that insults is a false religion."[4] Basavanna in Karnad's *Tale-Danda* says, "Some say this entire edifice of caste and creed, this poison-house of varnashrama, will come tumbling down. Every person will see himself only as a human being. As a bhakta. As a *sharana*. That is inevitable. . . . You know the most terrible crimes have been justified in the name of sanatan religion." (39) Arun Shourie, in his introduction to *Indian Controversies* (1993), states, "in each tradition there is much that is valuable, but also much that is malignant." (viii) Hence there is need of a new religion, a religion which can treat all human beings as equal. *sharanas* believe in this. In the words of Kakkayya, "There is no caste among *sharanas*, neither brahmin, nor cobbler." (38)

The major theme of Karnad's *Tale-Danda* is that of deconstruction of caste and religion to arrive at its real, proper meaning and to restructure the same for the benefit of the society and the country. In scene after scene Karnad gives new doses and fresh outlook to the set beliefs and rooted religious faiths. The traditional caste-system claims that a king is supposed to be a Rajput or a Kshatriya. The author gives a stunning dialogue taking place between Bijjala, the king and Rambhavati, the queen.

Bijjala: What is my caste? Tell me.

Rambhavati: We are Kshatriyas.

Bijjala: Your family—the Hoysalas, you may be Kshatriyas. But I am a Kalachurya. A barber. His Majesty king Bijjala is a barber by caste. For

> ten generations my forefathers ravaged the land as robber barons. For another five they ruled as the trusted feudatories of the emperor himself. They married into every royal family in sight. Bribed generations of Brahmins with millions of cows. All this so they could have the caste of Kshatriyas branded on their foreheads. (14)

Here Karnad achieves two aims. He shows that the king of Kalyan is not a kshatriya but a barber. Further he shows him full of insight and noble thoughts, perhaps to show that deep insight, noble character and ideal administration are not the inborn characteristics of one community only. Bijjala further adds, "In all my sixty-two years, the only people who have looked me in the eye without a reference to my lowly birth lurking deep in their eyes are the *sharanas*: Basavanna and his men. They treat me as—as what?—(Almost with a sense of wonder) as a human being. Basavanna wants to eradicate the caste structure, wipe it off the face of the earth. Annihilate the varna system. . . . Look at those he has gathered around him: poets, mystics, visionaries. . . . All hard-working people from the common stock. They sit together, indifferent to caste, birth or station." (15)

Treat everyone as 'a human being' only is the argument in *Tale-Danda*. Religion cannot ill-treat anyone, nor can it reduce any one from his being a human being. We know that greatest evils have been done in the name of God and deadliest wars have been fought in the name of religion. The existence of religion is like that of time. Both have the fluidity and the variance when seen through the human eyes, the eyes that have faith in science, a subject that deals with firm proofs, and Religion, which purely survives in faith. Now, when we know that the principles of science have also changed in certain cases; say for example Newton's gravitational laws have been superseded by Einstein, then Religious beliefs cannot have rigid unalterable sayings. Bijjala explains to his wife Queen Rambhavati the difference between God and a human being and the difference in him and God in the words: "But the one truth I know is that I exist and God doesn't." (15) Now, the question here is: if God doesn't exist, what about the relation or association between God and religion or between man and religion.

Once again Karnad breaks away with the rooted traditional beliefs regarding having a son and regarding birth, caste and creed.

Bijjala: A son is the final goal of human existence! It may be that he drinks your blood and chews your bones to mash. But he is the one who'll keep your soul fed till eternity.

Basavanna: For a *sharana*, physical parentage is of no consequence. A person is born truly only when the guru initiates him into a life of knowledge.

Bijjala: That's what you believe. As a child you tore up your sacred thread and ran away from home. Birth, caste and creed mean nothing to you. (20)

Karnad here disagrees with the established tradition of considering ı caste or creed on the strength of "physical parentage." Instead Knowledge' is the right canon to judge a human being. In *Chanlalika* Tagore presents a similar viewpoint. Ananda, a Buddhist nonk, says to a low-caste girl Prakriti, "As I am a human being, so ılso are you, and all water is clean and holy that cools our heat and atisfies our thirst." (148) The girl reports to her mother: "He said hat Janaki bathed in such water as this, at the beginning of her forst exile, and the Guhak, the Chandal drew it for her." (149) We ave seen earlier that every rule, be it of science or religion, needs ɔ be reviewed, restructured and deconstructed for better set up and or better strength. Through Manchanna Kramita, a Brahmin who vas an adviser to the king, Karnad shows his dissent with the ritual laughter of animals before the Vedic gods. When fire sacrifices or ıny other sacrifices are offered to God for religious purposes, it is mproper, inhuman, unworthy and beastlike; we cannot justify slaughtering of animals for our own purposes. In Act II, scene v, Madhuvarsa, a *sharana* who is a brahmin by birth, shows his willingness to sacrifice his daughter's life to forward the cause of their great movement. But Basavanna turns down the proposal saying, "No one has a right to sacrifice anyone—not even himself." (39)

In Act II, scene v, we find that Sheelavanta, a cobbler boy, is going to marry Kalavati, a brahmin girl. The author brilliantly develops this delicate matter and handles the situation in a masterly way to achieve new dramatic heights. Here the brahmin girl has no objection in marrying the cobbler boy. But the cobbler boy is hesitant to accept the brahmin girl because the girl "can't stand the smell of leather." (40) King Bijjala, who is a barber by birth, wants to forbid the marriage. Basavanna, a *sharana* saint poet, is not ready for such a kind of wedding because "the orthodox will see . . . mingling of castes as a blow at the very roots of varnashrama dharma." (38) Later he consents for this inter-caste wedding. But the king warns him that it will create an uncontrollable bloodshed. However, the king "staunched the wrath of the people and invited disaster on his own head." (65) The wedding procession also meets a success. Basavanna gives full credit to king Bijjala for this success.

The protection given to *sharanas* proves too costly to the king. His son, Prince Sovideva, conspires against him and imprisons him by bribing Bijjala's own men. Kallappa, who could not be bribed is killed. Basavanna, with his one hundred and fifty thousand *sharanas* fails to save the king. Jagadeva kills king Bijjala in the sanctum. In the words of Damodara: "On the one hand stands the Vedic Dharma, which has branched out in strength over the centuries and now shades the whole of Aryavrata. On the other, there is the *sharana* movement—a pestilence—but of a virulence not seen since the days of Buddha. These two face each other in implacable hostility." (64) Damodar Bhatta, the Queen's priest also states, "civilization has been made possible because our Vedic tradition controls and directs that self-destructive energy. How large-hearted is our dharma! To each person it says you don't have to be anyone but yourself. One's caste is like one's home—meant for one's self and one's family. It is shaped to one's needs, one's comforts, one's tradition. And that is why the Vedic tradition can absorb and accommodate all differences, from Kashmir to Kanya Kumari. And even those said to be its victims have embraced its logic of inequality." (56)

Basavanna knows king Bijjala's help to the *sharanas*. He knows that it was Bijjala's protection to the *sharanas* that made the inter-caste marriage possible. He hopes that "the king will receive his dues from the *sharanas*" (69) because he sings that "He who can turn space into form he alone is a *sharana*." (69) Basavanna, with all his ability and foresight fails to save king Bijjala against Prince Sovideva who wants to make the king and his men pay for defying him at the Treasury. And immediately on the verge of getting powers Sovi declares, "The king is father to his people and the people shall love him and obey him like his offspring. No tongue shall wag against the king or his family or his retinue or his officers. From this moment all *sharanas*, foreigners, and free thinkers are expelled from this land on pain of death. Women and the lower orders shall live within the norms prescribed by our ancient tradition, or else they'll suffer like dogs." (90)

Karnad's *Tale-Danda*, a tragedy, shows Basavanna's "principle of movement and progress in human enterprise"[5] ending in terror and bloodshed. Through conflict and confrontation which go side by side in the drama, Karnad deconstructs the meaning of caste and religion and shows a new community of *sharanas* who condemn idolatry and temple worship, reject anything that is static, believe in equality of sexes and hard work and oppose the caste system.

NOTES

1. A.K. Sinha, "Girish Karnad: Thematic Concerns and Technical Features," p. 54 in this book.
2. M.K. Naik, *A History of Indian English Literature* (New Delhi: Sahitya Akademi, 1982), p. 262.
3. Girish Karnad's preface to *Tale-Danda* (Delhi: Ravi Dayal Publisher, 1993).
4. Rabindranath Tagore, *Three Plays* (Madras: Oxford University Press, 1950), p. 154.
5. Preface to *Tale-Danda*.

Women without Voice: A Study of *Tale-Danda*

SUBHASH CHANDRA

If there is a commonality among the cultures of the world spanning the West and the East, it is the marginalization and inferiorization of women, which turns them into shadows of their male prototypes. The male has voice, presence and power, whereas the female is silent, absent and powerless. Taught to repress her own desires (this includes what has come to be known as *joi ssance*), and trained to practise self-effacement, woman has come to articulate a male-constructed definition, which she has internalized. Therefore, when she speaks it is patriarchy that speaks through her. She is not expected to go out and perform, but efficiently lurk around the threshold, supporting the male endeavour. Literature is replete with examples of women who met with destruction because they tried to cross the threshold and write their own definitions in the male-dominated social milieu: Flaubert's Emma Bovary, Ibsen's Dora, Namita Gokhale's Paro, Hawthorne's Hester and several heroines of Anita Desai. There are some who happened to cross the threshold and acquire voice, but were scared of the wide, dark, animalistic devouring world outside and beat an undignified retreat to get inside the threshold. Narayan's Savitri is the representative example of such women. But a large number of them remain committedly passive, servile and silent, bearing and rearing children, and gratifying the sexual needs of their husbands.

The representation of high-caste women in Girish Karnad's play *Tale-Danda*[1] is expectedly stereotypical: they are docile, shouted at, told to mind their own business, or worse still, rejected and packed off to their parents's. Let us consider two examples from the Royal household. The first example is that of Queen Rambhavati, King Bijjala's wife. What is her position? What does she think of her relationship with the King, her husband? Two statements by her made to her son, Sovideva, bring out her standing vis-a-vis Bijjala. When Sovideva is raging against the *sharanas*, who have made a fool of him in the treasury episode, she tells him: "Do as you wish. Just don't upset your father, that's all. *He turns his bad temper on me and I can't take it any longer.*" (8, my italics) When *Sovideva* accuses her of being in thrall to the *sharanas*'s mystic-saint leader, Basavanna, she says: "What am I to do? Do you think your father ever listens to me?" (8) There is hardly a hint of equality in the husband-wife relationship. She might be the queen of the kingdom, but her real standing is no better than any other servant of the palace, as far as the king is concerned. Bijjala's mercurial moods which make him arrogant and overbearing towards Rambhavati testify to her inferior status. And how does she get him to fulfill her wishes? She has to wail and cry and shed tears to persuade Bijjala to leave *sharanas* (who is a spoilt, unethical conspirator) alone. It is not that Bijjala does not love Rambhavati. He is fond of her and cares for her. But the deep-rooted patriarchal attitude made him feels superior and behave most of the time in a rude manner. Rambhavati seems to be devoid of her 'self,' or a 'will of her own.' Her very existence is defined and concretized with reference to her husband. Her not minding the inferiorized position is the outcome of the centuries of internalization of the patriarchal postulates by women in society. That she represents traditional women is also borne out by her unflinching allegiance to her husband through thick and thin. Though she is scolded and berated for her interference in the matter of the father-son antagonism, she willingly provides emotional succour to a suffering and tormented Bijjala, when he has been incarcerated by his son, Sovideva and his cohorts. Interestingly, even in this condition, Bijjala remains brusque with her. Elaine Showalter's words appropriately fit Rambhavati's situation: "We have seen our foremothers as mindless, downtrodden souls, accepting century after century the fetters of their lot with passivity, unheeding or incapable of perceiving their exclusion from society."[2]

The other woman in the palace is Sovideva's wife. What is Sovideva's attitude towards her? He has discarded her and sent her to her parents, not bothering to bring her back. She is absent both literally and metaphorically from the scene. She does not exist in her husband's scheme of things, who wantonly revels in the arms of a prostitute, Indrani. However, it is important to note that this absent, voiceless woman acquires value in the changed context. When Sovideva is confused and afraid and is in need of help in the aftermath of the beheading of Madhuvarasa and Haralayya, he is advised to visit his father-in-law for support and bring her queen back. The words spoken by Sovideva on this occasion are revealing for their irony and male egocentricities. When Manchanna says to Sovideva: "And then pay a brief visit to your father-in-law, sir? His support may come in handy," Sovideva answers: "Yes, And see our queen again! she *is* our Queen after all, *frigid bitch though she is*." (my italics) Woman is valued for her functional utility only, not for her intrinsic worth as a human being.

The most crucial event in the play which triggers catastrophic consequences, involving the death of the King and the beheading of Mahuvarasa and Haralayya is the wedding between a high-caste Brahmin's daughter and a cobbler's son. The marriage has become possible because both the families have embraced *sharana* religion. It is a momentous event which forces even Basavanna, the *sharana* saint-leader, to pause and reflect on the possible fall out.The girl's mother Lalitamba's reluctance has no weight or meaning, because it is her husband Madhuvarasa's decision which matters. A typical characteristic of patriarchy is that men are in control and it is they who wield power. Women remain voiceless. Lalitamba points to the practical problems, besetting the alliance of a Brahmin girl with a cobbler boy. But her objections and fears are not satisfactorily resolved: they are unceremoniously brushed aside by her husband, Madhuvarasa.

Basavanna's fears on account of this commingling of the high and the low caste through marriage turn out to be real; the words he speaks become prophetic. He says: "Until now it was only a matter of theoretical speculation. But this—this is real. The orthodox will see this mingling of castes as a blow at the very roots of varnashrama dharma. Bigotry has not faced such a challenge in two thousand years. I need hardly describe what venom will gush out, what hatred will erupt once the news spreads." (38)

Lalitamba's objections to the marriage sound justified: "Till the other day our daughter ran around barefoot. She was told it was unclean to touch any leather except deer-skin. How can she start skinning dead buffaloes tomorrow? Or tan leather?" And she goes on, "It's my child's life! She gets a splitting headache if she so much as smells burning camphor. She is so . . . so . . . tender." (41) The response of Madhuvarasa, the husband, is worth considering: "*Woman, I said hold your tongue.* You are insulting a *sharana*'s calling." (41, my italics) He sounds right, if one considers the essential tenets of the *sharana* religion. But his tone and attitude are overbearing and crushing. Expectedly, Lalitamba's objections are overridden, the marriage takes place. As a consequence, Madhuvarasa and Haralayya are brutally murdered in the aftermath of the violence that engulfs the city after the weddings. That Madhuvarasa has to pay the price for his foolhardiness and his ignoring the points raised by Lalitamba is beside the point. What is relevant here is that he acts as the representative of the stereotypical male in putting the woman's voice under erasure. Feminists, therefore, rightly believe that "the binary opposition has been skewed and the dichotomy between men and women has become not an equalized difference but a hierarchal one in which one member of the part is superior, in the centre, in control, while the other is subordinate, on the margin—invisible, inarticulate and ineffective."[3]

In the end, I would like to focus on the positioning of women within the *sharana* fold. A description of the religion, given on the blurb of the play is noteworthy: "A new religion, risen in revolt against the narrowminded, ritual-ridden Brahminism preaches equality of human beings. Caste does not add value or attach stigma to people. In the eyes of Lord Shiva, whom *sharanas* worship, all are equal." Much is made of this equality principle among them, which finds its culmination in the wedding between Sheelavanta, the son of Madhuvarasa and Kalavati, the daughter of Haralayya. But what about the principle of equality between the sexes? Let us examine the place the *sharana* women occupy in relation to their men. Basavanna's wife, Gangambika, does seem to enjoy a better position than many other women inasmuch as, she takes part in the conversations that occur at Basavanna's house. Basavanna himself is respectful towards her and regards her statements as worthy of consideration. She seems to have a voice. However, she performs within the four walls of the house. It is not for her to cross the threshold, and go out to lead the *sharanas.* Attainment of sainthood, the power to lead people, and the capacity to perform are rested in the male, Basavanna. Jane Tompkins succinctly articulates how women are conditioned in a certain way of thinking and behaving: "I saw that I had been socialized from birth to feel and act in ways that automatically excluded me from participating in the culture's most valued activities."[4] The most important question, however, is: What is the fate of Basavanna's wife eventually? Basavanna's leaving home and going nobody knows where in search of God and her spreading his message, ignore Gangambika's thoughts and feelings which are not shown in the play. Gangambika, like other women, suffers.

The most relevant example the shabby treatment meted out to women is provided by the *sharana* Jagadeva. It is for men to become achievers, gather laurels and revel in glory by attaining their coveted goals. In the process, they feel free to take their vows, make resolutions, and not to "look at" their womenfolk, what to talk of taking their permission to pursue their predetermined tasks. Marital responsibility does not matter. Considerateness be damned! Woman is treated as a worm who can be easily trampled upon. Jagadeva's wife's repeated visits to the venue where Jagadeva and his young companions (Kalayya, and Mallibomma) are practising marshall rituals, in order to have a word with Jagadeva because his own mother is seriously ill, and Jagadeva's dogged refusal to meet her are emblematic of the voicelessness of women, even among the *sharanas*. Told by Gundanna that she has come four times since the previous day, Jagadeva says haughtily: "I can't see her. Tell her to go away. She knows I have sworn not to look upon a woman's face till we have achieved our goal. . . . She has to attend to her mother-in-law." (71-72) In patriarchy, men command and it is women's lot to obey, silently, without so much as a protesting sound. She *will* attend to her mother-in-law no doubt, but what about Jagadeva's responsibility towards his very own mother. He is not bothered. There is his wife to do the job. Women's slavery leaves men free to pursue their wishes. Kate Millett seems right when she observes that "relations between the sexes are not solely matters of personal choice," as far as women are concerned.[5]

Such was the condition of women in the traditional Indian society, as the play depicts. Sociocultural and religious movements and revolution left out this significant segment of society. Women remained a marginalized and suppressed group, without voice, without power, and maybe even without consciousness of their peripheral position in society. I would like to conclude with the observation of Showalter who says that "women's relationships to themselves and society have been essentially static, as fixed as to render women of the past mute and dumb, unable to write, speak or even see the truth."[6]

NOTES

1. Girish Karnad, *Tale-Danda: A Play* (Delhi: Ravi Dayal, 1993).
2. Dona Bennet, "Naming the Way Home," *Amazing Space: Writing Canadian Women* (Longspoon/Newest), p. 229.
3. *Ibid.*, p. 233.
4. Jane Timpkins, "Me and My Shadow," in Linda Kaufman, ed. *Gender and Theory: Dialogues on Feminist Criticism* (Cambridge: Basil Blackwell, 1989), p. 124.
5. Kate Millett, qtd. Mary Eagleton, ed. *Feminist Literary Criticism* (London: Longman, 1991), p. 135.
6. Elaine Showalter, qtd. Bennet, p. 229.

Contributors

M. Sarat Babu, Government College, Srisailam Project
Suman Bala, S.B.S. College, University of Delhi
Subhash Chandra, S.B.S. College, University of Delhi
A. Jaganamohana Chari, Kakatiya University, Warangal
Veena Noble Dass, S.P. Mahila University, Tirupati
R.K. Dhawan, S.B.S. College, University of Delhi
Jaydipsinh Dodiya, Shardagram Arts & Comm. College, Mangrol
Savita Goel, Savitri Girls College, Ajmer
Christine Gomez, Tiruchirapalli
Jacob George C., Union Christian College, Alwaye
Santosh Gupta, University of Rajasthan, Jaipur
B. Indira, A.U. Engineering College, Visakhapatnam
S.R. Jalote, B.H.U., Varanasi
K.K. John, Kuvempu University, Shimoga
Pranav Joshipura, Uma Arts and Comm. College, Gandhinagar
Girish Karnad, the eminent writer
Geeta Kumar, S.P.M. College, University of Delhi
K. Ratna Shiela Mani, Nagarjuna University, Guntur
Pramod K. Nayar, Kuvempu University, Shimoga
Makarand Paranjape, I.I.T., New Delhi
P. Ramamoorthy, Madurai
P.H. Sethumadhava Rao, University of Poona
Shubhangi S. Raykar, Pune
P. Bayapa Reddy, S.K. University, Anantapur
A.R. Shukla, Navgujarat Arts College, Ahmedabad
A.K. Sinha, Patna University
Seema Suneel, Maharaja Agrasen College, University of Delhi
V.B. Vinod, St. Berchman's College, Changannassery

Index